THE POLISH-GERMAN FRONTIER
IN THE LIGHT OF INTERNATIONAL LAW

THE POLISH-GERMAN FRONTIER IN THE LIGHT OF INTERNATIONAL LAW

by
DR. BOLESŁAW WIEWIÓRA
Reader in Public International Law
at the University of Poznań

Preface by
Alfons Klafkowski, Professor
Head of the Department of International
Public Law at the University of Poznań

Poznań
Instytut Zachodni
1964

First Edition
GRANICA POLSKO-NIEMIECKA W ŚWIETLE PRAWA
MIĘDZYNARODOWEGO
Instytut Zachodni, Poznań 1957

First English Edition
POLISH-GERMAN FRONTIER FROM THE STANDPOINT OF
INTERNATIONAL LAW
Wydawnictwo Zachodnie, Poznań—Warszawa 1959

Second English Edition (Posthumous)
prepared and edited by
ALFONS KLAFKOWSKI
Professor at the University of Poznań
Head of the Department of International Law

Drukarnia Uniwersytetu im. Adama Mickiewicza—Poznań

CONTENTS

PREFACE TO THE SECOND ENGLISH EDITION

This monograph appeared first in the Polish language in 1957 as a doctor's thesis. Two years later, a full Russian translation was produced in Moscow. The same year, 1959, saw the publication of the first English language edition, revised and supplemented by the author. The present, second English edition is a posthumous one. It has been changed only in part, namely Chapter I of the first English language edition was elaborated by Bolesław Wiewióra at the beginning of 1963 and, on the basis of additional literature, re-made into the first two chapters of the present edition. Death interrupted Wiewióra's work of supplementing the whole of the present edition.

Bolesław Wiewióra died in February 1963 at the early age of 37. The bibliography of his writings comprises 12 type-written pages. In addition to the present book he wrote three other monographs: 1. *Granica na Odrze i Nysie Łużyckiej w polityce Zachodu* (The Frontier on the Oder and the Lusatian Neisse in the Policy of the West) Poznań 1958, 120 pp.; 2. *Niemiecka Republika Demokratyczna jako podmiot prawa międzynarodowego* (The German Democratic Republic as a Subject of International Law) Poznań 1961, 176 pp.; and 3. *Uznanie nabytków terytorialnych w prawie międzynarodowym* (Recognition of Territorial Acquisitions in International Law) Poznań 1961, 243 pp. Moreover, Wiewióra published 27 extensive studies and articles, numerous glosses and notes to gather with many reviews of scientific publications in foreign languages. In the present, posthumous edition the reader will find references to Wiewióra's principal writings published after 1956. His studies have been frequently reviewed and discussed with great attention.

It is difficult to present in a few sentences the portrait of this outstanding scholar. I must, therefore, confine myself to emphasizing those traits which are especially connected with the present monograph. Bolesław Wiewióra's work was marked by courage in the search for truth and boldness in its dissemination. He also showed determination and the ability to utilize scientific truth as an argument in the struggle for the right cause, a struggle conducted in the service of his nation. As regards Polish-German legal relations after the Second World War, both this book and all the other writings by Wiewióra demonstrate the best kind of applied knowledge, scientific truth serving the purposes of international practice. Although Wiewióra never expressed it openly, his publications show that what interested him particularly was the relationship between theory and practice. In a report published after a year's study at the University of Cambridge Wiewióra indicated the main differences between the English and Polish systems of law teaching. He wrote then that in Poland law was taught from the practical point of view, whereas the English universities stressed the theoretical aspects of the study. He explained that this theoretical tendency in the teaching of law did not mean any detachment from practice and pointed both to the selection of legal subjects and the methods of teaching to prove that there are close ties between the science of law and the needs of practice. In the work of this scholar it is difficult to separate Wiewióra, the theoretician of international law, from Wiewióra, the expert on international relations and outstanding specialist in the field of Polish-German legal relations. Some generalizations must, however, be made about his work, since this is also required by the second English language edition of his monography.

Wiewióra's research work comprises two great, basic problems: the problem of the Polish-German frontier and the problem of its recognition.

The first problem, that of the post-war frontier between Poland and Germany, has been thoroughly elaborated by him. He did it on the basis of a detailed and systematic analysis of legal acts as well as thorough research on theoretical literature and the practice of States. The present monograph shows the extent to which Wiewióra made use of documents and scholarly publications. He always emphasized that concrete norms of international law were for him the basis of legal interpretation. This did not mean, however, that ignoring the political foundations of the essential post-war international agreements regulating life after the Second World War. Being guided by this principle, Wiewióra strove to present the positive achievements of learning and avoided polemics. Where he engaged in a dispute, he did it in a concise and dry manner. He disarmed the opponent by irrefutable arguments.

The other problem is Wiewióra's research on the recognition of the Polish-German frontier in the light of legal acts, the practice of States and the theory of international law. He devoted considerable work and effort to a confrontation of present-day international recognition with the theory of international law. His extensive research work, presented in his habilitation thesis, is concentrated on three institutions of international law: recognition, sovereignty and territorial changes. According to Wiewióra, recognition of territorial acquisition seems to have certain particular characteristics which he tried to define in his writings. After profound research he came to the conclusion that recognition as a unilateral act on the part of a State was an institution mainly political in character. Recognition is also, of course, a legal action since it leads to definite legal effects in the relations between the State expressing recognition and the State recognized. Wiewióra regards the distinction between recognition *de jure* and recognition *de facto* as indicative of the political character of recognition. Perceiving the wide use of recognition in international relations, Wiewióra examined this institution and its role in the case of territorial changes. He came to the conclusion that recognition of territorial accessions was, above all, a political function. He also stressed that it was not a separate institution of contemporary international law.

This is of course but an outline of the opinions expressed by Wiewióra in his monographs and studies published between 1959 and 1963. In preparing the second English language edition of this monograph, Wiewióra wanted to include in at the conclusions he had reached in all his monographs. It would have been a synthesis of his imposing scholarly achievements. Death interrupted these ambitious plans and deprived science of a work which would have been a monograph of lasting value. The editorial footnotes inserted in the present, posthumous edition cannot of course reflect the wide range of Wiewióra's opinions. They indicate only where to look for the development and supplementation of the thoughts and opinions which Wiewióra expressed in the first English language edition of this monograph. A posthumous work must be marked by respect for the author's rights and this has been the aim of the present, second edition.

*

*		*

In 1959, at the request of Bolesław Wiewióra, I wrote a lengthy Preface to the first English language edition of this monograph. Upon his request, I formulated there the main divergencies between the Polish and the Western Powers' theories of international law as regards the interpretation of the legal acts regulating the frontier between Poland and Germany after the Second World War. The Preface grew to 32 pages. It concluded with a proposal, directed mainly to British experts on international law, to start a discussion on the subject. I presented my own point of view and tried to substantiate it by documents and literature concerning the problem. The aim of the Preface to the first English language edition was to facilitate the finding of a common language between the Polish and British experts on international law. The aim has not been achieved, since I do not know of a single review or polemical article that has taken up at least the majority of the problems raised by me in the preface. Maybe that the British and world scholars have had a different hierarchy of tasks and needs during that period. Maybe that the legal aspects of the Polish-German frontier were not then the most important task in the theory of international law. It may also be that the arguments presented in Wiewióra's monograph and the additional arguments included in my Preface have been recognized as true from the scientific point of view and, as such, legally irrefutable. I, for my part, have no doubt that from the legal point of view the problems documented by Wiewióra in the present monograph are no longer controversial and do not require any additional arguments.

I realize, of course, that one cannot complain of a lack of controversies in the theory of international law. Neither can one complain of such lack as regards the implementation of the norms of international law. I know that changes in State frontiers and the recognition of such changes are probably more controversial than any other aspect of international law. The lack of symmetry in the institutions of international law is nowhere more clearly apparent than in this field. As a lawyer I realize that neither the theory of international law nor its practice has so far elaborated any general and universally accepted criteria of legality of territorial acquisitions or their recognition. Nor is there any universal norm in international law regulating these problems. There are, however, international acts which in many concrete cases constitute, so to speak, individual legal solutions. A collection of such individual, uniform legal solutions is surely an adequate basis for generalizations.

Starting from these premises, I should like to present here several groups of legal acts regulating territorial changes after the Second World War. I have chosen the following groups: the armistice agreements providing for the cessation of hostilities, the peace treaties regulating the termination of the state of war, and some international agreements which, while putting an end either to hostilities or the state of war, are neither an armistice nor a peace treaty. I am now going to present these three groups of legal acts. I should like to stress once again that the aim and subject of my analysis is to find the criteria of legality of the territorial changes effected after the Second World War. The existence of such general criteria would, in my opinion, be an argument in favour of the legal finality of the settlement of the Polish-German frontier after the Second World War.

The armistice agreements terminating hostilities on the various fronts of the Second World War include provisions for territorial changes. A precise determination of these armistice provisions will enable us to follow their implementation in the peace treaties which were concluded after the armistice agreements and on the basis of those agreements. Following are the armistice agreements connected with the Second World War:

1) The armistice with Italy of September 3, 1943 did not re-gulate territorial questions, announcing only that the political, economic and other conditions would be communicated to Italy at a later date (Art. 12). Territorial problems were transferred to the Council of Foreign Ministers and its auxiliary organs. They were finally settled in the peace treaty with Italy.

2) The armistice with Rumania of September 12, 1944 restored the Rumanian-Soviet frontier of June 28, 1940 (Art. 4) and declared the so-called Vienna arbitrament concerning Transylvania to be in-valid and non-existent (Art. 19).

3) The armistice with Finland of September 19, 1944 assigned to the Soviet Union the region of Petsamo (Art. 7) and the base in Porkkala-Udd (Art. 8); it reinstated the status of the Aaland Islands as determined in the agreement with the Soviet Union of November 11, 1940 (Art. 9). The annex to the armistice agreement referred to the Finnish territories which were the subject of restitution or cession in the armistice agreement (Art. 7).

4) The armistice with Bulgaria of October 23, 1944 included indirect territorial clauses defining the conditions of Bulgarian withdrawal from the territories she had annexed or incorporated (Art.2).

5) The armistice with Hungary of January 20, 1945 included indirect territorial clauses defining the principles of Hungarian withdrawal from the Czechoslovak, Yugoslav and Rumanian territories occupied by her (Art. 2).

6) The capitulation of Japan of October 2, 1945 referred to the so-called Potsdam ultimatum of July 26, 1945 which contained territorial decisions. The act of capitulation defined which territories were to remain under Japanese sovereignty (Art. 8).

The armistice agreements regulating the cessation of hostilities in the Second World War can be divided into two groups. The first is represented by the agreements with Italy and the German Reich. It is characteristic of this group that the Great Powers which signed these agreements on behalf of the United Nations, having signed the military agreements on unconditional surrender, issued a number of additional legal acts announced in the military surrender documents.

These additional acts often regulate various problems, including territorial changes, in a pre-treaty manner. Armistice agreements of another type are those concluded with Rumania, Finland, Bulgaria and Hungary. What is characteristic of them is that the armistice act (together with annexes) contains all the military, territorial, economic and political provisions defining the mechanism of occupation. A confrontation of these armistice agreements with the peace treaties concluded after 1945 shows that the treaties, as a rule, take over, develop and make precise almost all the provisions of the armistice agreements. The peace treaties also confirm the territorial clauses of the agreements. The only exception is the peace treaty with Japan, signed in 1951. It should be remembered, however, that one of the Four Great Powers — namely the U.S.S.R. — as well as a number of countries members of the United Nations, did not sign the peace treaty. We can, therefore, say that this exception confirms the rule that after the Second World War the armistice agreements became a form of recognition of new State frontiers; this refers, of course, to those agreements which included territorial clauses.

The peace treaties regulating the termination of the state of war constitute the second group of legal acts dealing with territorial changes after the Second World War. This is how the problem appears in the various peace treaties:

1) The peace treaty with Italy restores Italy's frontiers of January 1, 1938 with some modifications in favour of neighbouring countries and changes resulting from the restoration of annexed regions and the different settlement of the African territories. The treaty refers to the additional provisions of the armistice agreement of September 29, 1943. The final settlement of all territorial questions was thus accomplished in the peace treaty. On the whole it can be stated that the treaty takes over the legal norms of the armistice agreement and its annexes.

2) The peace treaty with Rumania takes over the territorial decisions of the armistice agreement. Thus, the armistice with Rumania pre-judged the changes in Rumania's State frontiers in a pre-treaty manner.

3) The peace treaty with Finland takes over the territorial decisions of the armistice and confirms them. What is specific of this

treaty is that, as regards territorial changes, it refers to the peace treaty concluded by Finland and the U.S.S.R. in 1940.

4) The peace treaty with Bulgaria takes over and confirms the frontier changes provided for by the armistice agreement, and, exceptionally, introduces one additional change more.

5) The peace treaty with Hungary takes over and confirms the territorial clauses of the armistice.

6) The 1951 peace treaty with Japan refers neither to any legal act from the times of the Second World War nor to the agreement on Japan's unconditional surrender. Articles 2 and 3 enumerate the territories lost by Japan as a result of World War II. The peace treaty deprived Japan of more than 1,500,000 square km of territory and over 60 million people over whom she had exercised State sovereignty. It does not mention the legal acts which provided the basis for these changes. It is worth observing that Articles 2 and 3 do not mention the States in whose favour these territorial changes have been made. The commentary to the territorial clauses declares that Japan is losing territories which she did not acquire in the course of hostilities during the Second World War. Thus, the peace treaty with Japan introduced changes with regard to territories which until the commencement of hostilities in the Second World War had not been formally questioned. In this connection the opinion has been expressed that very often a peace treaty — the peace treaty with Japan being yet another proof of this — introduces territorial changes not possible to be made in normal, peaceful international relations.

An analysis of the above-mentioned peace treaties shows that as a rule they took over the pre-treaty settlement of State frontiers, effected by the armistice agreements. The peace treaties concluded after the Second World War are of a secondary, derivative character in comparison with the decisive settlement of State frontiers accomplished by the armistice agreements. This is a specific trait after the Second World War.

In addition to these two groups of legal acts — the armistice agreements and the peace treaties — there is also an international agreement which, without being either an armistice agreement or a peace treaty decisively regulates a number of problems connected with the termination of the state of war. I have in mind the settlement of the problems of the former German Reich after the Second World War. These problems were not typical and, consequently, had to be regulated by special acts of international law. Of particular importance among these acts is the Potsdam Agreement of August 2, 1945. The problem of changes in the territory of the former German Reich is raised several times in the agreement. Chapter VI states that pending the final determination of territorial questions at the peace settlement, the U.S.S.R. obtains a change of frontier in the section adjacent to the Baltic Sea. The Great Powers, signatories to the Potsdam Agreement, transferred ultimately to the U.S.S.R. the city of Königsberg together with an area defined in the agreement. At the same time, the President of the United States and the Prime Minister of Great Britain declared that "they will support the proposal of the conference at the forthcoming peace settlement". This is a typical pre-treaty decision concerning changes in the territory of the former German Reich. The future peace treaty with Germany can only confirm these decisions.

The problem of the Polish-German frontier is regulated in Chapter IX B of the Potsdam Agreement. It refers to the Yalta Agreement which included a general definition of the future Polish-German frontier. The Potsdam Agreement describes this frontier in detail. In view of the fact that France later declared adherence to the Potsdam Agreement, it may be stated that the Polish-German frontier has been established by the decision of the Four Great Powers acting on behalf of the United Nations. Neither Poland nor Germany — being the directly interested States — is a party to the Potsdam Agreement. Poland was, however, consulted during the Potsdam Conference, so that in relation to her the agreement is a *pactum in favorem tertii*. The Potsdam Agreement made a cession of territory to Poland, a fact reflected in the definition of the ceded territories as "former German territories". The ceded territories were placed under Polish administration and excluded from the Soviet zone of occupation. They were not under the jurisdiction of the Allied Control Council for Germany, being an integral part of the Polish State territory. These "former German" lands have been restored to Poland and placed under her sovereignty. Since the day when the Potsdam Agreement came into force they have been an integral part of the Polish State. The Potsdam Agreement supplemented these territorial decisions by imposing upon Poland the obligation to transfer the German population from Polish territory into the territory of the four zones of occupation in Germany. Section XIII of the Agreement provides detailed principles of this transfer. Poland fulfilled the duty imposed upon her by Section XIII of the Agreement and concluded agreements with representatives of the four occupying Powers, concerning the number of people to be transferred into the territory of the former German Reich and the international control over this transfer. Such is the legal state of this problem. If political doubts are raised, they by no means refer to the legality of the Polish-German frontier. These political doubts — devoid of a legal character — concern only the finality of this frontier and are connected with the future peace treaty with Germany.

On the basis of the above analysis of the armistice agreements and the peace treaties concluded after 1945, one can state that the future peace treaty with Germany can only confirm the legally existing Polish-German frontier. Poland is not responsible for the fact that there is still no peace treaty with Germany.

The general conclusions suggested by the aforesaid legal acts can be formulated in the following way:

Firstly: After the Second World War the peace treaties were concluded by the United Nations on whose behalf a considerable share of preparatory work had been done by the Great Powers, parties to the Potsdam Agreement. All these treaties refer to the Potsdam Agreement. There are only two cases in which a power signatory to the Potsdam Agreement did not sign the peace treaty with an enemy State from the times of the Second World War. The United States did not sign the peace treaty with Finland since they were not in a state of war with that country; the U.S.S.R. did not sign the peace treaty with Japan in 1951, for reasons explained at the San Francisco conference. On the whole it can be stated that the peace treaties took over the provisions of the armistice agreements and other legal acts drawn up during the war.

Secondly: The Potsdam Agreement is a formal legal foundation of the peace treaties. It was the main subject of discussion during the peace conference with Japan in September 1951. The drafts of the peace treaties were drawn up by the Council of Foreign Ministers, an international organ set up by the Potsdam Agreement. The lack of full documentation concerning the work of this organ makes a detailed analysis of its activity impossible. It is obvious that this organ is also entitled to elaborate a peace treaty with Germany.

Thirdly: All the peace treaties, except that with Japan, contain references to the numerous legal acts regulating the position of the former German Reich or other enemy States. Most of these references concern the Potsdam Agreement and other legal acts of 1945. In this way the peace treaties are linked with the whole system of legal acts of World War II, especially with the Potsdam Agreement.

Fourthly: All the peace treaties, except that with Japan, include a reciprocal recognition of the peace treaties concluded after 1945. These clauses are almost identical in all the treaties. The enemy States pledged themselves to recognize the peace treaties with Germany and Japan, which were to be concluded later. The details of these two treaties were not known to the enemy States in 1947 and in 1955 when the peace treaty concerning Austria was signed, since they had not yet been concluded. There is, therefore, no doubt that the pledge given by the enemy States was based on their recognition of the Potsdam Agreement as the basic, known foundation of a future peace treaty with Germany.

Such is the legal situation based on the definite acts of international law presented by me. Every international agreement can, of course, be subject to interpretation. It should be added, however, that the interpretation of an international agreement—that is the process of defining its content—is governed by definite rules and principles. Moreover, there are various divisions of interpretation. One of them distinguishes between legal interpretation and diplomatic interpretation.

The legal interpretation of an international agreement is strictly defined by universally recognized principles. It not only reflects legal skill but also follows the practice of courts, arbitrations and various international organs.

Diplomatic interpretation can conflict with legal interpretation and deviate from it considerably; however, it can neither replace nor cancel the legal interpretation of an agreement. It should be realized that diplomatic interpretation has no fixed rules. Statesmen often resort to diplomatic interpretation trying in this way to recover advantages they have sacrified by the conclusion of an international agreement. In this way diplomatic interpretation often becomes a means of revenge for the losses suffered at a peace conference; it becomes a means used by politicians to obliterate, be it only in part, what has with their participation and consent has been formulated in a given international agreement.

When analysing these problems we must therefore distinguish between legal interpretation and diplomatic interpretation. We must also remember who it is who is entitled to provide legal interpretation of any individual agreement. These rights are not the exclusive domain of the Great Powers.

In presenting my own point of view, I have sought to supplement and develope the arguments contained in this posthumous second edition of Bolesław Wiewióra's monograph.

Alfons Klafkowski, Professor
Head of the Department of International
Public Law at the University of Poznań

CHAPTER I

THE ANTI-FASCIST COALITION IN THE SECOND WORLD WAR

1. WAR AIMS OF THE ALLIES

The Second World War, started by Nazi Germany on September 1, 1939, became a turning point in the history of mankind. It brought about a basic change in the alignment of world political forces.

The powerful anti-Fascist coalition, developed in proportion to the spread of the war, embraced countries having different social systems. In addition to capitalist Powers—the United States, Great Britain and France—the coalition also included a Socialist country, the Soviet Union. Irrespective of their political systems, all countries were menaced by aggression from the Fascist States—Germany, Japan and Italy—bent on world domination. The plans of the Fascist countries were expressed in a treaty of alliance, called the Tripartite Pact, concluded in Berlin on September 27, 1940[1]. This treaty, originally signed by Nazi Germany, Italy and Japan, was later adhered to by the Fascist governments of Hungary, Rumania, Slovakia and Bulgaria, and, following the conquest of Yugoslavia in 1941, the Nazi sponsored puppet government of Croatia. The Tripartite Pact provided for mutual assistance and co-operation in establishing a "new order" (*Neuordnung*) in Asia and Europe. Japan acknowledged the "dominant" role of Germany and Italy in Europe, and Germany

---

[1] Text of the Tripartite Pact published in *Documents on American Foreign Relations*, ed. by L. M. Goodrich and M. J. Carroll, London, vol. III, pp. 304—305, (abbr. *Documents*).

and Italy reciprocated by conceding the "dominant" role of Japan in Asia. In the statements made at the ceremony of signing the Tripartite Pact, representatives of Nazi Germany, Italy and Japan openly announced that their aim was the conquest of the territories of other nations[2].

The Fascist countries implemented these aims by methods which were later recognized as crimes against peace and humanity, or war crimes. Consequently, after the war the main war criminals from the Axis countries were tried by Courts which based their judgments on international principles elaborated during the course of the war[3]. As regards Poland, her fate was German occupation after her defeat in September 1939; the criminal character of this occupation which defied international law has been documented in a comprehensive and all-inclusive manner[4]. The Fascist crimes, especially the crimes committed by the Nazis in the territories occupied by the Reich, shocked world public opinion. The peoples of the world began to exert pressure on the governments of the countries making up the

---

[2] *Ibid.*, pp. 305—309.

[3] See the book on Nuremberg materials by T. Cyprian and J. Sa-wicki, *Materiały norymberskie*. Warszawa 1948, p. 372.

[4] The basic documents for a legal evaluation of the occupation in Poland are included in the collection of source materials elaborated by K. M. Po-spieszalski, *Documenta Occupationis*, vols. I—VII, Instytut Zachodni, Poznań 1946—1959, and in the *Bulletin of the Chief Commission for the Investigation of Nazi Crimes*, vols. I—XIII. See also other source studies: T. Cyprian and J. Sawicki on Polish problems on the Nuremberg trial, *Sprawy polskie w procesie norymberskim*, Poznań 1956, and T. Cyprian and J. Sawicki on seven verdicts of the Supreme National Tribunal, *Siedem wyroków Najwyższego Trybunału Narodowego*, Poznań 1962, as well as the monographs: K. M. Pospieszalski, on Poland under German Law, *Polska pod niemieckim prawem 1939—1945 (Ziemie Zachodnie)*, Poznań 1946; A. Klafkowski on the German occupation in Poland in the light of the Law of Nations, *Okupacja niemiecka w Polsce w świetle prawa narodów*, Poznań 1946; J. Gumkowski and T. Kułakowski on German war criminals before the Supreme National Tribunal, *Zbrodniarze hitlerowscy przed Najwyższym Trybunałem Narodowym*, Warszawa 1961; S. Datner on the crimes committed by the *Wehrmacht* on war prisoners in World War II, *Zbrodnie Wehrmachtu na jeńcach wojennych w II wojnie światowej*, Warszawa 1961. These are but a few studies on the subject. A bibliography of the more important studies concerning the German occupation in Poland would comprise hundreds of volumes. Documents on Nazi crimes in Poland during the occupation are also included in a collection of documents published in the German Democratic Republic: *Polen, Deutschland und die Oder-Neisse Grenze*, ed. by R. Goguel, Berlin 1959, Chapter 2, pp. 119—219.

anti-Fascist coalition, demanding the elimination of the threat of renewed aggression after a victorious conclusion of the war.

While still engaged in the armed struggle, the anti-Fascist coalition began to formulate its post-war aims. The first act defining its purposes was the Atlantic Charter, a document drawn up at the conference held by the Prime Minister of Great Britain, Winston Churchill, and the President of the United States, F. D. Roosevelt, in August 1941, aboard a British battleship on the Atlantic off the Newfoundland coast[5].

The Atlantic Charter, signed on August 14, 1941, proclaimed "common principles" in the policies of the two countries "on which

---

[5] For the text see: *United Nations Documents 1941—1945*, published by the Royal Institute of International Affairs, London—New York 1946, pp. 9—10. The legal character of the document is controversial. In literature on International Law doubts have been expressed as to whether the Atlantic Charter is an international agreement, e.g. A. Leriche, *Quelques réflexions sur la Charte de l'Atlantique, Revue Générale de Droit International Public*, vol. XLVIII — 1 (1941—1945); F. A. von der Heydte — "Völkerrechtliche Lage der deutschen Ostgebiete", in: *Der deutsche Osten*, München 1956, p. 78, as also Oppenheim-Lauterpacht, *International Law*, 8th ed., vol. I (1955), p. 872, and J. Makowski in his article on the legal character of agreements concluded during the Second World War, "Charakter prawny umów zawartych podczas drugiej wojny światowej", *Państwo i Prawo* 1948, No. 5/6, p. 12 — all these are of the opinion that it was only after the adoption of the United Nations Declaration of January 1, 1942 — a legal act creating the anti-Fascit coalition—that the Atlantic Charter became a legally binding act. In the opinion of Makowski, the Atlantic Charter was previously an offer addressed to the Allies to accept its principles as binding upon the United Nations. L. Ehrlich in his study on Poland's sovereignty in the Recovered Territories, "Suwerenność Polski na Ziemiach Odzyskanych. Zagadnienia Prawne", *Zeszyty Naukowe Uniwersytetu Jagiellońskiego*, Prace prawnicze, fascicle No. 6, Kraków 1959, p. 19, does not clarify his opinion as to the legal character of the Charter. Neither does it S. Boratyński in his study on the Atlantic Charter and the Potsdam Agreement, "Karta Atlantycka a uchwały poczdamskie", *Przegląd Zachodni*, 1956, No. 9/10 and in the book on diplomacy during the Second World War, *Dyplomacja okresu drugiej wojny światowej. Konferencje międzynarodowe 1941—1945*, Warszawa 1957, pp. 69—130. In this book, the author undertakes a detailed analysis of the Atlantic Charter from the point of view of its political content but expresses no opinions as to its legal character. On the other hand, K. Skubiszewski in his study on the Potsdam agreement, "Umowa poczdamska jako jedyna podstawa prawna układu terytorialnego Niemiec", *Przegląd Zachodni* 1952, No. 7/8, pp. 516—520, and A. Klafkowski in his book on the Potsdam agreement, *Umowa poczdamska z dnia 2. 8. 1945. Podstawy prawne likwidacji skutków wojny polsko-niemieckiej*, Warszawa 1960, pp. 152—153, are of the opinion that the Atlantic Charter has the character of an agreement.

they base their hopes for a better future for the world". These principles were defined under eight points.

For the post-war territorial pattern of the world, of particular significance were the first two points of the Charter, which proclaimed: "... their countries seek no aggrandizement, territorial or other", and "They desire to see no territorial changes that do not accord with the freely expressed wishes of the peoples concerned".

At the London conference on September 24, 1941, other countries at war with Germany and Italy, including the U.S.S.R. and Poland, declared their adherence to the Atlantic Charter. Subscribing to the Charter some of these countries made statements explaining their expectations as regards the implementation of the Charter principles after the war. Thus, the U.S.S.R. representative, declaring "the most energetic support on the part of the Government and peoples of the Soviet Union, for the principles of the Charter", added that application of "these principles will necessarily adapt itself to the circumstances, needs and historic peculiarities of particural countries"[6]. The Czechoslovak representative expressed the view that the Charter should be applied "in accordance with the special circumstances and needs of the different parts of Europe and the world", and added that

"The application of the eight points should result in securing such international, territorial, political, legal, military and economic guarantees for all peace-loving peoples, but especially for the neighbours of Germany, as to enable them to defend peace for themselves and for the world against any future attempts at agression either by Germany or anyone else"[7].

The Polish representative at the London conference laid territorial claims against Germany, which though clear were imprecise as to details:

"The future frontiers of Poland should safeguard the country's security as a part of the general security of Europe: they should assure Poland's vital

[6] *Documents, op. cit.*, vol. IV, p. 216.
[7] *War and Peace Aims of the United Nations*, ed. by L. W. Holborn, Boston 1943—1945, vol. I, pp. 412—413 (abbr.: *War and Peace Aims*).

need of a wide access to the sea adequately protected from foreign interference as well as her economic development in proportion to the number of her population"[8].

Furthermore in a joint Polish-Czechoslovak declaration with reference to the Atlantic Charter, the two governments emphasized that safeguards against renewed German aggression should be sought also "in furnishing effective political and material guarantees", and expressed their conviction that the principles of the Atlantic Charter would be applied

"in the spirit of justice which does not admit the uniformity of treatment of those guilty of provoking world wars and of the victims of these wars"[9].

To these reservations should be added later ones, made in 1943 and 1944 by F. D. Roosevelt, President of the United States, Winston Churchill, Prime Minister of Great Britain, and other statesmen who denied to Germany the right to invoke the Atlantic Charter[10].

---

[8] *Documents, op. cit.*, vol. IV, p. 220.

[9] *Documents, op. cit.*, vol. IV, p. 221.

[10] In the parliamentary debate on February 24, 1944 Foreign Secretary Eden stated: "Germany would not, as a matter of rights, be able to claim to benefit from the Atlantic Charter in such a way as to preclude the victorious Powers from making territorial adjustments at her expense . . . we cannot admit that Germany can claim, as a matter of right on her part, whatever our obligation, that any part of the Charter applies to her". *Parliamentary Debates. House of Commons*, vol. 397, No. 35, pp. 936—7. On February 22, 1944, Prime Minister Churchill, explaining in the House of Commons the conception of unconditional surrender, stated: "There will be, for instance, no question of the Atlantic Charter applying to Germany, as a matter of right and barring territorial transferences or adjustments in enemy countries". *The War Speeches of the Rt. Hon. Winston Churchill*, p. 91. Speaking in the House of Commons on May 24, 1944, Churchill emphasized: "The Atlantic Charter in no way binds us about the future of Germany, nor is it a bargain or contract with our enemies. There is no question of Germany enjoying any guarantee that she will not undergo territorial changes if it should seem that the making of such changes renders more secure and more lasting the peace in Europe". *Ibid.*, pp. 151—152. The American Government formulated its reservations as regards the application of the Charter in a more general way. In his message to the Congress of the United States of February 12, 1943, President Roosevelt stated that not all the points of the Charter could be applied generally. On February 9, 1944, the American Secretary of State, Cordell Hull made a speech in which he explained that the Atlantic Charter was not a detailed code of laws, containing a solution to every problem. The Charter certainly did not exclude steps, including measures against enemy countries, necessary

The Atlantic Charter became the programme document of the anti-Fascist coalition. From the moment the United Nations Declaration was signed on January 1, 1942[11] as the legal expression of alliance in the struggle against the Fascist countries, every country wishing to join the coalition was required to accept also the Atlantic Charter. Even so, the statements quoted above clearly show that the Allies had no intention of applying the Charter principles mechanically to their enemies. This is further shown by the following facts:

1) the proposals presented by President Roosevelt and Prime Minister Churchill at the Teheran Conference, envisaging the dismemberment of Germany into a number of States[12];

2) the Morgenthau Plan, which also envisaged the dismemberment of Germany and was accepted · by President Roosevelt and Prime Minister Churchill at the second Quebec Conference on September 15, 1944[13];

3) the public and secret clauses of the Yalta Agreements, Chapter V of the communiqué on the results of the Yalta conference, published on February 12, 1945, includes a declaration on liberated Europe, which invokes the Atlantic Charter, even though Chapter VI of the communiqué promises large territorial accessions to Poland in the north and west. Chapter III of the unpublished full protocol of the conference includes the approved text of Article 12a concerning the conditions for Germany's surrender:

"The United Kingdom, the United States of America and the Union of Soviet Socialist Republics shall possess supreme authority with respect to Germany. In the exercise of such authority they will take such steps, including

---

to prevent aggression and to establish a system of world security. *Documents, op. cit.*, vol. VI, p. 210. These statements, which have the character of authentic interpretation, refute the thesis propounded by some West German authors (e.g. H. K r a u s, *Die Oder-Neisse Linie. Eine völkerrechtliche Studie*, Köln-Braunsfeld 1954, pp. 27—31) that the Atlantic Charter was valid also with regard to Germany.

[11] *United Nations Documents, op. cit.*, p. 11.

[12] *Foreign Relations of the United States. Diplomatic Papers. The Conferences at Cairo and Teheran 1943*, Washington 1961, pp. 600 and 602 (abbr.: *Conferences at Cairo and Teheran*).

[13] H. M o r g e n t h a u Jr., *Germany is our Problem*, New York—London 1945.

the complete disarmament, demilitarisation and dismemberment of Germany as they deem requisite for future peace and security"[14].

These facts show that the Allies intended to apply the principles of the Atlantic Charter in accordance with the fundamental aims of the coalition, the safeguarding of peace and international security. To implement these aims a number of steps had to be taken. First of all it was necessary:

1) to liquidate the political effects of the Fascist aggression;

2) to build a new political pattern in Europe and the world that would ensure permanence and take into account the changed alignment of forces resulting from the war;

3) to create an effective system of collective security that would eliminate aggression. A substantial territorial curtailment of Germany, and even her dismemberment were envisaged as a means of implementing these aims.

2. THE ROLE OF THE GREAT POWERS

It is understandable that these broad aims of the anti-Fascist coalition required a number of preparatory steps. If these aims were to be realized, they had to be supported by the Great Powers which had at their disposal an adequate political and military potential.

The Second World War clearly revealed the role of the Great Powers in the shaping of international relations.

The problem is not new. In the theoretical aspect, the problem of equality of States as subjects of international law has existed from the beginning of the history of international relations. Realism led theoreticians to put the problem in the form of the following di-

---

[14] *Foreign Relations of the United States. Diplomatic Papers. The Conferences at Malta and Yalta 1945*, Washington 1955, p. 978. (abbr.: *Conferences at Malta and Yalta*). The protocol was not published until 1947. The conditions of Germany's surrender were finally not presented. Also the far-reaching plans for the dismemberment of Germany into a number of States were abandoned at the decisive moment in 1945. See Ph. Mosely, "Dismemberment of Germany. The Allied Negotiations from Yalta to Potsdam", *Foreign Affairs*, April 1950.

lemma: equality of rights for all States, or equality of all States before law. In the majority of Polish studies devoted to this problem the opinion has prevailed that international law has given effect only to the principle of equality of States before law[15]. In view of the difference in political and economic potential, and consequently in influence on the development of international relations, the leading role of the Great Powers in international life is obvious. The Great Powers have as a rule assumed the role of organizers of the patterns of international relations following wars and political upheavals. Such was the case after the Napoleonic era and after the First World War. But it was only in the Covenant of the League of Nations that this political, privileged role of the Great Powers found its legal expression (permanent membership in the Council of the League, Article 4)[16].

The leading position of the Great Powers became particularly clearly apparent in the course of the Second World War. There were many reasons for this, above all the actual strength of these Powers, which was the only guarantee of the defeat of the aggressors[17]. Only the Great Powers could ensure lasting peace and international security to the world after the Second World War[18]. These aims were given prominence in the Four Powers' Declaration on General Security, signed in Moscow on October 30, 1943 by the U.S.S.R., the United States, Great Britain and China[19].

---

[15] R. Bierzanek in his study on the status of the Great Powers in International Law, "Stanowisko wielkich mocarstw w prawie międzynarodowym", *Państwo i Prawo* 1946, No. 5/6; M. Lachs in the article on unanimity of the Great Powers, "Zagadnienie jednomyślności wielkich mocarstw" (Aspekty prawne), *Myśl Współczesna* 1947, No. 12; K. Wolfke. *Great and Small Powers in International Law from 1814 to 1920 (From the Prehistory of the United Nations*), Wrocław 1961.

[16] Oppenheim-Lauterpacht, *op. cit.*, 8th ed., vol. I (1955), p. 276.

[17] R. Bierzanek, *op. cit.*, p. 66, writes that during World War II "out of more than 20 sovereign capitals of the European continent only six succeeded in preserving independence against German invasion".

[18] V. N. Durdienievsky — S. B. Krylov, *Miezhdunarodnoye Pravo*, Moskva 1947.

[19] Henceforward referred to as the Moscow Declaration. Text in *United Nations Documents, op. cit.*, p. 13. The legal character of this document as an international agreement is analysed by J. Makowski, "Charakter prawny umów . . .", *op. cit.*, p. 14.

The Moscow Declaration strongly emphasizes peace and international security as being the aims of the countries fighting against Fascism. It proclaims the establishment of "a general international organization. . . for the maintenance of international peace and security" (point 4). A fundamental feature of the Moscow Declaration is the emphasis placed on the role of the Great Powers at the head of the coalition, which "conscious of *their responsibility* to secure the liberation of themselves and the peoples allied to them from the menace of aggression" (preamble) "will take *all measures* deemed *by them* to be necessary to provide against any violation of the terms imposed on the enemy" (point 3, my italics — B. W.), and pending the establishment of a system of general security will "consult with each other, and, *as occasion requires*, with other members of the United Nations, with a view to joint action *on behalf* of the community of Nations" (point 5, my italics — B. W.). The Moscow Declaration also speaks of "unconditional surrender" by the Axis countries as a pre-requisite of the termination of war.

Interpretation of the Moscow Declaration as regards the problem of general security leads to the following conclusions:

1) As regards the post-war plans, the safeguarding of peace and international security has become the fundamental purpose of the coalition; in this connection the Declaration envisages the use of "all measures" to ensure against violation of the terms imposed on the enemy.

2) The Great Powers have definitely put themselves at the head of the coalition, justifying their leading position on the ground of their responsibility for their own liberation and that of other nations. In this connection, they reserved to themselves the right of final decision on all solutions concerning the post-war pattern of international affairs, and also the right to take appropriate action "on behalf of the community of Nations". Co-operation by lesser States was made dependent upon their own considerations (". . .measures deemed *by them* necessary", ". . .they will consult. . . *as occasion requires*")[20].

---

[20] J. Makowski, "Charakter prawny umów . . .", *op. cit.*, p. 13, sees the Moscow Declaration as a proclamation by the World Directorate of

The Moscow Declaration was thus a legal expression of the leading role of the Great Powers within the anti-Fascist coalition. It augured further legal differentiation of the status of the Great Powers in the United Nations Organization to be set up later. If we analyse the Moscow Declaration from this point of view, it was of great importance for the determination of the future Polish-German frontier that the problem was discussed at the Moscow Conference in October 1943 and that even agreement was reached as regards taking East Prussia away from Germany[21].

The Moscow Declaration comprises general decisions in the nature of a programme. In the light of current events the general nature of the formulations was completely comprehensible. However, in the decisions included in the Declaration, the programme of aims and means of the anti-Fascist coalition begins to take shape and it is therefore worth while to confront it with the Atlantic Charter. The Moscow Declaration formulated the principles by which the Great Powers were guided when making decisions at the Teheran, Yalta and Potsdam conferences, and when establishing the United Nations. At the same time, it emphasized the indispensable condition for achieving the aims of the coalition — namely co-operation by the Great Powers chiefly responsible for the restoration and preservation of peace.

Hence, the Declaration of December 1, 1943, published after the Teheran Conference, reads in part:

"And as to peace we are sure that our concord will make it an enduring peace. We recognize fully the supreme responsibility resting upon us and all the United Nations to make a peace which will command the good-will of the overwhelming masses of the peoples of the world and banish the scourge and terror of war many generations"[22].

In Section V of the Yalta Agreement (Declaration on Liberated Europe), we find the following decisions:

the Great Powers, which in this way gave expression to their leading role in the international community.
[21] Cordell Hull, *The Memoirs*, London 1948, vol. II, p. 1287.
[22] Text of the *Conferences at Cairo and Teheran*, p. 641.

"By this Declaration we reaffirm... our determination to build in co-operation with other peace-loving nations a world under law, dedicated to peace, security, freedom and the general well-being of all mankind"[23].

And in Section IX of the Agreement (Unity for Peace as for War) we find the following passage:

"Our meeting here in the Crimea has reaffirmed our common determination to maintain and strengthen in the peace to come that unity of purpose and of action which has made victory possible and certain for the United Nations in this war. We believe that this is a sacred obligation which our Governments owe to our peoples and to all the peoples of the world.
"Only with continuing and growing co-operation and understanding among our three countries and among all the peace-loving nations, can the highest aspiration of humanity be realized—a secure and lasting peace which will, in the words of the Atlantic Charter «Afford assurance that all the men in all the lands may live out their lives in freedom from fear and want».
"Victory in this war and establishment of the proposed international organization will provide the greatest opportunity in all history to create in the years to come the essential conditions of such a peace"[24].

The anti-Fascits coalition implemented its main aims by establishing the United Nations and creating a new political pattern in Europe. The new European political pattern comprised such changes in territorial division, population and political systems as would eliminate in future the threat of a new aggression on the part of any State, and would thereby create the prerequisites for an effective functioning of the United Nations, while it was the task of the United Nations to guard the stability of this pattern, and especially, to prevent any revival of aggressive tendencies as well as to ensure a peaceful and legal development of international relations. In order to leave no room for confusion, the Charter of the United Nations in Article 107 defines the relationship between the Charter provisions and the measures taken with a view to establishing the new political pattern:

---

[23] Text of *United Nations Documents*, p. 145.
[24] *Ibid.*, pp. 147—148.

"Nothing in the present Charter shall invalidate or preclude action in relation to any state which during the Second World War has been an enemy of any signatory to the present Charter, taken or authorized as a result of that war by the Governments having responsibility for such action "[25].

In this way the Charter of the United Nations, the fundamental document of contemporary International Law, approved all measures taken by the Great Powers in relation to the Axis States, including Germany. The terminology of Article 107 of the Charter is noteworthy. This Article refers to States *"having responsibility* for... action in relation to any state which... has been an enemy of any signatory to the present Charter". The States "having responsibility" are understood to be first and foremost the Great Powers leading the victorious coalition. The term "Governments having responsibility" emphasizes the role of the Great Powers in the victorious conclusion of war, as well as their responsibility for ensuring peace and security after the war[26].

The particular responsibility of the Great Powers is also emphasized in Article 106 of the Charter which until the Security Council is given powers envisaged to in Article 43 to carry out in accordance with Article 42 of the Charter an action for the purpose of maintaining peace and security, makes it incumbent upon the Five Great Powers to consult with one another "and as occasion requires with other Members of the United Nations with a view to such joint action on behalf of the Organization as may be necessary for the purpose of maintaining international peace and security"[27].

Article 106 of the Charter invokes the Moscow Declaration of 1943. The responsibility of the Great Powers justifies their special privileges in the United Nations.

---

[25] *Ibid.*, p. 174.

[26] See the interpretation of Article 107 of the Charter of the United Nations by L. Goodrich and E. Hambro, *Charter of the United Nations*, London 1949, p. 533 et seq. At the conference in San Francisco the delegate of Great Britain extended the term "Governments having responsibility" to governments of *all* victorious Allies.

[27] *United Nations Documents*, p. 174. Article 106 intended to be temporary is still binding, since agreements envisaged in Article 43 of the Charter have not yet been concluded.

The leading role of the Great Powers — the Soviet Union, the United States, Great Britain, France and China — which are principally responsible for international peace and security, finds its legal expressions not only in the U.N. system of security. As during the war, so also in the post-war period the Great Powers take part in solving all crucial international problems connected with the maintenance of peace and international security, irrespective of the degree to which they themselves are directly involved in the issue. A number of most important controversial international post-war problems may be quoted, the solution of which was wholly dependent upon agreement between the Great Powers: liquidation of the effects of the Second World War (the conclusion of peace treaties with a number of Axis States in 1946, the restitution of the State of Austria), world disarmament, peaceful settlement of conflicts which have arisen in the post-war period owing to national-liberation struggles and revolutionary movements (conflicts in Palestine, Korea, Indochina and the Carribean Sea)[28], the problem of a peace treaty with Germany etc. Some of these problems have already been solved — partly in the United Nations, and partly outside that Organization — others are still the subject of negotations between the Great Powers.

The practice to date warrants the conclusion that on the basis of the factual distribution of power the Great Powers at the end of World War II assumed responsibility for the restoration and preservation of peace and international security, and have borne this

---

[28] On the role of the Great Powers in solving the Indochina and other conflicts see: M. Lachs, *Układy indochińskie*, Warszawa 1955, p. 67 et seq. The Final Declaration of the Geneva 1954 Conference on Indochina (*Zbiór Dokumentów* 1954, a Collection of documents published by the Polish Institute of International Affairs No. 7/8, p. 1709) envisages reciprocal consultation of the parties if this should prove necessary in the discharge of obligations implied by the agreements. M. Lachs, *op. cit.*, p. 186, rightly construes this provision as an obligation resting especially on the Great Powers to see that the agreements are not violated. This was also what happened in practice. In connection with the restoration of the Austrian State too, the Great Powers made it obligatory for Austria to declare perpetual neutrality. See memorandum on the results of negotiations between the U.S.S.R. and Austria, April 15, 1955. *Zbiór dokumentów* 1955, No. 5, p. 991, and the decision on the neutrality of Austria of October 26, 1955, *Zbiór Dokumentów* 1955, No. 10, p. 2114.

responsibility also in the post-war period. They have become, so to speak, the executors of the aims of the anti-Fascist coalition as they were proclaimed during the Second World War.

The legal character of the Great Powers' decisions has been the subject of scientific comments. For example, territorial decisions concerning third States, taken by groups of States and the Great Powers have been defined as quasi-judicial[29] or arbitral decisions[30]. Generalizing international practice, the English doctrine distinguishes a separate category of treaty decisions, called "international settlements" defining them as

"an arrangement made by treaty between the leading powers, intended to form part of the International order of things, either defining the status or territory of particular states, or regulating the use of International waterways, or making other dispositions of general importance, and incidentally imposing certain obligations or restrictions on International conduct"[31].

The British scholar H. Lauterpacht also distinguishes international settlements

"whose essence is to make possible the creation of legal rights with an effect transcending the scope of the original parties to the treaty. International settlements are incipient international legislation"[32].

Sir Arnold Mc Nair in a separate opinion concerning the international status of south-west Africa stated:

"From time to time it happens that a group of Great Powers, or a large number of States both great and small, assume power to create by a multila-

[29] H. Lauterpacht, *Private Law Sources and Analogies of International Law*, London 1927, p. 108, footnote 3. The author speaks of the decision of the Concert of European Powers in 1913 awarding Skutari to Albania, and the decision of the Council of the League of Nations concerning the award of Memel to Lithuania and Mosul to Irak.

[30] J. Makowski, *Podręcznik prawa międzynarodowego*, Warszawa 1948, (abbr.: *Podręcznik*) p. 105 is inclined to assign to the Great Powers the powers of arbiter entitled to adjudicate a territory to a State; he emphasizes however that this requires an explicit or implied consent of the State losing that territory.

[31] R. F. Roxburgh, *International Conventions and Third States*, London 1917, p. 81. Cf. C. W. Jenks, *The Common Law of Mankind*, London 1958, pp. 96—97, who quotes a number of examples.

[32] Lauterpacht, *The Development of International Law by the International Court*, London 1958 (abbr.: Lauterpacht, *The Development*), p. 309.

teral treaty some new international regime or status, which soon acquires a degree of acceptance and durability extending beyond the limits of the actual contracting parties and giving it an objective existence"[33].

Although the theory of international law, recognizing that there can be agreements in favour of Third States, is reluctant to admit the possibility of agreements to the disadvantage of Third States[34], there have been numerous cases of decisions taken by groups of countries (especially Great Powers) introducing new territorial divisions without consulting Third States or consulting them only formally. Political evaluation of these decisions depends on circumstances. As regards the Second World War, the decisions taken by the Great Powers on behalf of the United Nations have not as a rule been questioned.

---

[33] *I. C. J. Reports* 1950, p. 153. Lauterpacht, *The Development, op. cit.*, p. 232, draws attention to the fact that in the Advisory Opinion on the Interpretation of the Treaty of Lausanne (*Publication de la Cour Permanent de Justice Jnternationale,* abbr.: *C. P. J. I.* Ser. B, No. 12, 1925) the Court in the Hague pronounced the decision of the Council of the League of Nations to have the character of judicial legislation, i.e. a final decision not liable to changes by one of the parties.

[34] J. G. Barsegov, *Tierritoriya v miezhdunarodnom pravie. Yuridichieskaya priroda tierritorialnego vierkhovienstva i pravoviye osnovanya rasporiazhenya tierritoriey,* Moskva 1958, p. 103 (with regard to territorial changes).

CHAPTER II

TERRITORIAL CHANGES AFTER THE SECOND WORLD WAR

1. THE PRINCIPLE OF SELF-DETERMINATION AND THE LEGALITY OF FRONTIER CHANGES

The history of international relations has recorded many changes in State frontiers. The overwhelming majority of these changes have been accomplished by way of war. Territorial expansion of States has been a normal phenomenon in all previous historical formations; it was regarded as quite normal by traditional international law which recognized the right of States to territorial acquisition through war. This has been stated explicitly by Vattel:

"By the voluntary Law of Nations, every regular war is accounted as regards its effects as just on both sides (par. 190), and no one has the right to judge a Nation as to the unfairness of its claims or as to the measures it deems necessary for its safety (Introd., par. 21). Every acquisition made in a regular war is, therefore, according to the *voluntary* Law of Nations, valid, independently of the justice of the cause and of the motives the victor may have in claiming the right to hold what he has taken. Accordingly, conquest has been regularly looked upon by Nations as conferring lawful title, and such title has scarcely ever been questioned, except when originating in a war not only unjust, but destitute even of a semblance of justice"[1].

Vattel also maintained that seizure of enemy property was "an equivalent for what is due from the enemy, for the expenses and

---

[1] E. de Vattel, *The Law of Nations or the Principles of Natural Law*, Washington 1916, vol. III, Book III, Chapter XIII, § 195, p. 307.

losses he has occasioned, and even, when there is cause for punishing him, as a commutation for the punishment deserved"[2].

The only restriction is the common sense of the victor.

"A just conqueror, scorning the suggestions of ambition and avarice, will form a fair estimate of what is due to him; that is, of the value of the object in dispute, if it can not be recovered in kind, and of the losses suffered and the expenses incurred in the war, and he will retain only so much of the enemy's property as is sufficient to form an equivalent. But if he is dealing with a perfidious, restless, and dangerous enemy, he will take from him, by way of punishment, certain of his towns and provinces, and will hold them as a barrier to protect his own territory"[3].

Thus classical writers on international law approved of territorial changes dictated by victors and demanded only that there should be at least "a semblance" of a just war. In practice it was not of course difficult to make a war appear justified. Later on, even this weak condition of legality was given up in positivist conceptions and in modern times normativists have ceased to concern themselves with the criteria of legality in frontier changes, leaving politicians and historians to worry about that. They themselves have dealt only with legal acts introducing changes in territorial sovereignty.

In contemporary legal opinions, the problem of justifying territorial acquisition has again come to the fore. This is undoubtedly due to the revival of ideological and political conflicts in the contemporary world. The conflicting attitudes in evaluating changes in the alignment of forces in the world — including changes in the territorial pattern — have revived the significance of such problems as a just or unjust war, justness or unjustness of territorial changes. The territorial pattern established by peace treaties was destroyed by the Second World War. The new post-war settlement of territorial problems has introduced a number of frontier changes, and

---

[2] *Ibid.*, § 193, p. 307.
[3] *Ibid.*, § 194, p. 307. Cf. the formulation by Grotius: "Furthermore, if any one should leave to a conquered people the right to form a state, he might still take for himself certain things which had belonged to the state. It rests with him to decide what he wishes the measure of his beneficence to be". (*De jure belli ac pacis libri tres*, Oxford 1925, Chapter VIII, § 4, Point 3, p. 700).

it is not surprising, therefore, that disputes have arisen as regards the justness or unjustness of the territorial solutions applied, especially after the division of the world into two blocs. The dispute has moved into the field of the theory of international law in the form of discussion as to whether there are any criteria of legality of territorial changes in international law, and if so what they are.

Attempts have been made to discovering the existence of some supreme principle to which all territorial changes might be subordinated. *The right of nations to self-determination* is often regarded as such a principle. These opinions are based on the assumption that territorial changes are legal only if they are in accordance with the right of self-determination.

I cannot, within the framework of the present work, outline the genesis of the right of self-determination; it must be stated, however, that in contemporary international law the problem of the right to self-determination is a complex phenomenon; the conception comprises several different elements which cannot be examined in an identical way.

In view of its genesis and content the principle of self-determination is of a *law-making* character, but if it is to become a positive norm of law (i.e. a norm providing a basis for concrete obligations and rights) it must be transformed into a definite institution of law.

In all cases where known to history, in which the principle of self-determination has been applied, the States — though invoking this principle — have always implemented it in the form of a definite institution which comprised concrete norms defining precisely the rights and duties of the parties concerned or of the addressees (e.g. plebiscites). Is there any conventional or customary duty to apply a particular form of this principle in particulars circumstances? The reply is negative. The States themselves decide which form of the principle of self-determination to apply in the given circumstances and whether to apply the principle at all. Such solution seems to be the only just one in contemporary international law, for the norms of international law come into being as an expression of the political needs and aims of States: the justification of these needs or aims will always be subjective, while the result (i.e.

a definite norm) will be a compromise between the needs and aims on the one hand, and the possibility of their being implemented on the other.

Attempts have been made by writers on international law to define the components of the right of self-determination. Sarah Wambaugh is of the opinion that the right of self-determination is "a factor in changes of sovereignty through separation, cession and annexation"[4]. She traces the beginning of the principle of national self-determination to the ideas of the French Revolution which were the first to proclaim the citizens' right to choose their rulers. She is of the opinion that "the doctrine of national self-determination is based on and inseparable from that of popular sovereignty"[5]. She says that:

"Title (to a territory — B. W.) rests for its final sanction on public opinion. History would seem to prove that, in questions of territorial sovereignty, public opinion bases its judgment on an unexpressed major premise, namely that no title acquired either through treaty, conquest or occupation, or based on economic, racial or historical arguments, or arguments of military necessity, is valid, no matter how many centuries it has run, unless it has behind it the consent of the majority of the inhabitants of the territory"[6].

Wambaugh is of the opinion that the application of the right of self-determination will lay foundations for stabilising of the international community, and consequently she recommends that plebiscites should be resorted to in any territorial changes.

In the contemporary doctrine of international law the West German writer Decker suggests that the conception of the right to national self-determination should comprise the following elements: 1) the right to national existence comprising the right to inhabit one's native land and to nationality (*Recht auf die Heimat und Nationalität*), the right to autonomy and the right to self-government; 2) the right to national independence comprising the right to secession and to the formation of a separate State, the right to

---

[4] S. Wambaugh, *A Monograph on Plebiscites*, New York 1920, p. 1.
[5] *Ibid.*, p. 2.
[6] *Ibid.*, p. 31.

national unity and to unification, as well as political, cultural, social and economic self-determination, and 3) equality of nations[7].

The role of the principle of self-determination in international law has been described as follows by Decker:

"The principle of national self-determination has become a fundamental principle (*Grundprinzip*) of international order and has been recognized as such; however, if it is to become a doctrine of international law it requires detailed elaboration"[8].

The formulation is not precise (what does a „fundamental principle of international order" mean?) and the author's attempt to define the conception of self-determination is tautological. Nevertheless, it is noteworthy that the author is ready to regard the right of self-determination as at least a norm o international law *in fieri*. Another West German theoretician, H. Kraus, enumerates five cases in which, in his opinion, the expressions of the people's will is demanded by *law*: 1) secession, 2) annexation, 3) cession, 4) existence of national minorities, and 5) the gaining of independence by colonies. According to Kraus, the principle of self-determination has the following common characteristics in all these cases: 1) it refers to all States, 2) it is not a subjective right — in the legal sense of the term of the population concerned, 3) the will of the people should be understood in a collective sense and not in the sense of personal rights of individuals, 4) it requires the expression of the will of the directly interested population, and not the whole population of the mother country or the population of the successor-State. Kraus regards plebiscite as the best, though not the only, way of ascertaining the will of the population, provided that a proper procedure is observed in the carrying out of the plebiscite[9].

[7] G. Decker, *Das Selbstbestimmungsrecht der Nationen*, Göttingen 1955, pp. 228—233. Decker's conception is an obvious attempt to provide theoretical justification for the postulates of the policy pursued by the German Federal Republic. The problem of the *Recht auf die Heimat* will be discussed on a later page.

[8] Decker, *op. cit.*, p. 342.

[9] H. Kraus, "Das Selbstbestimmungsrecht der Völker" (treatise included in the collective study: *Das östliche Deutschland. Ein Handbuch*, Würzburg 1959), pp. 63—67.

Another West German theoretician, R. Laun, discusses the right of self-determination as a conflict between people and States; he regards the demand for self-determination as a protest against foreign rule, expressed by a population, or a part of such population, subjugated by an alien State or by alien people[10]. As regards the application of the right of self-determination in territorial settlements, Laun recommends the adoption of the proposals submitted by the German Government at a conference convened by the League of Nations in Bern, in March 1919. These proposals referred to the peace conditions formulated by the Allies, and as regards to territorial decisions called for the adoption of two principles: 1) all controversial territorial problems should be settled by democratic plebiscites carried out separately in each commune in order to avoid a tendentious delimitation of plebiscite areas; 2) the frontier fixed on the basis of the results of these plebiscites should run in such a way as to leave an equal number of national minorities on either side[11]. Laun regrets that these proposals were not applied in the territorial decisions after the First World War and regards this as the source of various future conflicts. He admits that the right of nations to self--determination is not yet a conception adopted by general norms of international law. Plebiscites and protection of national minorities are only a subject of various treaties referring to particular regions and particular problems[12].

Another West German writer, E. Menzel, is of the opinion that in accordance with the recent development of international law "the application of the right of self-determination through plebiscite and option is generally appreciated as a solution most in harmony with democratic thought". He says, however, that in practice the procedure of plebiscite was not used after the Second World War, except on the territory ceded to France. This, according to him, resulted from the difference in the conceptions of the right of self-determina-

---

[10] R. Laun. "Le droit des peuples à disposer d'eux-mêmes", *Annuaire de l'Association des Auditeurs et Anciens Auditeurs de l'Académie de Droit International de la Haye* 1958 (No. 28), p. 91.

[11] *Ibid.*, p. 105.

[12] *Ibid.*, p. 102.

tion, which is presented in the Atlantic Charter and the Charter
of the United Nations (Article 1 § 2) rather as a right to choose the
form of government than as a right of ethnic groups to political
self-determination[13]. In this connection, Menzel concludes:

> "Even though there is no stronger justification for territorial changes than the
> implementation of the right to self-determination, it is certain that this
> principle will not be a binding legal norm unless it is contained in a proper
> contractual obligation"[14].

But there are also West German writers who deny that the principle of self-determination is a norm of positive law. Bieberstein,
for example, when dealing with only one aspect of this principle —
the right to choose a form of government — calls it a "supra-positive
norm of law" (*überpositive Rechtsnorm*)[15], thus emphasizing that its
character is more ideological than legal. A. H. Jellinek object to the
definition of plebiscite as a binding norm of international law and
calls it only a postulate of international law[16]. He also denies that
the statements made by the Allies during the Second World War
(the Atlantic Charter) and after the war (President Truman's statement of October 27, 1945)[17] give any ground for stating that there

---

[13] E. Menzel, "Gebietserwerb" (Strupp-Schlochauer, *Wörterbuch
des Völkerrechts*, vol. I) points out that from the American point of view there
is no advantage in holding plebiscites in territories inhabited by mixed populations, since the tendency prevailing in America is rapidly to assimilate
the separate national groups.

[14] Menzel, *op. cit.*, p. 622.

[15] W. F. Marschall von Bieberstein, *Zum Problem der völkerrechtlichen Anerkennung der beiden deutschen Regierungen*, Berlin 1959, p. 46, footnote 121.

[16] H. Jellinek, *Der automatische Erwerb und Verlust der Staatsangehörigkeit durch völkerrechtliche Vorgänge*, Berlin 1951, p. 48. The author
opposes the thesis that the territorial changes effected after the Second
World War are in view of the absence of a freely expressed will on
the part of the population concerned illegal; he says that this thesis would
imply that a wronged State has the right to *rei vindicatio*; since there is no
effective judicial system such an attitude, in the event of opposition by the
other party, would lead to the justification of war as a means of pushing
one's claims.

[17] In the third point of his statement President Truman declared that
the United States would not agree to territorial changes in any allied part
of the world if they were not in accord with a freely expressed will of the
population interested. Quoted after H. Jellinek, *op. cit.*, p. 44.

is a legal obligation to carry out a plebiscite in the event of territorial changes[18]. Bindschedler says quite clearly:

"it is not a plebiscite of the interested population which is a condition making annexation possible, even though in practice it has been applied since the middle of the nineteenth century"[19].

The Soviet theory of international law favours plebiscites its reasons being, however, completely different ideologically from the motives of certain West German writers. The most detailed explanation has been given by Barsegov. If one assumes that the nation is absolutely free to determine its existence then it also has the right to decide on the frontiers of its State:

"Establishment of frontiers in defiance of generally accepted principles of international law and in violation of the principle of self-determination is an act in open contradiction to law and as such is devoid of any legal justification"[20].

Barsegov is of the opinion that plebiscites are an organized form for a genuine and direct expression of the will of the population.

"The legal significance of the plebiscite consists in a free expression of the will of the nation which in a free vote takes its own decision on the inhabitants, its fate and territory. A free expression of will is an absolute and indispensable condition of the plebiscite"[21].

While stressing the right to self-determination as a fundamental principle in changes of State frontiers, Barsegov realizes that concrete historical circumstances must be taken into consideration:

"Analysis of the practice in international law confirms the rule formulated and accepted in the Socialist doctrine of international law; from the point

---

[18] This does not mean that the author concerned agrees to the loss by Germany of her eastern territories. See Jellinek, *op. cit.*, p. 97.

[19] R. Bindschedler, "Annexion" (Strupp-Schlochauer, vol. I, p. 69).

[20] Barsegov, *op. cit.*, p. 102.

[21] *Ibid.*, p. 123.

of view of the existing norms of international law, State frontiers should be
established in accordance with the sovereign will of the nation, due consideration being paid to the national composition, economic community and
historical past of the territory subject to delimitation; interests of mutual
security should be observed as far as possible. Such is the general norm of
law. At the same time two interdependent processes must be distinguished:
1) the formulation of a general norm of international law, regulating territorial changes, and 2) the application of this general norm in definite territories and conditions. *The practical application of the right of nations to self-
determination must be in full accord with the circumstances, needs and historical
peculiarities of both States*" (my italics — B. W.)[22].

Barsegov, like other Soviet writers[23], points out that in any change
of State frontiers all circumstances and concrete conditions must
be taken into consideration. The principle of self-determination is
only a general norm, and plebiscite one of the possible forms of its
application. This attitude shows that the Soviet doctrine of international
law regards plebiscite as a desirable though not always indispensable
condition for the legality of frontier changes. Its suitability depends
on concrete circumstances.

Similar is the opinion of French jurists. While the traditional
doctrine regarded plebiscite as "a basic instrument of the new order"
established by the Paris conference of 1919[24], the contemporary French
doctrine notices the inconsistency of States as regards the application of plebiscite in case of territorial changes, and says that there
is no written norm making plebiscite obligatory[25]. Rousseau is of
the opinion that the requirement to carry out a plebiscite is not
a binding norm in international law, but an additional clause —
not fundamental — of peace treaties[26].

---

[22] *Ibid.*, p. 154—155.
[23] See F. I. Kozhevnikov (editor), *Miezhdunarodnoye pravo*, Moskva
1957, pp. 183—184, and Durdienievsky-Krylov, p. 248 who also stress
the necessity of observing the principle of self-determination in the event of
frontier changes, but of course "with due consideration to the vital defence
interests of the given country". As regards plebiscite, the authors state
(p. 240): "Plebiscite is not a remedy for all diseases but in some cases it can
play a positive role".
[24] P. de Lapradelle, *La frontière*, Paris 1928, p. 103.
[25] M. Sibert, *Traité de droit international public*, vol. I, Paris 1951,
pp. 876—877.
[26] Ch. Rousseau, *Droit international public*, Paris 1953, p. 269.

Contemporary English writers unequivocally negate the obligatory character of plebiscite in territorial changes[27]. The same attitude has been adopted by the American doctrine. Hyde doubts whether the principle of self-determination can safeguard every State against the sacrifice of its territory — if for instance it was itself the transgressor — or whether the opposition of the occupants of a particular area can thwart a valid transfer: in other words he doubts whether a plebiscite can be regarded as a condition precedent to a valid operation[28]. Fenwick also states that plebiscite is not a rule of customary international law[29], and Gould calls plebiscite "so much the product of political expediency that it hardly represents either legal or moral principle"[30].

Other jurists confirm the absence of any obligation to hold a plebiscite when State frontiers are changed[31]. Polish writers, too, do not regard plebiscite as a necessary condition of legality of frontier changes[32].

The above survey of the doctrine of international law makes it possible to formulate the following conclusions:

1) the principle of self-determination, which as regards territo-

---

[27] Mervyn Jones, *International Law and Politics. The Transactions of the Grotius Society* 1955, p. 18, emphasizes that "as no criterion exists to decide where this principle begins or ends, it is manifestly too imprecise to have the character of a legal right". Oppenheim-Lauterpacht, 8th ed., vol. I, pp. 551—552, writes: "It is doubtful whether the Law of Nations will ever make it a condition of every cession that it must be ratified by a plebiscite", while McNair in *Legal Effects of War*, 3rd ed., Cambridge 1948, p. 389, says "the treaty may stipulate for the cession of particular pieces of territory to depend upon the result of a plebiscite" but it is not a general rule.

[28] Ch. Ch. Hyde, *International Law Chiefly as Interpreted and Applied by the U.S.*, 2nd ed., Boston 1945, vol. I, p. 378.

[29] Ch. G. Fenwick, *International Law*, 3rd ed., New York 1948, p. 363.

[30] W. L. Gould, *An Introduction to International Law*, New York 1957, p. 357.

[31] e.g. A. Verdross, *Völkerrecht*, Wien 1955, p. 214.

[32] J. Makowski, Textbook, *op. cit.*, p. 116, regards plebiscite as a postulate of international morality. C. Berezowski in his book on territory, specialized institutions, international co-operation, colonial and dependent territories and war in the air, *Terytorium, instytucje wyspecjalizowane, współpraca międzynarodowa, obszary kolonialne i zależne, wojna powietrzna*, Warszawa 1957, p. 16, maintains only that there is a possibility of making the cession dependent on the will of the population.

rial changes has been identified with plebiscite (that is, a vote by the people as to whether they want to remain with the given State or be under the sovereignty of another State), has often been advanced in international law as a general criterion of legality of territorial acquisition;

2) some West German writers support the idea of plebiscite as a prerequisite of legality of frontier changes; their attitude is motivated by political considerations—namely the desire to prove the illegality of the changes in Germany's frontiers after the Second World War;

3) the idea of plebiscite in case of changes in State frontiers is supported by Soviet jurists; their attitude is motivated by ideological reasons completely different from the German motives. However, the Soviet doctrine recognizes that application of a plebiscite must depend on concrete circumstances. The Soviet doctrine does not make plebiscite a prerequisite of legality of territorial changes;

4) the doctrine of other States (especially the Anglo-American doctrine) adopts for various political reasons a sceptical attitude to the plebiscite as a condition of legality of territorial acquisition.

It must be stated in conclusion that the requirement of plebiscite as a criterion of legality of territorial changes has not been confirmed in the theory of international law. Nor has it been confirmed in international practice. After the First World War plebiscites were stipulated by peace treaties in a number of cases[33], but the results turned out to be unsatisfactory from the political point of view, leaving many cockpits of future international conflicts[34].

According to the American writer I. L. Claude, the territorial

[33] The most important plebiscites were held in Warmia, Upper Silesia, the Klagenfurt district and Schleswig. For a detailed study of plebiscites before the First World War see: S. Wambaugh, *A Monograph on Plebiscites*, New York 1920, and *Plebiscites since the World War*, New York 1933. See also C. R. M. F. Cruttwell, *A History of Peaceful Change in the Modern World*, London-NewYork-Toronto 1937, p. 147 et seq.

[34] E.,Wiskemann, *Germany's Eastern Neighbours. Problems Relating to the Oder-Neisse Line and the Czech Frontier Regions*, London-New York-Toronto 1956, on p. 211, appears: "The frontiers of inter-war Poland, had been drawn in the closest possible accordance with the principle of self-determination; the result, viewed practically, had been a little fantastic".

changes made after the Second World War were motivated by other factors:

"It was clear that economic and strategic factors would enter prominently into determination of postwar boundaries. Calculated concern for world stability and the economic and military interests of national states made hardheaded statesmen unwilling to contemplate the full application of the principle of national self-determination. Moreover, the moral sanctity of the principle was challenged; it was generally regarded as merely one principle among many which ought to be considered" [35].

The peace treaties concluded in Paris on February 10, 1947 between the Second World War Allies on the one hand, and Italy, Finland and Hungary on the other, provided not only for restitution of the territorial status existing as in 1938, and for invalidation of all changes forcibly effected after that date by the Fascist States, but also for more far-reaching changes, establishing a new territorial pattern in Europe. Thus, the peace treaty with Finland provided (Article 2) for the cession by Finland of the province of Petsamo to the Soviet Union. The peace treaty with Hungary (Article 1, point 4) introduced small rectifications of frontiers in favour of Czechoslovakia. Article 2 of the peace treaty with Italy provided for the cession of certain territories to France; Article 3 introduced territorial rectification in favour of Yugoslavia; Article 4 stipulated the establishment of the Free Territory of Trieste; Article 14 provided for the cession of certain Dodecanesian Islands to Greece[36]. In settling the Austro-Italian frontier, the pre-war frontier was confirmed, despite Austria's demand for the cession by Italy of South Tyrol, inhabited by a compact German national minority. Moreover, the Austrian memorandum requesting a plebiscite on this territory was rejected[37]. Finally, the 1951 peace treaty with Japan—which the Socialist countries did not sign—provided (Article 2) not only for the restitution of Korea as an independent State, but also for the relin-

---

[35] I. L. Claude, *National Minorities. An International Problem*, Cambridge Mass. 1955, p. 93.
[36] Texts of the peace treaties concluded in Paris on February 10, 1947 published in *American Journal of International Law* 1948, vol. 42. Supplement.
[37] I. L. Claude, *op. cit.*, p. 128.

quishment by Japan of her rights to Formosa (Taiwan), Pescadores, southern Sakhalin, the Kuril Islands, and for the surrender of rights based on League of Nations mandates concerning certain Pacific Islands[38]. In the Soviet-Japanese declaration of October 19, 1956, whereby the parties decided to end the state of war between the two countries, the Soviet Union agreed to restore to Japan the Habomai and Shikotan Islands occupied following Japan's unconditional surrender[39], the *de facto* transference to be effected after the signing of a peace treaty between the Soviet Union and Japan. Territorial changes introduced by the peace treaties after the Second World War were as a rule effected without plebiscites[40].

2. THE PRINCIPLE OF TERRITORIAL INTEGRITY AND THE TERRITORIAL CHANGES AFTER THE SECOND WORLD WAR

One of the fundamental principles of international law is the principle of territorial integrity i.e. territorial inviolability. Territorial integrity is a static conception denoting inviolability of the status of territorial possession. This conception is by its very content opposed to the dynamic trend, constantly reviving in the history of international relations, towards changes in the territorial *status quo* which is usually established for an indefinite period by solemn legal acts after the conclusion of wars.

Whereas formerly States concluded agreements determining the territorial *status quo* "for all time" without envisaging the possibility of any change, in more recent times, following the experience

---

[38] Text of the 1951 peace treaty with Japan published in *American Journal of International Law* 1952, vol. 46, Supplement.

[39] Text of the Soviet-Japanese declaration of October 19, 1956, published in *Trybuna Ludu*, October 21, 1956, No. 293

[40] The only exception was the plebiscite held on the strip of territory ceded by Italy to France by virtue of Article 2 of the peace treaty with Italy. The plebiscite was carried out in accordance with Article 27 of the French Constitution of 1946. However, it was not determining in nature (i.e. it did not decide to what country the territory should belong), but merely ratifying (i.e. confirming) and was held after the cession had taken place. See Rousseau, *op. cit.*, pp. 269—270.

of history, attempts have been made to take into consideration the constantly reviving trend towards territorial changes[41], subjecting it however to the control of legal norms. The Covenant of the League of Nations was an attempt to combine protection of territorial integrity with the possibility of territorial changes; Article 10 of the Covenant made it incumbent upon all members "to respect and preserve as against external aggression the territorial integrity and existing political independence of all Members of the League", while Article 19 envisaged that

"the Assembly may from time to time advise the reconsideration by Members of the League of treaties which have become inapplicable and the consideration of international conditions whose continuance might endanger the peace of the world".

The Covenant of the League of Nations was an attempt to combine two contradictory functions: to protect the territorial pattern established by the peace treaties which terminated the First World War and to place under legal control the envisaged trend towards a revision of such treaties. Though this was not clearly formulated, Article 19 referred mainly to the possibility of changes in the territorial pattern brought about by the First World War[42]. It created a very general and rather imprecise legal framework for the application of the clause *rebus sic stantibus* and for a peaceful modification of the existing territorial pattern. It is characteristic, however, that the States which raised reservations against the Covenant (Japan, Italy and especially Germany) did not make use of the possibility provided for by Article 19 and chose instead the road of unilateral action which led to the outbreak of World War II.

In contemporary international law the problem of territorial integrity has been referred to in Article 2 § 4 of the Charter of the United Nations, which among other things makes it incumbent

---

[41] A comprehensive survey of territorial changes from the beginning of modern times up to 1936 is presented in the book by C. R. M. F. Cruttwell, *A History of Peaceful Change in the Modern World*, London-New York-Toronto 1937.

[42] L. P. Bloomfield, *Evolution or Revolution. The U. N. and the Problem of Peaceful Territorial Changes*, Cambridge Mass. 1957, p. 54.

upon all members to refrain in their international relations from the threat or use of force against the territorial integrity of any State. This rule is wider than Article 10 of the Covenant, since it outlaws the use of threat against the territorial integrity of any State (not only against the members of the Organization as was the case with Article 10 of the Covenant). The enlargement of the duty was undoubtedly the result of historical experience (the "peaceful" *Anschluss* of Austria and the seizure of Czechoslovakia by the Third Reich). Article 19 of the Covenant of the League of Nations has its counterpart in Article 14 of the Charter, which says that if a case has not been settled by the Security Council[43],

"the General Assembly may recommend measures for the peaceful adjustment of any situation, regardless of origin, which it deems likely to impair the general welfare or friendly relations among nations".

However Article 14 of the Charter, unlike Article 19 of the Covenant, has no clause concerning the possibility of revision of treaties, although the term "regardless of origin" (the origin of the situation) may be interpreted in various ways[44].

The Socialist doctrine has raised territorial integrity to the rank of a fundamental principle of contemporary international law[45].

The principle of integrity — i.e. of territorial inviolability — confronts us with a problem of utmost importance: *What* territorial status is subject to its protection. Historical experience shows that in the international community there are conflicting interests and a steady trend towards changing the territorial pattern existing at any given moment. The two world wars brought about fundamental changes in the territorial pattern. The principle of territorial

---

[43] "Subject to the provisions of Article 12. . ."

[44] L. P. Bloomfield, *op. cit.*, pp. 106—107. The author quotes a commentary by Senator Vanderberg that the omission of the clause concerning revision of treaties was deliberated so as not to encourage revision of the peace treaties terminating the Second World War. However, according to the American interpretation, the phrase "regardless of origin" comprises the possibility of revision of treaties.

[45] Kozhevnikov, *Miezhdunarodnoye pravo*, p. 13, Durdienievsky-Krylov, p. 22, Muszkat in his outline of public international law, *Zarys prawa międzynarodowego publicznego*, Warszawa 1955, vol. I, p. 16.

integrity proclaimed in Article 2 § 4 of the Charter of the United Nations protects a different territorial pattern from the one which was to have been protected by Article 10 of the Covenant. And even the contemporary territorial pattern is changing before our own eyes: new States are being established on former colonial territories, the range of the territorial sovereignty of the former colonial powers is shrinking. The question arises: If the principle of territorial integrity is not meant to petrify the territorial *status quo* what does it mean at present?

The reply is given in Article 2 § 4 of the Charter of the United Nations, which forbids all members of the United Nations *to use force or the threat of force* against the territorial integrity of other States.

Commentaries to the Charter of the United Nations stress that the protection of territorial integrity, as conceived in Article 2, paragraph 4 of the Charter, refers to the external relations of States. Goodrich and Hambro state cautiously that contrary to the provisions of Article 10 of the Covenant, the obligation of the members of the United Nations to respect the territorial integrity and political independence of other States is not accompanied by any obligation *to preserve* them[46]. Krylov goes further: he is of the opinion that Article 2, paragraph 4 of the Charter confirms the inadmissibility of aggression, without excluding voluntary changes of frontiers, a voluntary transference of bases on foreign territories and the granting of independence to some territories[47]. Ross says that the sense of Article 2, paragraph 4 of the Charter consists in the prohibition of an arbitrary use of force[48], and Ehrlich regards the pro-

---

[46] L. M. Goodrich—E. Hambro, *Charter of the United Nations*, *op. cit.*, p. 103. The authors add that there may be a case of a U. N. member sending his armed forces to the territory of another U. N. member for "protective" purposes with the declared intention of withdrawing them as soon as the threat to the weaker state has been removed. Hence, the rule on the duty to protect territorial integrity may be interpreted in two ways: as inviolability of territorial substance and as the right of a State to exercise exclusive jurisdiction within its own territory.

[47] S. B. Krylov, *Materialy k historii Organizatsi Obiedinionnykh Natsyi*, Moskva 1949, p. 108.

[48] A. Ross, *Constitution of the United Nations. Analysis of Structure and Functions*, New York 1950, pp. 128, 141.

vision of Article 2, paragraph 4 (including paragraph 3) as a more detailed formulation of the principles of the Briand-Kellogg pact[49]. In the contemporary Soviet doctrine Barsegov distinguishes the problem of a State's integrity from the problem of unchangeability of its frontiers:

> "In accordance with the norms of contemporary international law, the territory of any State is inviolable to external attack, and the validity of the title to territorial acquisition through *debellatio* comprising the use of arms is negated..."[50].

Barsegov also says:

> "Respect for the territorial integrity of States does not, by any means, signify the perpetuation and petrification of the political status and frontiers obtained by force and war. It is not infrequent that States attempt to protect such status, trying to subjugate territories which in the historical, ethnic, economic and geographical aspect strive for independence or are parts of other countries"[51].

Thus the Soviet doctrine also lays stress on the forcible inviolability of State frontiers, not negating however the possibility of territorial changes in principle, but only defining the limits of legality of such changes — i.e. their voluntary character.

Most of the commentators agree that Article 2, paragraph 4 of the Charter does not protect territorial immutability *as a rule* but forbids the carrying out of territorial changes by force or the threat of the use of force. Nothing however impedes peaceful territorial changes. And this gives the possibility of reconciling Article 2, paragraph 4 with Article 14 of the Charter. In other words, protection of the territorial integrity of States in the present international law does not mean *a prohibition of all territorial changes but denies the possibility of changes beeing effected by force.*

As regards the problem of recognition of territorial acquisition, this means that territorial accessions obtained by force are illegal.

---

[49] L. Ehrlich, *Karta Narodów Zjednoczonych*, Kraków 1946, p. 68.
[50] Barsegov, *op. cit.*, p. 82.
[51] *Ibid.*, p. 85.

Article 2, paragraph 4 does not tackle the essence of the problem—i.e. justification of territorial claims. *Modus procedendi*—i.e. the use of force — is a sufficient and necessary condition to make a change illegal. In the light of the present international law such territorial acquisition should not be sanctioned in accordance with the principle *ex iniuria jus non oritur*.

This statement does not however exhaust the problem. When asking the question as to what territorial pattern is at present protected by the principle of territorial integrity we must also take into account the factor of time. Article 2, paragraph 4 of the Charter of the United Nations provides for the protection of the territorial pattern established or accepted after the Second World War. It comprises the pre-war territorial solutions which survived the war and the territorial changes effected as a result of this war. This new post-war territorial pattern is protected by the principle of inviolability in the sense that any forcible change in this pattern would be illegal.

But the conception of the principle of territorial integrity as a principle protecting a definite territorial pattern against changes effected by force does not eliminate all the controversial problems: it does not solve protracted territorial disputes which were not settled when this pattern came into being, nor does it regulate new problems which arose when this new territorial pattern — in our case the post-war—territorial pattern — was being created.

When for instance two States have claims to a territory each of them can invoke this principle in defence of its title. But the elimination of force as a legal means of pushing one's claims greatly restricts the possibility of giving effect to these claims against the actual owner of the disputed territory. For every State which might pursue its claims by force—irrespective of the subjective conviction of being right—would commit an illegal act. In this sense the principle of territorial integrity—i.e. of inviolability—creates a more advantageous legal situation for the actual owner of a disputed territory.

Such a situation can in some cases protect an unlawful holder, but on the whole its *ratio legis* lies in a norm of higher order, namely the elimination of force from international relations. It is above all the weaker States which profit from this norm.

Another problem is whether the principle of territorial integrity —i.e. territorial inviolability—is also valid with regard to a State which has committed an act of aggression. In other words, whether within the framework of sanctions applied against the aggressor-State he may be deprived of certain territories.

This problem gave rise to no doubts as long as war was a legal means of solving disputes.

Vattel formulated this in a classical way:

"The right to security frequently authorizes a State to punish acts of injustice or violence, and is a further ground for depriving an enemy of some part of his property. It is more humane to punish a Nation in this way than to make the penalty fall upon the persons of the citizens. To this end the Nation may be deprived of valuable property, such as rights, towns, or provinces. But all wars do not give just grounds for inflicting punishment. A Nation which has supported a bad cause in good faith and with moderation is more deserving of the pity than of the anger of a generous conqueror; ...It is only where the injustice of his cause is clear and devoid of even a semblance of right, or where the conduct of the enemy has been marked by grievous outrages, that his opponent has the right to punish him; and on every occasion the punishment should be limited to what is required for the safety of the injured State and of other Nations"[52].

However, when war was declared to be an illegal way of solving disputes and when various legal acts were adopted forbidding the use of force, the problem arose as to the propriety of punishing the aggressor by depriving him of some territories.

The West German jurists have propounded a thesis groundlessly invoking the Atlantic Charter as a proof that the Allies had renounced the intention of territorial changes, and categorically prohibiting any territorial changes even as regards to the aggressor-State[53].

This attitude is of course contrary to the practice of States, especially to such practice after the Second World War. Nor is it confir-

[52] Vattel, *op. cit.*, vol. III, § 162, p. 291.
[53] This thesis has been formulated explicitly by E. Menzel in "Das Annexionsverbot des modernen Völkerrechts und das Schicksal der deutschen Ostgebiete", included in the collective work *Das östliche Deutschland. Ein Handbuch*, Würzburg 1959. The thesis is one of the basic premises of revisionist arguments directed against the Oder-Neisse frontier.

med in theory. Wehberg, who as a rule upholds the principle of inadmissibility of unilateral territorial changes effected by force, makes an exception, *expressis verbis*, as regards territorial changes effected in self-defence or by the use of collective measures to safeguard peace[54]. Bindschedler also says:

"It is only an unauthorized (*nicht autorisierte*) use of force which gives no legal title. But how does the problem appear in the case of a defensive war permissible in accordance with Article 51 of the Charter of the United Nations, or in case of military sanctions? To be logical one must acknowledge the right of annexation at the cost of the aggressor".

Bindschedler remarks, however, that this would be incompatible with the prohibition of forcible changes[55].

As regards the latest Soviet doctrine, Tunkin makes a distinction between "the right of the victor" which he considers illegal and territorial sanctions against the aggressor-State which are in conformity with international law.

"...According to contemporary international law the responsibility of the aggressor-State is not confined to a mere compensation for the losses inflicted. It also comprises sanctions against the aggressor which in particular can take the form of sequestration of a part of his territory in order to prevent aggression in the future. These considerations motivated the members of the anti-Nazi coalition in their attitude to the aggressor-States in the Second World War.

"The separation of certain territories from Germany and Japan, effected as a result of the Second World War, is basically different from the territorial annexation made previously on the basis of «the right of the victor». The measures taken by the Allies in relation to Germany and Japan were based above all on the responsibility of States before international law for the aggression committed by them"[56].

On the basis of this example Tunkin formulates a thesis to the

[54] H. Wehberg, *Die Stimson Doktrin. Grundprobleme des Internationalen Rechts. Festschrift für Jean Spiropoulos*, Bonn 1957, p. 439.
[55] R. Bindschedler (Strupp-Schlochauer, *Wörterbuch*, vol. I, p. 70).
[56] G. I. Tunkin, *Voprosy tieorii mezhdunarodnovo prava*, Moskva 1962, pp. 289—290.

effect that it is a binding principle of the law of nations that States are responsible for aggression; within the framework of this responsibility he fully approves of territorial sanctions against the aggressor-State.

In American literature Gould, generalizing contemporary practice says:

"The United Nations Charter includes an obligation resting upon all members to avoid the use of force against the territorial integrity of other States (Article II, paragraph 4). But at the end of both World Wars the transfer of territory was made possible by conquest, and so it would seem that any prohibition against acquiring or transferring title by conquest applies only to aggressors"[57].

Fenwick is still more explicit on the matter. If we presume that there is a principle in international law that territorial acquisition brought about by force should be denied validity, how is it possible, he asks, to reconcile this principle with the territorial arrangements resulting from the defeat of the Axis Powers and their satellites? He declares:

"The answer must be that these transfers of territory by the several treaties of peace are part of the punishment inflicted upon the defeated states for their own violation of international law. The constitutional guarantees of liberty are not violated when a criminal is denied his liberty or his property as a punishment of crime. The successive denunciations of conquest during the decade preceding the war were directed against act of aggression by individual states, not against the action of a group of states which, having banded together to restrain the aggressor, seek to protect themselves against future acts of aggression or to secure redress for wrong done"[58].

The thesis proclaiming territorial integrity of the aggressor-State has a political premise which cannot but arouse categorical opposition, since it demands equal rights for the aggressor and his victim.

---

[57] W. L. Gould, *An Introduction to International Law*, New York 1957, p. 354.

[58] Ch. Fenwick, *International Law*, 3rd ed., New York 1948, p. 361.

In other words the aggressor not only wants to secure impunity but even tries to place himself in a more favourable situation than the victim of aggression—an attempt which is hampered by the prohibition against ensuring future security by territorial changes.

The thesis concerning the territorial integrity of aggressor-States is contradicted by Article 107 of the Charter of the United Nations, which provides:

"Nothing in the present Charter shall invalidate or preclude action in relation to any State which during the Second World War has been an enemy of any signatory to the present Charter, taken or authorised as a result of that war by the Governments having responsibility for such action".

This article is unequivocally directed against the aggressive Fascist States. The principle of territorial integrity formulated in Article 2, paragraph 4 of the Charter does not apply to the aggressor-States; this has been confirmed both in Article 107 of the Charter and also in practice, in the territorial clauses of the peace treaties concluded so far.

3. THE CHANGE OF THE POST-WAR POLISH-GERMAN FRONTIER AND THE AIMS OF THE ALLIES DURING WORLD WAR II

Various principles have been advanced as the politico-judicial foundation of territorial changes effected as a result of the Second World War. Foremost among them is the *principle of security* from the threat of revival of aggresion by the Fascist States. This principle provided the main foundation for the changes of frontiers between Finland and the Soviet Union, between Italy and France, for Japan's renunciation of mandate rights to Pacific Islands, transference of the Kuril Islands to the Soviet Union. *Ethnographic principles* have also been applied, although on a restricted scale (modification of the Italo-Yugoslav frontier, cession of Dodecanesian Islands to Greece by Italy, but in the case of the Austro-Italian frontier this principle was ignored), finally, there was the *revindication* of certain territories previously taken by the Fascist countries by virtue of earlier treaties (renunciation by Japan of southern Sakhalin and adjoining islands[59], of Formosa and the Pescadores)[60]. Some territorial changes were also argued on the basis of *historical rights*.

It is significant that by contrast with the Treaty of Versailles, territorial changes were effected without plebiscites; on the contrary, recourse was taken to large-scale compulsory transference of population[61] or exchange of national minorities[62].

The territorial changes effected as a result of the Second World War were intended *to create indispensable conditions for the effective functioning of the international system of collective security* to be set up after the war. Hence the procedure of plebiscite was rejected in the solution of territorial problems. As is well known, the procedure of plebiscite was frequently used after the First World War but it gave unsatisfactory results in practice. Its application did not satisfy the States concerned—on the contrary, it kindled new conflicts. In the case of Poland, for instance, the frontier with Germany as drawn according to the results of the plebiscite, made her strategic position extremely difficult, which in view of Germany's obvious military superiority and intensifying revisionist tendencies, threatened not only Poland's territorial integrity but even her very existence as an independent State. Furthermore, plebiscites not infrequently ignored fundamental economic considerations, as witness the division of Upper Silesia.

Moreover, it is only in certain definite circumstances that plebiscite can be applied to implement the right of self-determination and upon the termination of hostilities in 1945—i.e. in the face of mili-

---

[59] The Russo-Japanese peace treaty signed in Portsmouth in 1905.

[60] The Sino-Japanese treaty signed in Simonoseki in 1895.

[61] See Section XIII of the Potsdam Agreements on the removal of German population from Poland, Czechoslovakia and Hungary. It is discussed later in the chapter.

[62] In March 1947, a Hungarian-Czechoslovak treaty was signed providing for an exchange of populations (i.e. 600,000 Hungarians from Czechoslovakia and 400,000 Slovaks from Hungary).

tary conquests of the Fascist countries—such circumstances did not exist. Inaugurating, in the interests of peace and security, a new political pattern of the world, the Great Powers were determined to take radical steps and rejected all halfmeasures and solutions which did not guarantee rapid and lasting results. This was in all likelihood the reason why plebiscites were completely left out of consideration as regards the planned territorial changes affecting the aggressive Fascist States. The aim pursued by the Great Powers—which in the words of the Moscow Declaration of October 30, 1943 concerning general security were responsible for "ensuring rapid and orderly transit from war to peace" — was to establish such a territorial pattern in Europe as would make possible the efficient functioning of the proposed system of collective security—i.e. the United Nations. In this connection it was necessary to find a radical solution to the problem of national minorities which after the First World War supplied the Fascist countries with a convenient pretext for launching aggression. Hence, the territorial changes effected as a result of the Second World War, and confirmed in peace treaties, did not involve the procedure of plebiscite.

The problem of the post-war Polish-German frontier was a point intimately linked with questions concerning lasting peace and security, which confronted the Allies after the Second World War. Public opinion in the countries fighting against the Fascist States urged governments to take radical measures which would make impossible a future resurgence of aggressive forces and the outbreak of a new war. That public opinion demanded the application of measures capable of paralysing the expansionist tendencies of countries which had been centres of aggression. In Europe, this demand was aimed especially against Germany. It will be right and pertinent to quote here a principle laid down by a group of experts who during the war studied the German problem. This group formulated the principle that as regards territorial questions, the "overriding factor in doubtful cases would be the needs of Europe as a whole". Transference of certain German territories to other States claiming them "should serve the purpose of making Germany unable to threaten the security of others, provided that there were a reasonable prospect of permanence for the new arrangements"[63].

The new pattern of European relations, intended to ensure peace and security to all nations, called for the application of a number of special measures against Germany, whose imperialistic policies had twice within the twentieth century led to aggression and whose expansionist ambitions, expressed by the slogan *Drang nach Osten*, had over a period of centuries caused hardships to the nations of Central and Eastern Europe[64]. Poland has been a special victim of such policies and it is apt here to recall Bismarck's thesis to the effect that no rebirth of the Polish State should be permitted, and also the statement by General Seeckt that the very existence of Poland is intolerable to Germany[65].

The problem of ensuring Poland's security was so obvious that there was complete unanimity among the Great Powers chiefly responsible for ensuring world peace and security as to the necessity of changes in the pre-war Polish-German frontier. This conclusion is confirmed by the entire history of the conception of the post-war frontier between Poland and Germany.

Thus, President Roosevelt in his report on the Yalta Conference stated *inter alia*:

[63] *The Problem of Germany*, Royal Institute of International Affairs, London 1945, p. 33, quoted after Z. Jordan, *Oder-Neisse Line. A Study of the Political, Economic and European Significance of Poland's Western Frontier*, London 1952, p. 110 (abbr.: Jordan I).

[64] The aggressive German policies of the past are well characterized in the words of the former Chancellor Bülow: "Vergrösserungstrieb und Ländergier waren allen deutschen Fürsten und Dynastien seit Jahrhunderten eigen und flackerten kurz vor ihrem Zusammenbruch noch einmal auf, nicht nur im Westen, sondern auch im Osten, wo Kurland, Finnland, Litauen die Begierden reizten". B. Bülow, *Denkwürdigkeiten*, vol. I. Berlin 1930, p. 142.

[65] "Polens Existenz ist unerträglich, unvereinbar mit den Lebensbedingungen Deutschlands", F. von Rabenau, *Seeckt. Aus seinem Leben 1918—1936*, Leipzig 1940, p. 316. An analogical statement was made with reference to Czechoslovakia by General Beck, one of the leaders of the anti-Hitlerite attempt of July 20, 1944, who writes in his memorandum of May 30, 1938: "Es ist richtig, dass die Tschechei in ihrer durch das Versailler Diktat erzwungenen Gestaltung für Deutschland unerträglich ist". J. Wheeler-Bennett, *The Nemesis of Power. The German Army in Politics 1918—1945*, London 1949, p. 399 ("It is true that Czechoslovakia in the form imposed by the Dictate of Versailles is unbearable for Germany. . .").

"Throughout history Poland has been the corridor through which attacks on Russia have been made. Twice in this generation Germany has struck at Russia through this corridor. *To ensure European security and world peace* (my italics — B.W.) a strong and independent Poland is necessary to prevent a recurrance"[66].

A still more unequivocal statement was made on the subject in the House of Commons on March 1, 1945 by Clement Attlee, leader of the Labour Party and subsequently Prime Minister of Great Britain:

". . . if it is found necessary to take certain areas (from Germany — B.W.) in order to enable the Polish people to lead a free, full life. I shall not complain — and I do not think that the Germans have a right to complain. *I shall judge all these changes,* not by whether they fit into past history or whether they are performing an act of revenge, but entirely as to whether they will *make for a peaceful Europe in future*" (my italics — B.W.)[67].

The universal trend to prevent any future aggression by German and Japan was repeatedly expressed in official political declarations made by representatives of the Great Powers in 1942 and 1943[68]. Similar arguments in support of Polish claims were also advanced by Poland's official representatives. In a speech made in the Polish National Council on July 21, 1945, the Polish Prime Minister emphasized that:

"One of the conditions of European and world peace is a strong and independent Poland. And one of the ways to creating a strong and independent Poland is to settle, as promptly as possible, our just Western frontiers on the Western Neisse, Oder (including Szczecin) and the Baltic"[69].

---

[66] *Zbiór Dokumentów* 1946, No. 12, p. 415.
[67] *Parliamentary Debates*, vol. 408, No. 41, p. 1617.
[68] A broadcast by the United States Secretary of State Cordell Hull on July 23, 1942, and a speech by the British Foreign Secretary Anthony Eden in the House of Commons, on December 2, 1942. (*War and Peace Aims of U. N.*, vol. I, pp. 105 and 269—270). In a speech of November 6, 1943, made on the occasion of the 26th anniversary of the Great October Revolution, Stalin declared: "Together with our Allies we shall have . . . to introduce in Europe such a state of affairs as will completely exclude the possibility of a new German aggression". J. V. S t a l i n, *O Vielikoi Otiechestviennoi Voinie Sovietskovo Soyuza*, Moskva 1952, p. 125.
[69] *Records of the proceedings of the Polish National Council* (in Polish), Session VIII, pp. 11—12.

While the President of the Polish National Council declared:

"For democracy, a stable world peace is essential. But this cannot be achieved without a new organization of the distribution of power in Europe, without breaking the imperialist expansion of German Fascim. An increase in the importance of a reborn democratic Poland in the new pattern of European relations is one of the conditions for a lasting peace in Europe. There will be no lasting peace in Europe if Poland is internally weak, as she was before September 1939, if she is unable to resist the threat of a German avalanche. The problem of Poland's western frontiers cannot be considered merely from the point of view of redeeming the age-old wrongs suffered by the Polish nation. East Prussia, the centre and stronghold of Germany's most rapacious class, the Junkers, which has alwys been the mainstay of German imperialism and reaction, must — in the interests of peace and world security — be transformed from a cockpit of aggression into a bridge linking the peaceable countries of Eastern Europe with the sea. In the interests of peace and world security, the power of Prussia — the focus of German Fascism and lust for conquest — must be broken once and for all. Prussia must be pushed back to the edges of her cradle, Brandenburg. The lands up to the Oder and Neisse must be transformed from a springs board for attack into an area of peaceful labour and of work for the peace of all Europe"[70].

The concept of the Oder-Neisse frontier as a means of ensuring peace and security to Europe was confirmed by the transference of the German population from all the territory of Poland as marked by her new boundaries. Transference of the German population was effected with a view to eliminating future international conflicts over the issue of national minorities and was therefore also a means of safeguarding peace within the new pattern of post-war relations. The transfer of population involved not only the territory of Poland within her new boundaries, but also the German population in Czechoslovakia and Hungary, and further, though this was not explicitly sanctioned by the Great Powers, the German population living in Rumania and Yugoslavia. The Czechoslovak Government, remembering the diversive role of the Sudeten Germans in 1938, presented to the Great Powers in 1943 a plan for transfering that minority from Czechoslovakia. This plan was approved by the governments of the Great Powers. Although there was a risk that the transfer

---

[70] *Ibid.*, Session VI, p. 27.

of over two million Germans from Czechoslovakia might have entailed serious economic and demographic difficulties, the desire for security prevailed[71]. Similar motives determined the transfer of the German population from post-war Polish territories, the initiative for such removal having in this case lain with Western Powers.

It must be emphasized that the lands east of the Oder and Neisse were not alien to Poland. When making her territorial claims, Poland invoked also her historical rights. Those lands had been lost to Poland under pressure from age-old German expansion, carried out under the slogan *Drang nach Osten*[72]. Poland's historical rights were recognized by the Soviet Government[73].

In spite of intensive Germanization of these lands, large, ethnically Polish groups survived and resisted all attempts at denationalization. The existence of what are called autochthonous groups[74] confirms the historical basis of Poland's rights to these territories.

[71] J. B. Schechtman, *European Population Transfers 1939—1945*, New York 1946, pp. 457—458. Cf. E. Wiskemann, *op. cit.*, pp. 228 et seq., 250 et seq.

[72] The present work is not concerned with historical arguments proving Poland's historical rights to the territories east of the Oder-Neisse line. This problem has been widely discussed by Polish writers. From among the more recent works the following may be quoted by way of example: K. Piwarski, "Polskie Ziemie Zachodnie w rozwoju historycznym" included in the collective work *Polskie Ziemie Zachodnie*, Poznań 1959; G. Labuda, "The Territorial, Ethnical, and Demographic Aspects of Polish-German Relations in the Past (X—XX centuries)", *Polish Western Affairs* 1962, No. 2; Z. Kaczmarczyk, "Polska granica zachodnia w perspektywie tysiąca lat historii", *Przegląd Zachodni* 1960, No. 6, and the collective work edited by G. Labuda, *Ekspansja wschodnia Niemiec w Europie środkowej. Studia nad tzw. niemieckim "Drang nach Osten"*, Poznań 1963.

[73] The statement issued by T.A.S.S. on January 11, 1944 read in part: "Poland's western frontiers must be enlarged by the inclusion of ancient Polish lands previously seized by Germany, since otherwise it would be impossible to unite the whole Polish nation in a State which should also receive the necessary access to the Baltic Sea" (*Vnieshnaya politika Sovietskovo Soyuza v pieriod vielikoi otiechestviennoy voiny*, Moskva 1946, vol. II, p. 61). During the session of the Council of Foreign Ministers in April 1947, the Soviet Foreign Minister stated: "In the west Poland has returned to her ancient lands which were once the cradle of the Polish State. Her present territory corresponds to the historical areas Poland possessed under the Piast dynasty". (*Vnieshnaya politika Sovietskovo Soyuza*, 1947, Moskva 1952, p. 491).

[74] Totalling roughly 1,067,000. See "Materiały syntetyczne do zagadnienia Ziem Odzyskanych", *Myśl Współczesna* 1947, No. 1, p. 132.

The post-war change of the Polish-German frontier was also based on — in addition to the principle of security and historical rights — the principle of responsibility of the aggressor-State for the effects of aggression.

The Nazi invasion of Poland inflicted enormous economic and especially biological losses upon the Polish nation. According to the estimates of the Polish War Reparations Office, during the Nazi occupation in the years 1939—1945 Poland's biological losses totalled 6,028,000 individuals — that is 22.2 per cent of the total number of the Polish and Jewish population inhabiting Poland at that time. Poland's economic losses have been estimated at 16,882 million dollars. As a result of the war the Polish national income fell in 1945 to 38.2 per cent of the pre-war level. The extent of the Polish losses can best be gauged if we realize that they amounted to 75 per cent of the national income of Great Britain in 1939[75].

In the traditional doctrine of international law war losses were regarded as a legal basis for territorial claims[76]. The conception of compensation for war losses in the form of territorial concessions was also considered by the participants in the Yalta conference with regard to the Netherlands for the destruction wrought by the Germans[77]. This conception was the basis of territorial claims submitted against Germany in November 1946 by the Netherlands and Luxembourg[78].

---

[75] These figures are based on the *Report on Poland's War Losses and Damage in the Years 1939—1945*, Office for War Reparations of the Presidium of the Council of Ministers, Warszawa 1947. See J. Szafrański, "Straty biologiczne i gospodarcze" included in the collective work *Straty wojenne Polski w latach 1939—1945*, Poznań—Warszawa 1962.

[76] See footnotes Nos. 3 and 56 of this chapter.

[77] The "Briefing Book Paper" of January 12, 1945, entitled "The Testament of Germany", prepared by the American delegation for the Yalta conference, included the following passage in Chapter III, "Frontier Settlements": "... (2) that the water-boundary between the Netherlands and Germany be moved to the main channel of the Ems Estuary and that further consideration be given to any Netherlands claim on German territory as compensation for war damage..." (*Conferences at Malta and Yalta*, p.179).

[78] Keesing's *Archiv der Gegenwart*, 1946—7, 917 G, 935 B. By virtue of the London Agreement of Six Powers (the United States, Great Britain, France, Belgium, the Netherlands and Luxembourg) concerning changes in Germany's western frontiers, signed on March 28, 1949. The communique provided for provisional frontier rectifications and strongly emphasized that the frontier may be changed in the final peace settlement. For the text see: *Europa-Archiv* 1949, p. 2028. See commentary by Jellinek, *op. cit.*, p. 103,

In political literature it has been recognized that the Polish post-war territorial accessions have been justified by the losses which Poland suffered during the occupation as a result of the German aggression[79]. This view was also shared by the French Foreign Minister when he stated at the Moscow session of the Council of Foreign Ministers in April 1947 (fourth session) that although the territorial changes in favour of Poland and the Soviet Union had a provisional character, they were difficult to change. He added:

"*In view of the enormous losses suffered during the war by Soviet Russia and Poland* (my italics — B.W.), France abandons any further discussion on this matter"[80].

Moreover, from the point of view of international law it must be stated that the German aggression as well as the unparalleled crimes committed by the Germans in Poland during the occupation, the unlawful incorporation of some Polish regions into the Reich (*eingegliederte Ostgebiete*), the unlawful expropriations and transfers of the Polish population, as well as the announcement of the *debellatio* of Poland show that Germany did not feel herself bound by international law with regard to Poland, a fact which — in accordance with the principle of reciprocity — released Poland from any obligations towards Germany[81]. Germany's responsibility to Poland for the aggression and the enormous biological and material losses is indubitable. It was on this basis and in accordance with the aims of the anti-Fascist coalition — to ensure future peace and security for herself and other nations — that Poland put forward territorial claims to the territories east of the Oder and Western Neisse against the German aggressor-State.

---

who regards this decision as an agreement to the disadvantage of a third State (without the participation of wronged Germany). In the direct agreements concluded by the German Federal Republic with Belgium (September 24, 1956), Luxembourg (July 6, 1957) and the Netherlands (April 8, 1960), the changes of Germany's western frontier were annulled.

[79] E. Wiskemann, *op. cit.*, p. 134, J. Giertych, *Poland and Germany*, London 1958.

[80] B. Meissner, *Russland, die Westmächte und Deutschland*, Hamburg 1954, p. 108.

[81] L. Ehrlich, *Suwerenność Polski na Ziemiach Zachodnich i Północnych. Zagadnienia Prawne*, Śląski Instytut Naukowy, Biuletyn No. 34, Katowice 1962, pp. 7—9.

CHAPTER III

THE YALTA AND POTSDAM AGREEMENTS AS THE LEGAL BASIS OF THE SYSTEM OF INTERNATIONAL RELATIONS AFTER THE SECOND WORLD WAR

1. THE CONSTITUTIVE CHARACTER OF THE YALTA AND POTSDAM AGREEMENTS

At the beginning of 1945, the imminent end of the war faced the victorious Allied Powers with the necessity of determining the foundations of post-war international relations.

Decisions of vital importance for Europe and the World were taken at two international conferences attended by the Heads of Government of the Three Main Powers — the United Kingdom, the United States and the Soviet Union. These conferences were held at Yalta and Potsdam.

The results of the Yalta Conference were published in the report dated February 11, 1945. That report constitutes a joint statement signed by the Heads of Government of Great Britain, the United States and the Soviet Union[1]. The document, referred to as the Yalta Agreement is in spite of some doubts raised by certain authors concerning its formal aspects[2], by most considered as legally binding[3], a fact fully confirmed by the practice of States.

---

[1] *United Nations Documents*, pp. 142—148.

[2] H. W. Briggs, "The Leader's Agreement of Yalta", *American Journal of International Law* 1946, p. 376; S. C. Y. Pan, "Legal aspects of the Yalta Agreement", *Am. Journal of International Law* 1952, p. 40; K. Marek, *Identity and Continuity of States in Public International Law*, Genève 1954, pp. 486—487. Among Polish authors, J. Makowski in his book on the legal character of agreements concluded during the Second World War, (*Charakter prawny umów*), p. 17, distinguishes in the Yalta Agreement several acts differing as to legal character.

Since the decisions reached at Yalta, and subsequently at Potsdam determined the foundations of the new political pattern and trends in European development after the Second World War, those decisions impart to the two agreements extraordinary political and legal significance, comparable only with that of such a document as the Charter of the United Nations[4].

It was a peculiar feature of the Yalta Agreement that it concerned also Third Party States, not participating in the Agreement and not attending the Conference[5]. However, such agreements have precedents in the history of international relations. These were political agreements between Powers dominant at a given time, their purpose being to regulate on a new basis the international relations prevailing in a specific area. Such agreements have usually been concluded after great wars — as for instance the Final Act of the Congress of Vienna (1815), the Paris Treaty (1856), the Versailles Treaty (1919); alternatively, they have made arrangements for a new distribution of colonial possessions, as for instance the Berlin Treaty (1878). Such agreements have not infrequently granted certain rights to, or imposed certain obligations on, smaller States, not being party to the agreement and not even consulted. This type of

---

[3] Oppenheim-Lauterpacht, *op. cit.*, vol. I, p. 788. Wł. Namysłowski, in his article discussing Poland's western fronties from the standpoint of International Law ("Granice zachodnie Polski z punktu widzenia prawa międzynarodowego") *Przegląd Zachodni* 1946, No. 10, p. 812; A. Klafkowski, *Podstawy prawne, passim*; M. Lachs in his article on imperialistic tendencies in the bourgeois doctrine of International Law ("Imperialistyczne tendencje burżuazyjnej nauki prawa międzynarodowego"), *Państwo i Prawo* 1951, No. 3; R. Maurach, P. H. Seraphim, G. Wolfrum *Ostwärts der Oder und Neisse*, juridical part compiled by R. Maurach, Hannover 1949, p. 112 (abbr.: R. Maurach); R. Nadolny, *Völkerrecht und deutscher Friede*, Hamburg 1949, p. 12; *Ost-Handbuch*, Deutsches Büro für Friedensfragen, Stuttgart 1949, part 15, pp. 75—77; K. Marek, *Identity and Continuity of States in Public International Law*, Genève 1954 p. 488.

[4] H. Kraus, *op. cit.*, p. 36, considers the Yalta Agreement as a "gentlemen's agreement", binding not the States, but only personally the Heads of Government of the Great Powers; R. Laun, *Das Recht auf die Heimat*, Hannover-Darmstadt 1951, pp. 17—18, belittles the importance of the Yalta and Potsdam Agreements and refers to them as particular law, binding on the parties only. This is manifestly refuted by the contents of the acts, which are of constitutive consequence for Third States as well.

[5] Attention is rightly drawn to this by J. Makowski, *Charakter prawny umów*, p. 17.

agreement is occasionally considered in literature as a special category[6]. The subject matter of the Yalta and Potsdam Conferences comprised the basic principles of post-war international relations as intended to prevent the resurgence of forces of aggression in Europe.

The fact that the Yalta Agreement and, subsequently, the Potsdam Agreement recorded certain decisions affecting Third Party States, not attending the Conferences, emphasizes the paramount role of the Great Powers which, during the Second World War, carried the main burden and the main responsibility for the liberation of the conquered nations from Axis occupation, and after the war became — in the words of the Moscow Declaration of the Four Nations on General Security (October 30, 1943) — responsible for a rapid and orderly transit from war to peace and for maintaining international peace and security.

An analysis of the Yalta Agreement shows that the Third States concerned in the Agreement are not treated on an equal footing.

The Great Powers reserved to themselves special rights as to deciding the future fate of Germany. The relevant programme outlined in Section II of the Yalta Agreement envisages the intended temporary incapacitation of Germany as regards undertaking legal acts. This status of Germany in the Yalta Agreement is understandable in view of the plan, agreed upon beforehand, "for enforcing the unconditional surrender terms"[7] upon Nazi Germany.

Different is the situation of other Third Party States concerned in the Yalta Agreement. Such States are left free to decide their attitude to the decisions taken at Yalta. This refers first and foremost to France, which "should be invited by the Three Powers,

[6] British doctrine distinguishes a separate category of agreements and refers to them as international settlements, which it defines as follows: "An International Settlement is an arrangement made by a treaty between the leading Powers intended to form part of the international order of things, either defining the status of territory of particular States, or regulating the use of international waterways, or making other dispositions of general importance, and incidentally imposing certain obligations or restrictions on international conduct" — R. F. Roxburgh, *International Conventions and Third States*, London 1917, p. 81; cf. also Pitt Cobbett, *Cases and Opinions on International Law*, London 1909, pp. 12—13.

[7] Section II of the Yalta Agreement, *United Nations Documents*, p. 143.

if she should so desire, to take over a zone of occupation and to participate as a fourth member of the Control Commission"[8]. The invitation to France to take part in the occupation of Germany had far reaching consequences. France accepted the invitation, which was duly expressed in the Statement (June 5, 1945) on control machinery in Germany issued by the United States, Great Britain, the Soviet Union, and France. The result was that France participated in the occupation of Germany.

Polish questions were referred to in the Yalta Agreement, under Section VI, headed "Poland". The most important decisions concerning Poland's western frontier read as follows:

"The three Heads of Government consider that the eastern frontier of Poland should follow the Curzon Line with digressions from it in some regions of five to eight kilometres in favour of Poland. They recognize that Poland must receive substantial accessions of territory in the North and West. They feel that the opinion of the new Polish Provisional Government of National Unity should be sought in due course on the extent of these accesions and that the final delimitation of the western frontier of Poland should thereafter await the Peace Conference"[9].

With the moment of the Nazi Army's unconditional surrender, the victorious Allied Powers had to determine the further fate of Germany. Inseparably interwoven with the question of Germany was that of the Polish-German frontier. All these questions were considered during the third meeting of the Big Three, and the conclusions were summed up in the Potsdam Agreement. An American author writes on the role of the Agreement in the following words:

"The second phase of the process of shaping a new world order was initiated at the Tripartite Conference of Berlin, commonly referred to as the Potsdam Conference, from 17 July to 2 August 1945. The prewar European *status quo* had been supplanted by the Hitlerian New Order, which had in its turn been overthrown by the invading armies of the United Nations. In the interregnum which followed, with Europe suspended between war and peace, political control of the Continent was divided between the govern-

---

[8] *Ibid.*
[9] *United Nations Documents*, pp. 146—147.

ments of resurrected national states and authorities of the great powers — the United States, the United Kingdom and the Soviet Union — which had led the coalition to victory. The Big Three constituted a kind of European directorate, a latter-day Concert of Europe, with *de facto* competence to exercise leadership in the interim between the demolition of the old order and the construction of a new one. This was a period of transitional arrangements and preliminary settlements. Yet, however tentative and provisional the policies put into operation during this period may have been in theory and intent, they in fact set into motion trends which could not easily be reversed, and thereby contributed significantly to the determination of the ultimate form of the postwar European system"[10].

At the Potsdam Conference, attention was focussed on the same problems as at Yalta — that is, broadly speaking, on foundations for the post-war system and development of international relations in Europe. This coinciding of the subject matter of the two conferences was duly reflected in the texts of the resulting agreement.

In addition to formal similarities — both acts are headed "Report", are similarly arranged, and were signed by the Heads of Government of the Three Great Powers — the two agreements are intimately related as to content. While the Yalta Agreement laid down certain general principles, the Potsdam Agreement develops them, and defines them in a number of more detailed decisions. The core of the Yalta decisions was the agreement on the future status of Germany. This is dealt with in greater detail in the Potsdam Agreement, especially as regards the following points:

1) The Yalta Agreement defines in Section II the general principles of the occupation of Germany (zones of occupation, Control Commission, and its composition), and the aims of the occupation. The Potsdam Agreement refers to the former and defines in Section III the political and economic principles which were to govern Germany's treatment "in the initial control period" (detailed aims, and the control machinery, viz. Control Council).

2) The Yalta Agreement lays down in Section III the general principles of reparations (compensation in kind to the greatest extent possible, establishment of a Commission for the Compensation of

---

[10] Claude, *op. cit.*, p. 114.

Damage); the Potsdam Agreement refers in Section IV to the Yalta decisions, and develops and defines the principles in greater detail.

3) There is also a link with the Yalta Agreement in Section IX of the Potsdam Agreement. There, the Great Powers refer three times to Yalta — twice as regards the establishment of the Provisional Government of National Unity in Poland (Section IX, paragraph A), and once in the decisions on Poland's western frontier (Section IX, paragraph B)[11].

In addition to developing and defining more precisely the Yalta decisions, the Potsdam Agreement also decides certain questions not referred to in the Yalta Agreement. This primarily concerns questions that had matured in the intervening period. Some of them — for instance, the transfers of German populations from Poland, Czechoslovakia, and Hungary — are known to have been discussed at Yalta, since the Western Powers clearly considered transfers to be closely related to the question of Polish territorial accessions in the West and North. Also, the Soviet Government was manifestly in agreement with the transfers. Thus, even here the Potsdam Agreement set out in greater detail a viewpoint already agreed by the Great Powers which, although not reflected in the text of the Yalta Agreement, was nevertheless settled at the Conference.

The correlation already referred to between the Yalta and the Potsdam Agreements warrants the conclusion that the decisions of the latter should be interpreted in conjunction with the former[12].

---

[11] Also Molotov, *Voprosy Vnieshniey Politiki*, Moskva 1948, p. 425 stressed the executive character of the Potsdam Agreement in relation to the Yalta Agreement.

[12] Wl. Namysłowski, *op. cit.*, pp. 810—811, writes: "While the decisions made at the Crimean Conference could still be worded in general terms owing to the not yet clear military situation of Germany, and while these resolutions may be considered from the legal point of view *as an agreement on a future definite international accord* (my italics—BW), the Postdam Agreement on the other hand, as an execution of the Crimean obligations, cannot contain generalities and hints and must embody quite definite decisions".

2. THE POLISH-GERMAN FRONTIER ON THE EVE OF THE YALTA CONFERENCE

Towards the end of 1944, as a result of an extensive exchange of views, the Great Powers defined their attitude in relation to the future Polish-German frontier as follows:

The Soviet Union supported quite unequivocally and unreservedly the Polish demands for a post-war Polish-German frontier on the Oder and Western Neisse. Among the occasions on which this became manifest was Mikołajczyk's visit to Moscow in October 1944[13]. It is worth emphasizing that — as was reported by Harriman, the United States Ambassador — the Moscow negotiations (October 1944) between Premier Stalin and Prime Minister Churchill led to an agreement to grant to Poland a part of East Prussia west and south of Königsberg and to accept the Oder, together with Stettin, as a Polish-German frontier[14]. Great Britain's positive attitude towards Polish claims had already been expressed in Cadogan's confidential letter.

On February 2, 1944, Sir Alexander Cadogan, Under-Secretary of State at the British Foreign Office, wrote a letter to Tadeusz Romer, then Minister of Foreign Affairs in the Polish London Government, in which he replied to a question put by Mikołaczyk to Churchill[15]. The relevant part of the letter reads as follows:

"... you enquired whether His Majesty's Government were definitely in favour of advancing the Polish frontier up to the line of the Oder, to include the port of Stettin. The answer is that His Majesty's Government do consider that Poland should have the right to extend her territory to *this* extent". (my italics — B.W.)[16].

---

[13] Stettinius, *Roosevelt and the Russians, The Yalta Conference*, London 1950, p. 155.

[14] *The Conferences at Malta and Yalta*, pp. 202—203.

[15] The question addressed to Churchill by Mikołajczyk as Premier of the Polish London Government was: "Does Great Britain support the extension of Poland's post-war western frontiers as far as the river Oder and including Stettin?"

[16] Cadogan's letter published in *Zbiór Dokumentów* 1947, No. 10, pp. 223—224.

The attitude of the British Government was publicly confirmed by Churchill in a speech in the House of Commons (December 15, 1944). That speech included the following statement:

"The Poles are *free* (my italics — B.W.), so far as Russia and Great Britain are concerned, to extend their territory at the expense of Germany to the West. I do not propose to go into exact details, but the extensions, which will be supported by Britain and Russia... are of high importance"[17].

Furthermore, Churchill declared:

"It is asked: Why cannot all questions of territorial changes be left over till the end of the war? I think that is a most pertinent question and it is, in fact, the answer which I and the Foreign Secretary gave in almost every case that has been presented to us... Why cannot that be said in this case? It can be said in every case, or almost every case, except in that of Poland"[18].

Still in the same speech, Churchill announced the decision to transfer the German population from the territories to be given to Poland:

"The transference of several millions of people would have to be effected from the East to the West or North, as well as the expulsion of the Germans (because that is what is proposed — the total expulsion of the Germans) — from the area to be acquired by Poland in the west and the north. For expulsion is the method which, so far as we have been able to see, will be the most satisfactory and lasting. There will be no mixture of populations to cause endless trouble, as has been the case in Alsace-Lorraine[19]".

Simultaneously Churchill said quite openly:

"I am not alarmed by the prospect of the disentanglement, nor even by these large transferences, which are more possible in modern conditions than they ever were before"[20].

---

[17] *Parliamentary Debates, House of Commons, Official Report*, vol. 406, No. 1, p. 1483.
[18] *Ibid.* p. 1487.
[19] *Ibid.* p. 1484.
[20] *Ibid.*

Let it be added that Churchill was by no means isolated in holding this view concerning transfers. The attitude of the British Labour Party is expressed in the programme of the Party's National Executive Committee, presented to the Annual Conference in London (May 29 — June 3, 1944). The Programme includes:

"«national minorities» in Central Europe left outside the boundaries of their own nation, should be encouraged to rejoin it. In particular all Germans left outside the post-war frontiers... should go back to Germany... The organized transfer of population in the immediate post-war period, may, indeed, be one of the foundations of better international relations in a later phase... there will be a unique opportunity, which will not recur, to make a permanent settlement of this vexed question"[21].

The Labour Party Programme not only encouraged transfers of Germans from outside Germany's post-war boundaries, but justified it on the following grounds: the Party believed that the transfer would settle permanently the question of national minorities in Europe in the interests of future peace and international security.

As will be seen from what has gone before, Great Britain unequivocally approved in 1944 of Polish demands for a Polish-German frontier on the Oder, and was inclined to reach decisions even before the peace conference.

The Government of the United States left the initiative concerning the Polish-German frontier in British hands. At the same time, it follows clearly from the facts referred to that the British Government acted in close consultation with the United States Government. Towards the end of 1944, the American Government also declared its attitude to the question. This was expressed in a letter by President Roosevelt to Mikołajczyk (November 17, 1944). The letter made it clear that if the question of Polands' territorial accessions in the west should be agreed upon between the Polish, Soviet and British Governments, the Government of the United States would offer no objection. Furthermore, the letter said:

---

[21] *The International Post-War Settlement*. Report by the National Executive Committee of the Labour Party to be presented to the Annual Conference to be held in London from May 29th to June 2nd 1944".

"If the Polish Government and people desire in connection with the new frontiers of the Polish State to bring about the transfer to and from the territory of Poland of national minorities, the United States Government will raise no objection and as far as practicable will facilitate such transfer"[22].

President Roosevelt's attitude was subsequently confirmed in somewhat different terms in an official statement by Secretary of State Stettinius (December 18, 1944). Point 2 of the statement ran as follows :

"It has been the consistently held policy of the United States Government that questions relating to boundaries should be left in abeyance until the termination of hostilities. As Secretary Hull stated in his address of April 9, 1944, «This does not mean that certain questions may not and should not in the meantime be settled by friendly conference and agreement.» In the case of the future frontiers of Poland, if a mutual agreement is reached by the United Nations directly concerned, this Government would have no objection to such an agreement which could make an essential contribution to the prosecution of the war against the common enemy. If, as a result of such agreement, the Government and people of Poland decide that it would be in the interests of the Polish state to transfer national groups, the United States Government in cooperation with other governments will assist Poland, in so far as practicable, in such transfers. The United States Government continues to adhere to its traditional policy of declining to give guarantees for any specific frontier. . ."[23].

The United States Government reiterated its adherence to the principle of not guaranteeing any frontiers in Europe and of postponing territorial decisions to the peace conference, but it did not exclude exceptions to such postponement. A document prepared by the special Government Committee for Post-War Plans (July 28, 1944) urged that even if that policy were to assume a postponing of solutions until termination of hostilities, it should admit

---

22 Excerpt from Roosevelt's letter to Mikołajczyk quoted after Hoffmann from a collection of Official Documents covering the years 1944—1948, published by the Polish Embassy in London under the title *Poland, Germany, and European Peace*, p. 107. See also E. Wiskemann, *op. cit.*, p. 81.

23 *Documents*, vol. VIII, p. 898, The United States replied by way of this statement to a memorandum by Mikołajczyk who requested, among other things, American guarantees for future Polish frontiers.

that it may be useful to have certain controversial territorial problems settled beforehand. In these cases, the solution adopted ought to be based as far as practicable, on the same permanent features, which, according to the Committee's anticipations, would determine post-war territorial decisions. The Committee felt that the United States was not strictly bound by the formula requiring that questions relating to boundaries be left in abeyance until the termination of war. The Committee declared that in preparing plans for the treatment of Germany after her surrender, the United States Government may be compelled to take part in settling certain German territorial questions which may prove to require immediate attention[24].

The above documents clearly shown that on Polish questions the United States left the initiative in British hands. However, it follows from both Roosevelt's letter to Mikołajczyk and Stettinius's statement, that the American Government did indirectly express agreement to a Polish-German frontier on the Oder. Furthermore, the United States was, like Great Britain, prepared to agree to decisions being made on the subject even before the termination of hostilities. Such a possibility is clearly envisaged in the document prepared by the Committee for Post-War Plans. Special attention should be devoted to the question of transfers, in which the United States Government unequivocally declared itself willing to help Poland.

France's attitude in 1944 to the Polish-German frontier was of no decisive effect, since France was at that time only recovering politically from the defeat of 1940, and her influence on the shaping of Europe's post-war political system was negligible. But since France subsequently joined the Great Powers, it is important to note that General de Gaulle, in his capacity as Head of the French Provisional Government, expressed in Moscow (December 1944) his agreement to a Polish-German frontier on the Oder and *Western Neisse*[25]. This French attitude was publicly expressed by Minister

---

[24] *Quellen zur Entstehung der Oder-Neisse-Linie.* Ed. by G. Rhode und W. Wagner, Stuttgart 1956, p. 154 (abbr.: *Quellen*).
[25] The information was confirmed by Harriman, United States Ambassador, on December 19, 1944. *Quellen*, pp. 158—160.

of Foreign Affairs Bidault shortly after the Moscow visit, in a statement in which he announced his Government's agreement to the granting to Poland of East Prussia, Silesia, and Pomerania[26].

Thus, towards the end of 1944, all the Great Powers leading the coalition of the United Nations officially approved the principle of fixing the post-war Polish-German frontier on the Oder, and some of them (the Soviet Union and France) even a frontier on the Oder and Western Neisse.

The second meeting of the Big Three — that is the Yalta Conference, attended by the Heads of Government of the Three Main Powers engaged in the struggle with the Axis Countries — took place at a time when the war was drawing to a close and the Powers were faced with the necessity to make immediate decisions on the foundations of the post-war world political system.

The situation at the front indicated that the decisive factor in smashing the Nazi war machine was the Soviet Union, which at that time had already liberated from German occupation the countries of Eastern, South-Eastern, and partly even Central Europe. The Soviet Armies were advancing towards Berlin and almost the whole of Poland was liberated.

In Poland, as well as in other areas liberated by the Red Army, profound historic transformations were in the making. A system involving social, political, and economic changes was becoming more and more firmly established in those countries. These developments were largely responsible for the change in the attitude of the United States and Great Britain with regard to Poland's western frontier. When the question was taken up at Yalta, the delegations of the two Western Powers strove to withdraw the support they had given earlier to the claims made by Poland on Germany.

The attitude of the Western Powers is strikingly illustrated by Secretary Eden in the report he wrote (February 1, 1945) to Prime Minister Churchill, on talks he had on Malta with the American Secretary of State Stettinius. The talks sought to produce agreement

---

26 *Journal Officiel*, Paris 1944, No. 85, p. 571, quoted after *Quellen*, p. 161.

on a common attitude to be adopted by the American and British Delegations at the Yalta Conference. Point 9 of the report referred to reads as follows:

"We were prepared last October in Moscow to let Mr. Mikołajczyk's Government have any territories they chose to claim up to the Oder, but this was conditional upon agreement then being reached between him and the Russians and there was no question of our agreeing to the Western Neisse frontier. I also think that we should keep our position fluid as regards the Oder line frontier, and take the line that H. M. G. cannot be considered as having accepted any definite line for the western frontier of Poland, since we need not make the same concessions to the Lublin Poles, which we were prepared to make to Mr. Mikołajczyk in order to obtain a solution of the Polish problem"[27].

As will be seen from the quotation, the British and American Governments clearly discriminated between the Polish emigré circles in London and the leftist forces grouped around the Polish Committee of National Liberation; while on behalf of the former they were prepared to support territorial claims — cf. such documents as Cadogan's letter already referred to, or Roosevelt's letter to Mikołajczyk — as regards the leftist forces they denied support to *any* territorial claims, even if the scope of such claims overlapped those made by the London emigré circles.

3. THE MOTIVES OF THE GREAT POWERS AND THE INTERPRETATION OF THE YALTA AND POTSDAM AGREEMENTS

The foregoing outline of the attitude of the Great Powers to the post-war Polish-German frontier warrants certain conclusions in interpreting the Yalta and Potsdam decisions.

It is evident that a certain change did take place on the eve of the Yalta Conference in the attitude of the United States and Great

---

[27] *The Conferences at Malta and Yalta*, p. 509, see also E. Wiskemann, *op. cit.*, p. 83.

Britain. At the same time, the legal significance of the difference between the attitudes of the Anglo-Saxon Powers and of the Soviet Union should not be unduly stretched. The fact that there appeared a divergence of views between the parties attending the Conference, by no means excluded a compromise at Yalta.

Since West German literature, bent on demonstrating, by means of so-called historical interpretation, divergencies in the intentions of the parties to the Conference, places great reliance on such differences, it may be worth while to consider the question from the point of view of theory.

To begin with, let it be clearly understood that historical interpretations (i.e. analysis of the will of the parties on evidence of circumstances attending or preceding a given agreement) is of no more than supplementary significance in interpreting the agreement[28].

A Polish author very appropriately writes that sources relating to circumstances preceding or attending a treaty

"are never so carefully collected and published as the norms of positive law, and may therefore be incomplete, while in other cases it may happen that at the moment of the judicial emergence of the norm the lawmaker was guided by motives other than those operative during the preliminary discussion or even changed his view to a diametrically opposite one"[29].

In classifying sources of knowledge concerning the will of makers of norms in International Law, the same author gives priority to the text of the norm; next come other norms included in the same treaty, followed, by the norms incorporated in other treaties between the parties, and only then, the circumstances attending or

---

[28] L. Ehrlich in his work on interpretation of treaties, (*Interpretacja traktatów*), p. 77, defines historical interpretation thus: "Examination of the will of the parties may call for historical investigations in order to determine either the meaning attached to a word or term at the time of the drawing up of the treaty, or the historical circumstances that may explain the purpose of the treaty or certain of its provisions". In the same work (pp. 175—212) L. Ehrlich discusses in considerable detail the practice of States, of the Permanent Court of International Justice, and the International Court of Justice, on the admissibility of "preliminary documents" as an aid in interpreting an agreement.

[29] M. Król in his book on interpretation of International Treaties (*Wykładnia traktatów międzynarodowych*), Wilno 1932, p. 17.

preceding the establishing of the norm; in the fifth place he puts unpublished documents, concealed intentions of the contracting parties and all other circumstances that may have influenced some of the authors of the norm, but which are known neither to the other co-authors, nor to those affected by the norm. The author quoted believes the latter source of knowledge of the will of the parties to be altogether inadmissible in interpreting an agreement, since nobody can be forced to bear the consequence of a state of affairs created without his will and knowledge[30].

This view is confirmed by the resolution of the Permanent Court of International Justice concerning the territorial competence of the Oder International Commission. In this resolution, the Hague Tribunal barred from inclusion as evidence documents unknown to some parties to the dispute[31].

In interpreting the Yalta and Potsdam Agreements it should be noted that a certain revision on the eve of the Yalta Conference of the Anglo-American attitude with reference to the question of the Polish-German frontier — the product of specific political reasons — — was kept secret. The United States and Great Britain did not overtly reveal the motives of their opposition, and they still officially supported Polish territorial claims. Furthermore, attention is drawn to the fact that complete records of the Yalta and Potsdam Conferences have not yet been published[32].

---

[30] M. Król, *op. cit.*, p. 16.

[31] *Publ. de la Cour Permanente de Justice Internationale*, Ser. C. No. 17, vol. II, p. 42 (abbr.: *C. P. J. I.*).

[32] The American State Department publication issued under the title *Conferences at Malta and Yalta*, Washington 1955, represents no such record and contains only incomplete notes of the United States Delegation.

Many leading British and American political personalities having retired from the posts they had occupied have published memoirs not infrequently containing valuable information relating to the genesis of the Oder-Neisse frontier. Memoirs, however, must be handled with circumspection, since they have not infrequently been written as a matter of political expediency and in the interests of the current policies. Therefore, while not denying the informational value of memoirs, the material must be sifted and evaluated with considerable care; certain it is that they can by no means be regarded as fundamental in interpreting the most important legal acts relating to the Oder-Neisse frontier. All these legal acts embody a compromise between various—and in some instances conflicting—political interests of the Powers, and cannot be interpreted in the light of the wishes, plans and thwarted

[*Ed. note*: Since the first edition of B. Wiewióra's monograph, documents of great importance for the study of the problem have been made public. Foremost among them are the two volumes of documents published in Moscow and translated into Polish under the title *Korespondencja Przewodniczącego Rady Ministrów ZSRR z Prezydentem Stanów Zjednoczonych i Premierem W. Brytanii w okresie Wielkiej Wojny Narodowej 1941—1945* (The Correspondence of the Chairman of the U.S.S.R. Council of Ministers with the President of the United States and the Prime Minister of Great Britain during the Great National War of 1941—1945). These two volumes have been elaborated by the Commission for Diplomatic Documents at the U.S.S.R. Ministry of Foreign Affairs. The 687 closely printed pages contain 900 full documents from the archives of the Soviet Ministry of Foreign Affairs. The preface to this publication notices the absence of six documents which have been referred to in official British and American publications or quoted in the memoirs of western statesmen. So far none of the 900 documents has been questioned in the United States or Great Britain. No attempt has yet been made to confront the Soviet documents with the American papers concerning the Potsdam conference, included in the two-volume publication *Foreign Relations of the United States. Diplomatic Papers. The Conference of Berlin (The Potsdam Conference) 1945.* (vol. I, 1960, 1088 pp.; vol. II, 1960, 1645 pp.). Some aspects of the Soviet documents have been discussed by Wiewióra. See, for instance the article by Jerzy Krasuski and Bolesław Wiewióra on the problem of the Polish-German frontier in the correspondence of the heads of State of the U.S.S.R., Great Britain and the United States, published in *Przegląd Zachodni* 1958, No. 1, pp. 99—104.]

All this adds up to the conclusion that interpretations of the Yalta and Potsdam Agreements must be based first and foremost on the

---

hopes of certain only of the contracting parties. In particular, memoirs cannot be viewed as material, which is included in so-called preparatory work. Such material is usually understood to comprise documents illustrating the aims and intentions of the contracting parties, as expressed in the course of discussions on the legal wording of the final act. The records of the Teheran, Yalta and Potsdam conferences have not been published, and memoirs of participants in those conferences are no substitute for them, since memoirs are not of the character of official documents, and therefore they cannot serve as a basis for historical interpretation.

Their role in interpreting the Yalta and Potsdam decisions on Polish-German frontiers is far from being so weighty as is suggested by revisionist west German doctrine concerned with International Law, which takes advantage of the political, and not infrequently clearly biassed character of such materials and uses them as the foundation for legal constructions. Memoir material can be regarded as merely a supplementary source of information, whereas interpretation must be unequivocally based on definite legal standards, the essence of which has in many instances been defined in practice by the contracting parties.

texts of the documents, as well as on authentic and practical interpretation[33], while all other sources of information on the will of the parties, dating back to a period preceding the Conference, can be relevant from the viewpoint of International Law only to the extent to which they were revealed to the other parties. Mental reservations of some of the Great Powers, determined by political reasons, cannot afford a basis for interpretation, especially if such reservations were opposed to the essence of the legal norms and execution of such norms.

---

[33] See Chapter VIII.

CHAPTER IV

THE QUESTION OF THE POLISH-GERMAN FRONTIER AT THE YALTA CONFERENCE

1. DISCUSSION AT YALTA

The question of the Polish-German frontier to be agreed upon after the Second World War was an important item on the agenda of the Yalta Conference.

The discussion on that question can be reconstructed only on the evidence of the material available, with the explicit reservation that such material is incomplete and gives a one-sided view — that is the standpoint of the Western Powers.

The post-war Polish-German frontier was referred to for the first time on February 5, 1945, incidentally to a discussion on the possible dismemberment of Germany. On that occasion, Prime Minister Winston Churchill declared, *inter alia*, that all the Powers taking part in the Conference had agreed that Germany was to lose certain territories conquered by the Red Army, and that such were to become a part of Polish settlement territory[1]. The question was however discussed in full somewhat later. At a meeting on February 6, 1945, the Soviet Delegation proposed that the Polish-German frontier be drawn along a line running from Stettin to the south, following the course of the Oder and Western Neisse[2]. At the same time, Stalin appealed to the Governments of the United States

---

[1] *Die offiziellen Jalta-Dokumente des US State Departments*, Wien—München—Stuttgart—Zürich 1955, p. 88. (abbr.:Jalta-Dokumente)
[2] Leahy, *I was there*, London 1950, p. 359; Stettinius, *op. cit.*, p. 166; *Quellen*, p. 178. In these works the term "Western-Neisse" has been used, by which obviously was meant the Lusatian Neisse.

and Great Britain to support the Soviet Union in its effort to establish the Polish-German frontier on that line even if this should slightly prolong the war[3]. Minister Molotov also referred to the fact of the Provisional Polish Government having requested that the Polish western frontier be settled along the line proposed by the Soviet Government[4]. Ignoring the general acceptance of the Polish claim, as expressed in Roosevelt's letter of November 17, 1944, the United States Delegation made a counter proposition limiting Polish territorial acquisitions in the west and north to East Prussia, a minor part of Pomerania and Upper Silesia[5]. The American Delegation argued their proposal on the grounds of the great difficulties that would be entailed by the transfer of between 7 million and 10 million Germans inhabiting the lands east of the Oder--Neisse line[6]. This attempt to link the transfer of German population and the settling of the Polish-German frontier is characteristic of the attitude of the Western Powers[7]. It is especially conspicuous in the British propositions, which were as follows:

"Poland in the west would include Danzig, the regions of East Prussia west and south of Königsberg, the district of Oppeln in Silesia and the lands desired by Poland to the east of the Oder. All Germans in these regions were to be repatriated to Germany and all Poles in Germany, if they wished, would be repatriated to Poland"[8].

[3] J. Byrnes, *Speaking frankly*, New York—London 1947, pp. 29 ff.
[4] Stettinius, *op. cit.*, p. 191.
[5] Stettinius, *op. cit.*, pp. 47, 85, 188; *Quellen*, p. 181; *Jalta Dokumente*, p. 53.
[6] Stettinius, *op. cit.*, p. 44; Leahy, *op. cit.*, pp. 351, 363. Obviously the Lusatian Neisse was meant. It is clear from the approximate data (available at the Conference), that the representatives of the Three Great Powers did not know the exact number of Germans who would have to be transferred after the assignment of the territories on the Oder to Poland.
[7] Even during a meeting between Foreign Secretary Eden and Secretary of State Stettinius at Malta, before the Yalta Conference, this problem was discussed. The results were summed up by Eden in his report to Churchill of February 1, 1945, as follows: "The cessions upon what we and the Americans are agreed would involve the transfer of some 2¼ million Germans. The Oder frontier without Breslau and Stettin would involve a further 2¼ million. The Western Neisse frontier with Breslau and Stettin would involve an additional 3¼ million making 8 million in all". E. Wiskemann, *op. cit.*, p. 83.
[8] Stettinius, *op. cit.*, p. 190; *Quellen*, p. 182.

These British proposals were not altogether clear; in particular, the formulation "east of the Oder" called for an explanation.

During the course of the discussion, the Western Powers emphasized the difficulties involved in a transfer of German population from the territories to be taken over by Poland. On this point, Churchill strove to restrict the scope of the transfer and proposed to apply it only to East Prussia[9]. The Soviet representatives replied that the majority of the German population were fleeing before the advancing Red Army[10]. From the American Delegation, doubts were raised on two occasions as to whether President Roosevelt was constitutionally competent to make decisions on the Polish-German frontier without reference to the Senate[11]. Finally, an equivocal attitude was taken by Churchill who while he said that he did not object to the Oder line if that was what the Poles wanted[12], also declared his conviction that the British Government, would not accept the line of the Western Neisse[13].

The attitudes adopted by the United States and Great Britain on the question of the Polish-German frontier stood in glaring contradiction to the declarations they made towards the end of 1944[14]. Owing to these attitudes of the American and British diplomacies, Section VI of the Yalta Agreement, concerning Poland, failed to give a more detailed definition of future Polish territorial accessions

---

[9] In this connection, W a g n e r, *Die Entstehung der Oder-Neisse Linie*, Stuttgart 1953, p. 121, points out that the term East Prussia "...ist im Englischen zweideutig; es kann sowohl Ostpreussen als auch das östliche Preussen (jenseits der Oder) gemeint sein. Aus dem Zusammenhang ergibt sich, dass in diesem Fall das Gebiet östlich der Oder und nicht nur Ostpreussen gemeint ist. Oder sollte Churchill daran gedacht haben, Millionen von Deutschen in den Gebieten östlich der Oder, die Polen übergeben werden sollten, unter polnische Herrschaft kommen zu lassen? Nach allen vorangegangenen und nachfolgenden Äusserungen des Premiers ist dies sehr unwahrscheinlich".

[10] S t e t t i n i u s, *op. cit.*, p. 168.

[11] Roosevelt mentioned this on Feb. 8 and 10, 1945, L e a h y, *op. cit.*, pp. 363, 370—371.

[12] S t e t t i n i u s, *op. cit.*, p. 240. For an account of the entire discussion see *Quellen*, pp. 173 ff.

[13] S t e t t i n i u s, *op. cit.*, p. 291.

[14] G. M. S l a v i n, *Borba Sovietskovo Soyuza za diemokraticheskoye rieshenie polskovo voprosa v nachale 1945 g.* — Moskva 1952, p. 122, rightly stresses that Churchill behaved at Yalta as if Cadogan's letter did not exist.

and did not go beyond an expression of the general principle that "Poland must receive substantial accessions of territory in the North and West".

2. THE QUESTION OF COMPENSATION

Polish questions are dealt with in Section VI of the Yalta Agreement entitled "Poland". The most important decisions relating to Polish frontiers read as follows:

> "The three Heads of Government consider that the eastern frontier of Poland should follow the Curzon line with digressions from it in some regions of five to eight kilometres in favour of Poland. They recognized that Poland must receive substantial accessions of territory on the North and West. They feel that the opinion of the new Polish Provisional Government of National Unity should be sought in due course on the extent of these accessions and that the final delimitation of the western frontier of Poland should thereafter await the Peace Conference"[15].

In connection with that formulation, western literature, taking as a basis declarations by political personalities among the Western Powers, claims that the decisions of the Yalta Agreement as regards Polish frontiers are based on the principle of compensation. In support of this attitude it is emphasized that formulations concerned with Poland's eastern frontier are in immediate proximity to formulations referring to Poland's western frontier.

The notion of compensation cropped up in formulations by the Western Powers — strictly speaking in the terminology of British diplomacy — which imparted to it a political meaning. That notion was repeatedly advanced by Churchill in negotiations between the Great Powers and with the Polish London Government[16].

---

15 *United Nations Documents*, pp. 146—147.
16 According to Sasse, "Die Ostdeutsche Frage auf den Konferenzen von Teheran bis Potsdam", *Jahrbuch für die Geschichte Mittel- und Ostdeutschlands*, Tübingen 1953, vol. II, p. 226, Churchill formulated it even before the Teheran Conference, that is in the autumn of 1943. Compensation was also referred to in a memorandum by the Polish London Government dated

The political implications involved can be reduced to the following two main points:

1) they were to serve the Anglo-Saxon political leaders in explaining to their own nations the decisions on Polish frontiers as a whole;

2) they were calculated to persuade the Polish London Government to accept the proposed changes in Poland's eastern frontiers which, though approved by the Powers, met with resistance on the part of that Government.

Acceptance of this conception was calculated to remove the obstacles in the way of a resumption of diplomatic relations between the Polish London Government and the Government of the U.S.S.R., which would confirm the exclusive right of the former to represent the Polish State.

In view of the fact that the first implication was intended to convey the impression that the Western Powers agreed to a shifting of the Polish-German frontier eastward because Poland ought to be compensated for the lands ceded to the Soviet Union, the Soviet Foreign Minister declared on April 9, 1947, at the Moscow meeting of the Council of Foreign Ministers:

". . . at Potsdam, the point in question was not that of a simple compensation to Poland for the territories in the east she transferred to the Soviet Union. That would be an oversimplification. To the Soviet Union were ceded only lands inhabited by Ukrainians and White-Ruthenians united as of right with their brethren in the Soviet Ukraine and Soviet White-Ruthenia"[17].

In addition to the political implications, the compensation concept also has a judicial sense. In earlier practice of States, compensation

November 16, 1943 and submitted to Roosevelt and Churchill before the Teheran Conference. Furthermore, the compensation concept was mentioned in points 1 and 2 of the proposition submitted to the Polish London Government by Churchill on his return from Teheran in January 1944 (*Oder-Neisse*, p. 64), in an exchange of letters between Churchill and Stalin in February 1944 (XXX *Pierepiska*, vol. I, p. 204), in a speech in the House of Commons on May 14, 1944 (*Parliamentary Debates, House of Commons, Official Report*, v. 400, pp. 778 ff.), during talks in Moscov in October 1944 (*Oder-Neisse*, p. 67), and in a speech on February 27, 1945. (*Parliamentary Debates*, vol. 408, No. 31, pp. 1277—8).

[17] V. M. Molotov, *op. cit.*, pp. 427—428.

in the form of a cash transaction had appeared in connection with territorial changes[18]. Towards the end of the Second World War, the concept of compensation appeared in two instances in connection with contemplated territorial changes concerning Germany:

1) the intended shifting of Polish frontiers towards the west, and

2) the contemplated indemnities to the Netherlands for damage inflicted by German occupation[19].

The concept of compensation in the form of territorial concessions, for damage inflicted by German occupation, appeared after the war in reparation claims made by the Netherlands and Luxemburg against Germany, as defined in November 1946[20]. Also, as regards the taking over by Poland of the lands east of the Oder and Neisse, there were those who motivated Polish accessions as being compensation for losses suffered as a result of German occupation[21]. This idea appears to have been adopted also by the French Foreign

---

[18] The Paris Treaty (1899) between the United States and Spain concerning cession of the Philippine Islands to the United States, for which Spain was to receive 20 million dollars as compensation. Coleman Phillipson, *Termination of War and Treaties of Peace*, London 1916, p. 280.

[19] The *Briefing Book*, referred to above, formulated the United States State Department's viewpoint on that problem in section A, "Recommendations". In point 2 of the recommendations it was stated that the water frontier between the Netherlands and Germany should have been shifted from the western banks in the estuary of the river Ems to the main canal; furthermore, Dutch claims to the German territory on the grounds of indemnities for damage of Dutch lands, should have been considered. *Quellen*, p. 162. In this connection, President Roosevelt referred during the Yalta Conference, in the course of a talk with his advisers, to the problem of giving to Dutch farmers access for a period to certain west German territories by way of compensation for Dutch territories flooded by the Nazis, *Quellen*, p. 173.

The same attitude was adopted with regard to the Netherlands by Clement Attlee, then Britain's Deputy Premier, who, in a debate in the House of Commons on March 1, 1945, said: "...if it is necessary to take some German soil, to make it up to the entirely innocent Dutch people who have seen their land destroyed. I shall not complain". It is significant that he said in the very next sentence that: "if it is found necessary to take certain areas in order to enable the Polish people to lead a free, full life, I shall not complain — and I do not think that the Germans have a right to complain". *Parliamentary Debates*, vol. 408, No. 41, p. 1617.

[20] Keesing's *Archiv der Gegenwart*, 1946-7, 917G, 935B.

[21] E. Wiskemann, *op. cit.*, p. 134, and *Oder-Neisse*, pp. 62 and 166. Also J. Giertych, *Poland and Germany*, London 1958.

Minister Bidault at the Moscow Meeting of the Council of Foreign Ministers, in April 1947, as mentioned before[22].

Considering the differences indicated as to attitudes to compensation, and to the meaning given to the formula, the following observations suggest themselves:

1) as a basis for territorial claims against Germany, the concept of compensation was either rejected (U.S.S.R.) or treated as a political formula (Great Britain and United States), or, finally, regarded as an alternative form of reparation claim (France, Holland, Luxemburg, United States, Great Britain);

2) the fact that two adjacent sentences of Section VI of the Yalta Agreement deal with post-war Polish frontiers in the east and west does not imply any judicial correlation between the two decisions[23]. Since the *political* concept of compensation, though frequently referred to (especially by the Western Powers) in negotiations preceding the Yalta Conference, was ignored in the text of the Agreement, it is reasonable to assume that the Great Powers deliberately neglected to raise this political concept to the rank of a basis for the Polish-German frontier;

3) the fact that certain parties to the Yalta Agreement adopted this concept as a political basis for explaining changes in the German-Polish frontier, does not affect the legal consequences which follow from the Agreement concerning that frontier. (The more so since, essentially, the concept was not "addressed" to Germans, Poles or Russians, but to their own, or "third party" nations).

3. CONCLUSIONS FROM AN INTERPRETATION OF SECTION VI OF THE YALTA AGREEMENT

Section VI of the Yalta Agreement constitutes a *recognition of the principle* that Poland must receive *substantial* accessions of territory in the north and west. This recognition is binding on the

---

[22] See Chapter II, p. 63
[23] Contrary to A. Klafkowski, *Podstawy prawne*, p. 34.

signatories to the Yalta Agreement — the United States, Great Britain and the Soviet Union.

At the Yalta Conference, the Great Powers agreed in principle on the foundations of post-war Polish-German frontiers[24]. This is proved at least by the declarations made by the Heads of Government of the Western Powers after the Conference. President Roosevelt's report on the results of the Yalta Conference, included the following passage:

". . . it was *agreed* (my italics — B.W.) also that the new Poland, will have a large and long coastline and many new harbours. Also that East Prussia, most of it, will go to Poland. . . Also. . . I think Danzig would be a lot better if it were Polish"[25].

Further Prime Minister Churchill said in his report to the House of Commons on February 27, 1945:

". . . the three Powers have now *agreed* (my italics — B.W.) that Poland shall receive substantial accessions of territory both in the North and in the West. In the North she will certainly receive, in the place of a precarious Corridor, the great city of Danzig, the greater part of East Prussia west and south of Königsberg and a long, wide sea front on the Baltic. In the West she will receive the important industrial province of Upper Silesia and, in addition, such other territories to the East of the Oder as it may be decided at the peace settlement to detach from Germany after the views of a broadly based Polish Government have been ascertained"[26].

Furthermore, Churchill declared:

"We need not fear that the task of holding these new lines will be too heavy for Poland, or that it will bring about another German revenge or that it will, to use a conventional phrase, sow the seeds of future wars. We intend to take steps far more drastic and effective than those which followed

---

[24] Confirmed by L e a h y, *op. cit.*, p. 378, who said in referring to the results of the Yalta Conference: "These three men agreed . . .to transfer territory from Germany to Poland that would *necessitate* (my italics — BW) the deportation of between 7 million and 10 million inhabitants (if that many survived)".

[25] *Zbiór Dokumentów* 1946, No. 12, p. 416.

[26] *Parliamentary Debates*, vol. 408, No. 31, pp. 1277-8.

the last war, because we know much more about this business, so as to render all offensive action by Germany utterly impossible for generations to come"[27].

In addition to the demilitarization and denazification of Germany, the measures, referred to by Churchill and designed to prevent a recurrence of German aggression, undoubtedly included the transfer of the German population. This must be specially emphasized because as the materials quoted make clear, the Anglo-Saxon Powers linked the question of transfer with that of Polish territorial accessions in the west; the extent of the agreed transfer of German population was of fundamental importance to the final setting of Poland's western frontier in the Potsdam Agreement.

In the light of the decisions in Section VI of the Yalta Agreement Poland's situation was as follows:

1) Poland, not herself a party to the Yalta Agreement, was empowered to demand that the Three Powers should obtain for her substantial territorial accessions in the west and north. This demand could not be satisfied until after the Great Powers were in a position to decide the fate of Germany and to start putting into practice the programme of rebuilding Germany as outlined in Section II of the Agreement — that is after unconditional surrender.

2) Poland was assured that she would be consulted prior to any decisions being taken by the Great Powers as regards Poland's western frontiers. Poland's right to demand that she be consulted on issues in which she has an interest is implied also by the general decisions in Section V of the Yalta Agreements: "The three Governments will consult the other United Nations and provisional authorities or other Governments in Europe when matters of direct interest to them are under consideration"[28].

3) Analysis of the text makes it clear, that the opinion of the Provisional Government of National Unity on the extent of Poland's territorial accesions would be sought by the Great Powers "in due

[27] *Ibid.* p. 1278.
[28] *United Nations Documents*, p. 147.

course", but that "the final delimitation of the western frontier of Poland should *thereafter* (my italics — B. W.) await the Peace Conference". The parties to the Yalta Agreement thus envisaged the possibility of a break in time between the moment of decision on the course of the frontier and its final delimitation. Since final delimitation was to take place during the Peace Conference, the Polish-German frontier could already be substantially decided *even before the Peace Conference*. This was, after all, in agreement with the attitude of the United States and Great Britain formulated as early as 1944.

In concluding an analysis of the part of the Yalta Decisions dealing with Polish questions, reference must be made to the decisions concerning the transformation of the Provisional Polish Government into the Provisional Government of National Unity, and the question of elections in Poland. These decisions would call for a separate legal analysis which, however, *would bear no relation to the question of Polish-German frontiers*. Nevertheless, since in German revisionist literature there have appeared — based on clearly indicated tendencies among the Western Powers to make their attitude towards Polish territorial claims dependent on Poland's political system[29] — views suggesting that Great Britain and the United States agreed to Polish accessions in the west *on the condition* that there should be established "a free and democratic Poland", and further that, the condition not having been fulfilled[30], the Western Powers stand released from their obligation to support Polish territorial claims, some comment is important.

The revisionists' arguments, based on the construction referred to above, are of course completely illfounded. The Western Powers were indeed inclined to support the territorial claims of the Polish London Government with far greater vigour than the claims of leftist forces, however:

---

[29] Eden's letter to Churchill, February 1, 1945.

[30] E. W i s k e m a n n, *op. cit.*, p. 112, sums up the views of German revisionists as follows: "The Germans claim that the British and Americans only agreed to the expansion of Poland to the West on condition that a free and democratic Poland was established, a condition which was certainly not fulfilled by appointing Mikolajczyk as a Vice-Premier in circumstances which he soon discovered to be intolerable".

1) the Polish London Government, as also the Polish Committee of National Liberation, and the subsequent Polish Provisional Government acted as organs representing Poland in international relations [31];

2) as organs representing the Polish State in relations with other States, both the Polish London Government and the Polish Provisional Government accepted obligations and acquired rights in the name of the Polish State as being a subject of International Law;

3) irrespective of whether the Western Powers expressed their support for Polish claims to this Government or that, such support was given to Poland *as being a subject of International Law.*

The significance of the Yalta Agreement as regards the question of post-war Polish-German frontiers lies first and foremost in the fact that the Great Powers, acting on behalf of the Second World War Allies, decided for the first time, in the interests of international peace and security, to assume the obligation to recognize Polish territorial claims in the west and north. The question of the Polish-German frontier ceased to be a subject of negotiation and became a subject of legal obligation. Polish rights acquired by virtue of the Yalta Agreement make the decisions in Section VI of the Agreement a *pactum in favorem tertii* [32]. The significance of the obligations of

---

[31] Here I am not concerned with the question of the representative nature of the two Governments, since that is irrelevant to the matter in question.

[32] A. Klafkowski in his work on legal foundations of the Oder-Neisse frontier (*Podstawy prawne*) pp. 25—26, emphasizes that the Yalta Agreement conferred also certain benefits on France, in addition to those conferred on Poland. The construction of *pactum in favorem tertii* is not, with reference to Poland, admitted by J. Makowski in his work on the legal character of agreements concluded during the Second World War (*Charakter prawny umów*, p. 19); he sees Section VI of the Yalta Agreement as containing an offer made to, and accepted by, the Polish Government. This view is contradicted by the text of the Yalta Agreement which does indeed contain an offer, but an offer to France, to "be invited by the Three Powers, if she should so desire, to take over a zone of occupation and to participate as a fourth member of the Control Commission" (Section II of the Yalta Agreement). There is no analogical invitation to Poland in Section VI. Makowski refers to conditions fulfilled by the Polish Government and identifies the conditions with an offer accepted. In actual fact, the conditions concerned only a reconstruction of the Polish Government, which, thereupon, was to be recognized by all the Great Powers. The question of the western frontier was in the exclusive competence of the Great Powers and was independent of any conditions. Thus, when the Polish Government

the Great Powers towards Poland was all the greater because the Powers planned to reshape Germany — after her unconditional surrender — from a totalitarian State into a democratic and peaceful one, and were to determine, in the interest of international peace and security, the new political pattern of Europe. The Polish-German frontier was not however defined in greater detail at the Yalta Conference. Reasons for this were the Western Powers' diplomatic action, referred to above, and in part the military operations still in progress. A final settlement of the Polish-German frontier took place during the subsequent meeting of the Big Three, that is, at the Berlin Conference.

---

made a declaration accepting the Yalta Agreement in its entirety — *Documents*, vol. VII, p. 904 — this was above all tantamount to an acceptance of the obligation to reorganize the Government. By virtue of general formulations in Section VI of the Yalta Agreement, Poland acquired merely a recognition of her claim to "substantial accessions of territory in the North and West", and this was a classical "purchase of hope" (*emptio rei speratae*), since the object of the obligations assumed by the Great Powers was not yet defined in detail. Furthermore except for France, which was mentioned *expressis verbis*, the Yalta Agreement did not envisage the possibility of accession by any other State; France's accession was a typical discretionary act of the Great Powers acting on behalf of the victorious Allied Nations.

CHAPTER V

THE POTSDAM AGREEMENT AS THE LEGAL BASIS OF THE POLISH-GERMAN FRONTIER

1. POLAND'S LEGAL STATUS IN THE POTSDAM AGREEMENT

Before analysing the Potsdam Agreement as regards the part it played in settling the post-war Polish-German frontier, it is necessary to define the status of particular countries implicated in the Agreement.

[*Ed. Note*: Since the publication of the first English edition of Wiewióra's book three monographs on the Potsdam conference have been produced. The first was the study by Fritz Faust, *Das Potsdamer Abkommen und seine völkerrechtliche Bedeutung* (Frankfurt a/M — Berlin 1959, 201 pp., 2nd ed. in 1960). The same year saw the publication of Herbert Feis's book *Between War and Peace. The Potsdam Conference* (Princeton — New Jersey 1960, 367 pp. This is a diplomatic history of the Potsdam conference, including a section concerning the Polish-German frontier (pp. 203—235) and a number of annexes hitherto unknown. At the same time a monograph by Alfons Klafkowski was published in Poland under the title *Umowa Poczdamska z dnia 2.VIII. 1945 r. Podstawy prawne likwidacji skutków wojny polsko-niemieckiej z lat 1939—1945* (The Potsdam Agreement of August 2nd, 1945. Legal Foundations of the Liquidation of the Effects of the Polish-German War of 1939—1945) (Warszawa 1960, 629 pp.). A revised edition of this monograph, supplemented by further source materials and documents, has been published in English under the title *The Potsdam Agreement* (Warszawa, Polish Scientific Publishers, 1963, 340 pp.). It is thus possible to compare the results of research on the Potsdam conference on the basis of monographs published at the same time in the German Federal Republic, the United States and Poland. The problem of the Polish-German frontier occupies a leading place in these publications. Since the previous English edition of Wiewióra's book appeared in 1959, it naturally could not mention the three monographs].

The first legal status to be defined is that of Poland. Poland was not a signatory to the Potsdam Agreement as a whole or to any of its provisions. However, the Potsdam Agreement decided problems so vital for Poland as the settling of her western frontier.

In the Yalta Agreement, the Great Powers guaranteed to Poland the right to express her opinion as to the extent of her territorial accessions from Germany. During the Potsdam Conference, Poland availed herself of this right, as was duly reflected in Section IX of the Potsdam Agreement.

The decision concerning the post-war Polish-German frontier was taken by the Great Powers in consultation with the Polish Provisional Government of National Unity. However, the opinion of the Polish Government influenced only the *extent* of Polish territorial accessions in the west and north; it had no effect on the decision *per se* which settled the new Polish-German frontier. This was a decision exclusively taken by the Great Powers responsible for a rapid and orderly transition from war to peace and for ensuring to the post-war world peace and security.

Hence the conclusion that in defining Poland's legal status in the Potsdam Agreement a legal construction must be adopted analogical to that referring to the Yalta Agreement — that is that of *pactum in favorem tertii*[1].

Agreements conferring certain rights upon a third country, not party to the agreement are — although rare — nevertheless known in International Law[2]. The question as to whether a *pactum in favorem tertii* is admissible has been not infrequently discussed in literature concerning International Law[3]. But the existence of such agreements (or clauses in agreements) has been confirmed by the

---

[1] A. Klafkowski, *Podstawy prawne*, p. 26; this conclusion is further supported by the executive character of Section IX, paragraph B, of the Potsdam Agreement in relation to Section VI of the Yalta Agreement. Poland's legal status in the Yalta and Potsdam Agreements *had to be identical*. In both acts Poland appeared as a *third party State* benefiting from certain rights granted to it.

[2] Liszt-Fleischmann, *op. cit.*, p. 259.

[3] See Roxburgh *op. cit.*, *passim*. Cf. the viewpoint of Soviet doctrine: I. S. Pereterski, "Znachenie miezhdunarodnovo dogovora dla tretievo gosudarstva", *Sovietskoye gosudarstvo i pravo*, 1957, No. 4.

practice of States (for example, Art. 109 of the Treaty of Versailles gave territory in Schleswig to Denmark, although that country did not take part in the First World War). That agreements in favour of third party States are admissible is also stated in an award by the Permanent Court of International Justice on the free zones of Upper Savoy and Gex[4]. But to acquire such rights, it is necessary for the third party State to express agreement[5]. Agreement of the third party State may be either distinct or implied (*per facta concludentia*)[6]. Once a third party State, not a party to the agreement, has acquired the rights accorded to it, such rights cannot be varied without its consent[7].

Poland demanded that her western frontier be established on the Oder and Western Neisse. A delegation of the Provisional Government of National Unity submitted this demand to the Heads of Government of the United States, Great Britain and the Soviet Union during the Potsdam Conference. To exert any further influence on the decision concerning the Polish-German frontier was not possible to Poland. Agreement on this subject was reached between the Three Powers, agreement which accorded to Poland the right to draw her western frontier on the Oder-Western Neisse line. Once

---

[4] *C.P.J.I.*, Ser. A/B, No. 46, pp. 147—148.

[5] J. Makowski, in his textbook on International Law, pp. 454—455 also quotes a number of cases; L. Ehrlich, *Prawo narodów*, p. 216.

[6] J. Makowski, *op. cit.*, p. 455. In literature concerning International Law, there has appeared also the view that a third party State may by what is called tacit adherence become party to an agreement from the moment when it begins to give effect to the provisions of the agreement (*adhésion postérieure tacite*). See Despagnet, *Cours de droit international public*, 4th edition, 1910, § 59, p. 448, quoted after Roxburgh, *op. cit.*, p. 25. It was very likely this view which prompted certain Polish authors to formulate the concept that Poland became a party to the Potsdam Agreement *per facta concludentia* (Wł. Namysłowski, *op. cit.*, p. 813). L. Gelberg goes still further, describing the Potsdam Agreement as an open treaty to which Poland adhered, acquiring all the privileges of a party (expressed in a paper read at a scientific conference of the Polish Institute of International Affairs on March 23, 1948). The paper is condensed in a report by St. Nahlik on the work of the International Law Section of the Institute published in the *Rocznik Prawa Międzynarodowego* — Year-book of International Law, 1949, pp. 282—293.

[7] Oppenheim-Lauterpacht, *op. cit.*, vol. I, pp. 832—833. L. Ehrlich, *op. cit.*, p. 216.

Poland — as a *tertius* — availed herself of that right, any alteration of the present western frontier would require her consent.

The decisions of Section IX, § B, of the Potsdam Agreement thus contain a clause in favour of a third party State — viz., Poland. As previously stated, such clauses are not frequent in international agreements. But there is an element incorporated in the Potsdam Agreement which makes it an agreement without precedent: it grants to Poland, as a third party State, certain rights in relation to another third party State, which also took no part in the Potsdam Conference — Germany.

2. THE LEGAL STATUS OF GERMANY IN THE POTSDAM AGREEMENT

In traditional international jurisprudence the general principle is laid down that no agreement can impose any obligations on a State which is not a party to the agreement, since such would be incompatible with its sovereignty[8]. However, this principle was not always respected in the practice of States, and hence certain authors have been inclined to distinguish a category of agreements imposing obligation on third States[9].

The legal status of Germany in the Potsdam Agreement calls for a somewhat more detailed explanation. Two points are of special interest:

---

[8] Vattel, *Le droit des gens*, Paris 1863, "Préliminaires" § 24; Heffter, *Le droit international public de l'Europe*, 1866, § 83; Fiore, *Nouveau droit international public*, 2nd edition 1885, vol. II, p. 389; Calvo, *Le droit international*, Paris, 1896, vol. I, § 5, p. 143 and § 92, p. 16; Hall, *A Treatise on International Law*, Oxford 1909, pp. 8, 130; Pradier-Fodéré, *Traité de droit international public*, Paris 1885—1906, vol. I, p. 86, vol. II, pp. 477, 816; Bonfils, *Manuel de droit international public*, Paris 1912, pp. 53, 849; Despagnet, *Cours de droit international public*, 1910, p. 696; Pitt Cobbett, *op. cit.*, pp. 7, 10; Westlake, *International Law*, 2nd edition, Cambridge 1910—3, vol. I, pp. 130—131. A survey of views compiled by Roxburgh, *op. cit.*, p. 19. The principle is also confirmed by Oppenheim-Lauterpacht, *op. cit.*, vol. I, p. 834.

[9] Liszt-Fleischmann, *op. cit.*, p. 259; Guggenheim, *Lehrbuch des Völkerrechts* vol. I, pp. 88—89; Muszkat, *op. cit.*, vol. II, p. 105, quotes very recent examples of such agreements.

1) what were the legal foundations underlying decisions concerning German territory made by the participants in the Potsdam Conference?

2) whether the decisions of the Potsdam Agreement were permanently binding on the German State, and specifically, whether and to what degree the German State should be bound by the territorial clauses of the Potsdam Agreement for the future.

In this section let us analyse the first problem.

As regards the legal foundations of the dispositions of the Great Powers concerning German territory, there exist two fundamental views in Polish jurisprudence:

a) by signing an unconditional surrender, Germany gave so to speak *a priori* her consent to the Potsdam Agreement[10];

b) having assumed supreme authority as regards Germany, the Great Powers also assumed the right to effect changes in German territory[11].

---

[10] L. Gelberg in an article on tendencies in modern German international jurisprudence ("Tendencje we współczesnej niemieckiej literaturze prawa międzynarodowego"), *Państwo i Prawo* 1949, No. 1, p. 95; A. Klafkowski and W. Morawiecki in their work on collective security and the German problem (*Bezpieczeństwo zbiorowe a sprawa Niemiec, Zagadnienie bezpieczeństwa zbiorowego w Europie*). Materials of the Polish Academy of Sciences Session, Warszawa 1955, p. 179. A similar view was expressed by M. Muszkat in his article on the role of defence in the K.P.D. trial ("Rola obrony w procesie przeciw K.P.D."), *Państwo i Prawo* 1955, No. 6, p. 890. In western German literature, Wagner, *op. cit.*, p. 31, claims that the formula of unconditional surrender embodied also a desire to change German territory: „Nur von einem Deutschland, das bedingungslos kapituliert hatte, konnte man ohne Schwierigkeiten die Reparationen, die Zahlungen und die *Gebietsabtretungen* (my italics — B.W.) erreichen, die zu seiner dauernden Schwächung beitragen sollten".

[11] K. Skubiszewski in his paper on Paris Agreements (Umowy paryskie), p. 71, footnote 28, elaborating on the concept in the article by Y. R. Jennings, "Government in Commission", *British Yearbook of International Law*, vol. 23, 1946, p. 137. It is worth while to quote also a view formulated during a discussion at the 41st Meeting of the American Society of International Law in April 1947. In the discussion on Ch. Fairman's paper, *Military Occupation and the Development of International Law*, Major G. B. Crook declared: "In Germany the victorious powers did everything but annex German territory. In fact we specifically renounced annexation in the declaration of 5 June made in Berlin. However, we did place ourselves in the position of having undertaken to transfer certain German territory to the control of another government. I refer to the transfer of the territory lying east of the *present German border* (my italics — B.W.), to Polish Administration.

These two views are not at variance as to the essence of the problem, but only as to the meaning of unconditional surrender. The first view links with unconditional surrender far-reaching political and legal consequences, since it holds that Germany surrendered sovereign authority to the victorious Powers. The other view arises from the assumption that unconditional surrender is a purely military act having no legal consequences, whereas the assumption of supreme authority as regards Germany springs from *debellatio*[12]. The essence of the matter, on which there is in Polish literature an agreement of views is that the *decision concerning Germany's future —* consequently, also, the future of German territory — *was entirely within the competence of the victorious Great Powers.* This is further confirmed by the decision in Section I of the Potsdam Agreement, referring to the Council of Foreign Ministers, which provides in § 3, point 1: "The Council shall be utilised for the preparation of a peace settlement for Germany, to be accepted by the Government of Germany when a government adequate for the purpose is established"[13].

The legal status of Germany was determined by the following elements:

1) unconditional surrender,
2) the lack of an all-German Government,

Perhaps I should not use the term "present German border" as theoretically at least the eastern border of Germany is yet to be determined by treaty. Nevertheless, when we turned over Silesia and parts of Prussia, Brandenburg, and Pomerania, we were as a practical matter effectively disposing of this German territory. Further, we also reserved the right to transfer other German areas to Allied sovereignty if it should be decided at a later time that such a step was available. Under these circumstances, as we reserve the right of disposition though we renounce the right of annexation, I believe that we have a legal basis for claiming the power to exercise complete sovereign authority or its equivalent over Germany". *Proceedings of the American Society of International Law, at its Annual Meeting, April 24—26, 1947,* held in Washington, 1947, p. 144.

[12] An interesting evolution of views may be followed in the works by A. Klafkowski, who, in his *Podstawy prawne,* pp. 7—19, associates with unconditional surrender very important political and legal consequences, but accepts in his work on the problem of Treaty (*Sprawa Traktatu*), p. 19, the view formulated by K. Skubiszewski, in his paper on the problem of the German State (*Zagadnienie państwa*), p. 333, to the effect that unconditional surrender agreements involve purely military consequences. The latter view is shared by H. Kraus, *Die Oder-Neisse Linie,* p. 15.

[13] *United Nations Documents,* p. 194.

3) the plans of the Allies to transform Germany from a totalitarian into a democratic and peaceful State.

An analysis of these elements warrants the following conclusions:

As to the first point, the unconditional surrender insisted on by the Great Powers during the war meant, in the first place, that the victors refused to enter into *any* negotiations *with Nazi Germany*[14]. Furthermore, according to American views, unconditional surrender involved something more than narrow legal consequences: the point in question was reasonably to ensure universal peace for generations, liquidate German and Japanese military power, and eliminate in Germany, Italy and Japan the ideology based on conquests and subjugation of other nations[15]. In this declaration it is not difficult to trace the foreshadowing of a number of special measures to be applied to Germany and intended to transform that country into a peaceful State.

As to the second point, since, at the moment when military operations ceased, there was in Germany no other authority save the Nazi Government (the Government of Doenitz was not different in character from its predecessor), with which the victorious Powers refused to enter into peace negotiations[16] there was no possibility for Germany to participate in any negotiations with those Powers. By refusing to negotiate with the only organized authority in Germany, the Great Powers temporarily deprived Germany of the capacity to

---

[14] President Roosevelt's view on the significance and consequences of surrender are presented by Sherwood, *The White House Papers of Harry L. Hopkins*, London 1949, vol. II, pp. 693—694.

[15] *Quellen*, p. 50; cf. A. Klafkowski, *Sprawa traktatu*, p. 12.

[16] It is of interest to quote Art. II of the Treaty of Alliance between the Soviet Union and Great Britain (May 24, 1942), which reads: "The High Contracting Parties undertake not to enter into *any* (my italics — B.W.) negotiations with the Hitlerite Government or any other Government in Germany that does not clearly renounce all aggressive intentions, and not to negotiate or conclude except by mutual consent any armistice or peace treaty with Germany or any other State associated with her in acts of aggression in Europe".
This Article entails two obligations: 1) not to enter into any negotiations with aggressive Germany; 2) if there were a change of government in Germany and the new government denounced policies of aggression, negotiations would be possible only by mutual consent of the contracting Governments.

conclude legal acts, since there was no organ capable of making a declaration of will on behalf of the German State which would be valid in International Law.

As to the third point Germany was deliberately temporarily deprived of her capacity to undertake legal acts. This was involved in the fundamental aim of the Allied Nations — destruction of the totalitarian Nazi State machinery. This distinction made between Germany and the Nazi system is of fundamental importance. It was also expressed in the Yalta Agreement, Section II: "It is our inflexible purpose to destroy German militarism and Nazism and to ensure that Germany will never again be able to disturb the peace of the world"[17]. But further on appears the following: "It is not our purpose to destroy the people of Germany, but only when Nazism and militarism have been extirpated, will there be hope for a decent life for Germans, and a place for them in the comity of nations"[18]. A further expression of the endeavours of the Allied Nations to liquidate the Nazi State machinery and to uproot Nazi ideology will be found in the decisions of Section III of the Potsdam Agreement, where are formulated the principles of the occupation of Germany "during the period of Allied control". The aim of the agreement concerning "The political and economic principles to govern the treatment of Germany in the initial control period" was set out in the introductory paragraphs:

"The purpose of this agreement is to carry out the Crimean declaration on Germany. German militarism and Nazism will be extirpated and the Allies will take in agreement together, now and in the future, the other measures necessary to assure that Germany never again will threaten her neighbours or the peace of the world. It is not the intention of the Allies to destory or enslave the German people. It is the intention of the Allies that the German people be given opportunity to prepare for the eventual reconstruction of their life on a democratic and peaceful basis. If their own efforts are steadily directed to this end it will be possible for them in due course to take their place among the free and peaceful peoples of the world"[19].

---

[17] *United Nations Documents*, p. 143.

[18] *Ibid.*, pp. 143—144.

[19] *Ibid.*, pp. 195—196.

Germany was deliberately deprived by the victorious Powers of a central authority, since the reshaping of Germany was to start from the bottom, from a democratization of local administration. Absence of a central government *made it impossible for Germany to become a party to the Potsdam Agreement*, since she found herself in the position of a subject of International Law temporarily deprived of capacity to conclude legal acts. The State, as subject of International Law, acts through its organs. In the absence of such organs qualified to represent the State internationally, the State is incapable of acting with legal consequences.

The fact that Germany was deprived by the victorious Powers of a central authority, and thereby legally incapacitated in International Law, was a preliminary stage in the process of democratizing Germany and transforming her from an aggressive into a peaceful State. This process was to ensure that "Germany never again will threaten her neighbours or the peace of the world". In order to give effect to this aim, recourse had to be taken to various means: temporary assumption of supreme authority with respect to Germany by the victorious Powers[20], the laying down of such principles of occupation and control as would make effective the policies of transforming Germany into a peaceful State[21] and giving Germany a new territorial and ethnic pattern.

---

[20] "Declaration regarding the defeat of Germany and the assumption of supreme authority with respect to Germany by the Governments of the United Kingdom, the United States of America and the Union of Soviet Socialist Republics and the Provisional Government of the French Republic" of 5 June 1945, *Unconditional Surrender of Germany*. Germany, No. 1 (1945), H. M. Stationery Office.

[21] The principles are defined by Section III of the Potsdam Agreement. Their fundamental purpose was "to destroy potential sources of aggression by fundamental democratization and demilitarization of Germany". See Polish Government's note to the Governments of the United States, Great Britain and France, October 8, 1949, in connection with the setting up of a West German State. *Zbiór Dokumentów*, 1949, No. 10, p. 841. The purpose of the Potsdam Agreement was similarly formulated by Minister Gromyko, who said, as a representative of the Soviet Union at the preliminary conference of Deputy Foreign Ministers in Paris on June 21, 1951: "It is known that in the Potsdam Agreement, Four Powers pledged themselves not to permit of any revival of German militarism, to ensure the security of European nations, and to prevent future German aggression", (translated from Russian) *Zbiór Dokumentów*, 1951, No. 11, p. 2031. In order to secure these ends,

3. BERLIN DECLARATION OF JUNE 5, 1945

In defining the qualifications of the Great Powers special importance attaches to the Declaration by the Four Powers, June 5, 1945, regarding the assumption of supreme authority with respect to Germany which includes:

"The Governments of the United Kingdom, the United States of America and the Union of Soviet Socialist Republics, and the Provisional Government of the French Republic, will hereafter determine the boundaries of Germany or any part thereof and the status of Germany or any area at present being part of German territory"[22].

It clearly follows from the excerpt quoted from the Declaration that within the scope of supreme authority over Germany the Great Powers conferred on themselves *full competence to settle future German boundaries, and the right to dispose of German territory.* Revisionist West German jurisprudence — by laying primary emphasis on the fact that, in the Declaration referred to, the victorious Powers announced that the assumption of supreme authority did not effect the annexation of Germany, as also on the Statement by the Governments of the Great Powers of the same date, June 5, 1945, concerning the zones of occupation in Germany, in which we read: "Germany, within her frontiers as they were on the 31 December, 1937, will, for the purposes of occupation, be divided into four zones . . ."[23]

---

it was necessary — as A. Klafkowski emphasized in an article on the concept of a uniform German State ("Konstrukcja jednolitego państwa niemieckiego", *Przegląd Zachodni* 1948, No. 7/8, p. 103) — to base the occupation of Germany not on the IV Hague Convention, but on special principles defined in Section III of the Potsdam Agreement. A similar attitude was adopted by Soviet jurisprudence: F. I. Kozhevnikov, "Niekotoryie voprosy tieorii i praktiki miezhdunarodnovo dogovora", *Sovietskoye gosudarstvo i pravo* 1954, No. 2, p. 72, argues that the occupation of Germany had the special character of an international safeguard against renewed aggression and violation of International Law by Germany.

[22] *Unconditional Surrender of Germany*, Germany, No. 1 (1945), His Majesty's Stationery Office, p. 2.

[23] *Ibid.* p. 7.

— strives to draw the conclusion that the Great Powers had assumed an obligation to preserve German frontiers of 1937[24].

This conclusion is completely unfounded. The statement that the assumption of supreme authority as regards Germany did not effect the annexation of Germany merely emphasized that Germany did not cease to exist as a State in spite of the occupation of the entire German territory and liquidation of the central government. On the other hand, it did not signify an automatic acknowledgement of Germany's 1937 frontiers. On the contrary, the distinct statement that the Allies would themselves determine the future "boundaries of Germany or any part thereof" proves that the Great Powers reserved to themselves liberty to determine such frontiers, and clearly envisaged changes. In the light of these decisions, the division of Germany "within her frontiers of December 31, 1937" into zones of occupation was unquestionably a temporary arrangement made merely for technical administrative reasons. That arrangement was replaced by subsequent decisions of the Potsdam Agreement in respect of both the Polish-German frontier and the surrender to Soviet Russia of the Königsberg region. The Statement of the Powers "on the zones of occupation in Germany" in no sense established any rights for Germany; on the contrary, it subjected the whole territory as at December 31, 1937, to the authority of the occupying Powers which were to define Germany's future boundaries.

In this connection, it is necessary to define the attitude to be taken with reference to the concept current in West German literature concerning the annexation by Poland of the provinces east of the Oder and Neisse. The revisionists' argument runs as follows: annexation is an act prohibited in contemporary International Law; Poland has effected annexation, and, therefore, Poland has violated International Law[25].

---

[24] *Ost-Handbuch*, Part 15, p. 66, and other revisionist works; the West German weekly *Der Spiegel* of April 17, 1957, No. 16, makes the following comment on these views: "Dass selbst diese Rechtsposition auf etwas schwankendem Boden steht, wird intern von zahlreichen Politikern und Völkerrechtlern zugegeben, weil es sich bei der alliierten Erklärung nur um eine verwaltungstechnische Massnahme «zum Zwecke der Besatzung» handele".

[25] E.g., H. Kraus, *op. cit.*, *passim*, v. d. Heydte, *op. cit.*, p. 85. This

[*Ed. note*: Wiewióra studied the West German revisionists'
claims against the Polish-German frontier and presented the
results of his research in the article "West German Territorial
Claims Against Poland and International Law", published in
Polish Western Affairs, Poznań 1961, No. 1, pp. 3—30.]

The concept completely ignores the role of the Great Powers,
which, after all, conferred on themselves authority to define future
German boundaries. Poland did not effect annexation which consists
in the armed conquest of specific territories[26], but took over the
Recovered Territories by virtue of the decision of the Potsdam Conference. The legal basis for the taking over by Poland of these territories is provided not by alleged Polish conquest but by a decision
of the Great Powers.

The Great Powers — conducting, in agreement with the announcement made in the Moscow Declaration on general security,
October 30, 1943, a "joint action on behalf of the community of
nations"[27] and "acting... in the interests of the United Nations"[28] — were competent to determine German frontiers and
to make far reaching changes in the structure of Germany and Europe
by transferring German minorities from States neighbouring on Germany. Thus *Germany's legal status in the Potsdam Agreement particularly in the Sections concerning German territory, is defined by the
fact that the Great Powers*, being responsible for carrying into effect
the aims of the Allied programme, i.e. for ensuring peace and security
after the war, *have themselves defined German frontiers in the interests
of peace and security in Europe and with a view to establishing a future
peaceful German State.*

The conclusions arising out of an analysis of the legal basis on
which were founded decisions by the Great Powers concerning German territory, also give a partial answer to the question, posed in
the preceding section, as to whether the Potsdam Agreement was
binding on the future German State. It must be appreciated that it

argument was also used by Carroll Reece in his speech in the United States
Congress, May 16, 1957, entitled *On German Provinces East of Oder-
Neisse Line, and Economic, Historical, Legal, and Political Aspects Involved*,
U. S. Government Printing Office, Washington 1957, pp. 19—22.

[26] Liszt-Fleischmann, *op. cit.*, p. 150.
[27] Point 5 of the Moscow Declaration, *United Nations Documents* p. 13.
[28] *Unconditional Surrender of Germany*, Germany No. 1, p. 2.

is not merely territorial stipulations which are in question, but the *principle*, that is the binding power of the Potsdam Agreement with reference to Germany. The temporary incapacity of Germany as regards undertaking legal acts, the assumption of supreme authority by the Great Powers in order to carry through the programme of democratization, and the taking of several measures designed to establish a new territorial, ethnic, and political pattern of Germany in all this leads to the conclusion that the Potsdam Agreement afforded a legal framework for the programme of reshaping Germany into a democratic State and determined the direction and the ends of such reshaping. It also determined the scope of qualifications, aims and apparatus of the Great Powers' occupation authority in Germany.

Any German Government established on German territory was obliged to adopt as the starting point for its operations the principles laid down in the Potsdam Agreement, and to act within the framework it provided — since the Agreement alone regulated the situation in Germany, it alone defined the scope of the qualifications of the allied occupation authorities (Allied Control Council), and, finally, it provided a basis for mutual intercourse between a new German Government and the occupation authorities. In other words, no government could be created in Germany which would ignore the relevant legal status arising out of the Potsdam Agreement.

4. AN ANALYSIS OF SECTION IX OF THE POTSDAM AGREEMENT

At the Potsdam Conference, another controversy ensued owing to differences between the Soviet and the Anglo-American concepts regarding the post-war Polish-German frontier. The Western Powers again opposed the Soviet Delegation's proposition to establish the frontier on the Oder and Western Neisse.

Developments in Poland — the establishment and the composition of the Provisional Government of National Unity — thwarted the political plans of the Western Powers as regards Poland. The prospects for the taking over of control in Poland by political groupings supported by the United States and Great Britain were visibly dwindling[29]. Revolutionary changes in Poland reached to the very roots of the economic and social system. There was every indication of the process being irreversible. Therefore, the Western Powers lost interest in supporting Polish territorial claims.

On the other hand, the Potsdam Conference was considered a moment decisive for establishing the Polish-German frontier, since the problem was most intimately linked with the question of the future fate of Germany. It was impossible to determine the direction and principles to be followed in reshaping Germany without deciding her territorial boundaries. This clearly follows from the American propositions for the Potsdam Conference:

"Assuming that a Peace Conference with any German government would be indefinitely postponed, it would appear proper, and the President proposed to recommend, that the Conucil of Foreing Ministers after consultation with the Provisional Government of Poland, recommend to their respective governments an agreed delineation of the frontiers of Poland"[30].

These propositions were an attempt to postpone a decision, but they prove simultaneously that the Western Powers were prepared definitely to settle the Polish-German frontier even before a peace conference, at a special meeting of the Council of Foreign Ministers[31].

The attempts to postpone a decision concerning Poland's western frontier were opposed by the Soviet Union. Owing to the Soviet Delegation's opposition, the Western Powers gradually abandoned

---

[29] This matter was always an especial concern to the Western Powers. This was expressed by, among others, Churchill in his speech in the House of Commons, February 27, 1945: "To establish a free Polish nation, with a good home, to live in, has always far outweighed, in my mind, the actual tracing of the frontier line, . . ." (*Parliamentary Debates*), vol. 408, No. 31, p. 1275.

[30] Leahy, *op. cit.*, p. 457.

[31] Cf. Churchill's declaration on December 15, 1944, already quoted, concerning the necessity to determine Poland's frontiers before the end of the war, and the results of the studies of the American Post-War Plans Committee.

their attitude [32]. Eventually, after hearing on July 24, 1945, the opinion of the Polish Delegation, the Three Powers came, towards the end of the Conference, to an agreement the text of which can be read in Section IX, paragraph B of the Potsdam Agreement:

"The following agreement was reached on the western frontier of Poland: In conformity with the agreement on Poland reached at the Crimean Conference, the three Heads of Government have sought the opinion of the Polish Provisional Government of National Unity in regard to the accession of territory in the north and west which Poland should receive. The President of the National Council of Poland and members of the Polish Provisional Government of National Unity have been received at the Conference and have fully presented their views.

"The three Heads of Government reaffirm their opinion that the final delimitation of the western frontier of Poland should await the peace settlement.

"The three Heads of Government agree that, pending the final determination of Poland's western frontier, the former German territories east of a line running from the Baltic Sea immediately west of Swinemünde, and thence along the Oder River to the confluence of the Western Neisse River and along the Western Neisse to the Czechoslovak frontier, including that portion of East Prussia not placed under the administration of the Union of Soviet Socialist Republics in accordance with the understanding reached at this Conference and including the area of the former free city of Danzig, shall be under the administration of the Polish State and for such purposes should not be considered as part of the Soviet Zone of occupation in Germany"[33]

The text of the Agreement shows, above all, the executive character of the decisions relating to Section VI of the Yalta Agreement [34].

---

[32] The course of the discussion at the Potsdam Conference confirms the fact that the Oder-Neisse frontier was established as a result of the attitude of the Soviet Union — see *Quellen*, pp. 231—266; cf. Leahy, *op. cit.*, pp. 466, 474, 477—478, 493—494; J. Byrnes, *op. cit.*, pp. 79 ff. On July 29, 1945, the American Delegation proposed to settle the Polish-German frontier on the Eastern Neisse. The proposal was opposed by Minister Molotov. This fact refutes the claims of certain German revisionists to the effect that there was a fatal ignorance of geography among western political leader taking part in the conference. For example E. W. Meyer, *Die Grundlagen für den Frieden mit Deutschland*, Wiesbaden, p. 70. Above all, the suggestions are refuted by the text of Section IX of the Potsdam Agreement which explicitly refers to the Western Neisse.

[33] *United Nations Documents*, p. 273.

[34] This is also emphasized by J. Makowski in his work on the legal

The Yalta Agreement envisaged consultation with the Polish Government "in due course" as to the extent of Poland's territorial accessions in the north and west. "Due course" was to mean the moment when the time should be thought ripe for settling the Polish-German frontier. The fact that the opinion of representatives of Poland on that question was sought at the Potsdam Conference proves that *the moment considered by the Great Powers as "due" for settling the line of the Polish-German frontier was precisely the moment of this Conference.* The only task left to the peace conference was *formally to affirm the substance of the decisions,* which decisions were themselves intended by the Powers to be taken earlier, after hearing the opinion of the Polish Delegation [35].

Furthermore, it follows from the text of the Agreement that the Three Powers consented to Poland taking over former German provinces east of the Oder and Western Neisse line. Interpreting Section IX § B, attention should be paid to the following:

1) Introductory sentence to Section IX § B, refers to agreement having been reached "on the western frontier of Poland" [36]. If this were to be a provisional line of demarcation, the fact would undoubtedly have been expressed in the terminology which, however, uses the term "frontier".

2) In the text, the term "*former* German territories" is used. This means that the parties to the Agreement consider the territories east of the Oder and Western Neisse line as no longer belonging to Germany [37]. An aid to interpretation may be found in the fact that with reference to Gdańsk (Germ. Danzig) the analogical term —

---

character of agreements concluded during the Second World War (*Charakter prawny umów*) p. 22.

[35] Cf. Meister, *op. cit.,* p. 46.

[36] Cf. A. Klafkowski, *Podstawy prawne,* p. 33.

[37] A. Klafkowski, *ibid.*; Wł. Namysłowski, *op. cit.,* p. 813; O. Grotewohl, *Der Kampf um die einige Deutsche Demokratische Republik,* Berlin 1954, vol. II, p. 152, states: "Wenn Worte überhaupt einen Sinn haben, dann besagt die Formulierung "die früher deutschen Gebiete" vollkommen klar und eindeutig dass die. . . Gebiete nach Unterzeichnung des Potsdamer Abkommens nicht mehr als deutsche Gebiete gelten", quoted after Meister, *op. cit.,* p. 47. Also the note by the Polish Military Mission to the Allied Control Council for Germany of July 11, 1946, emphasizes the term "former German territories". *Zbiór Dokumentów,* 1948, No. 10, p. 683.

"*former* free city of Danzig" — is used, and Prime Minister Churchill and President Roosevelt made repeated assertations that the great city of Danzig would be given to Poland[38].

3) The greatest doubts may be occasioned by the wording "that the final delimitation of the western frontier of Poland should await the peace settlement". West German doctrine confronts this formulation with the statement that the territories east of the Oder and Western Neisse line "shall be under the administration of the Polish State and for such purposes should not be considered as part of the Soviet Zone of occupation in Germany". Comparing the two formulations, an attempt is made to conclude that the Potsdam decisions concerning the Polish-German frontier are merely provisional, and that from the legal point of view, German territory is, pending the signing of a peace treaty, defined by the 1937 frontiers[39]. This matter will be dealt with separately[40] and here we shall limit ourselves to an analysis of the meaning and scope of the term "administration", for which purpose the territories east of the Oder and Western Neisse were given to Poland.

What is this term to be taken to mean? An aid to interpretation will be found in the formulation that "for *such* purposes . . . (the territories) . . . should not be considered as part of the Soviet Zone of occupation". Since the system of uniform occupation, including the Soviet Zone of occupation, was to cover the whole of Germany[41], exclusion of the territories east of the Oder and Western Neisse

---

[38] Churchill asserted twice that Poland would receive Gdańsk in speeches on December 15, 1944, and February 27, 1945 — *Parliamentary Debates, House of Commons, Official Report*, vol. 406, No. 1, p. 1483 and vol. 408, No. 31, p. 1277 respectively; Roosevelt referred to this in his report on the Yalta Conference, *Zbiór Dokumentów* 1946, No. 12. German revisionists strive to put aside this argument by claiming that the formulations "former German territories" and "the area of the former free city of Danzig" are mere publishing errors — *Ost-Handbuch*, part 15, pp. 23-24.

[30] E. Kaufmann, *Deutschlands Rechtslage unter der Besatzung*, Stuttgart 1948, p. 23; Maurach, *op. cit.*, p. 113; Hoffmann, *Die Oder-Neisse Linie. Ihre politische Entwicklung und völkerrechtliche Lage*, Frankfurt am Main 1949, Nachtrag für 1950; *Ost-Handbuch*, part 15, p. 16; Wagner, *op. cit.*, p. 159.

[40] See Chapter VII.

[41] A. Klafkowski, *Podstawy prawne*, pp. 70—71. Cf. Section II of the Potsdam Agreement.

line is tantamount to their exemption from the principles of occupation laid down for the whole of Germany. From the above premises, two conclusions may be drawn:

1) Territories east of the Oder and Western Neisse line are not part of Germany, and 2) "administration" by Poland has nothing in common with the occupation extended to cover the whole of Germany[42].

Thus the question arises: if "administration" by Poland does not mean occupation, what then does it mean in fact?

In Polish literature, attention has been drawn to the fact that an analysis of the concept of "administration", based on linguistic studies and English dictionaries, leads to the conclusion that "administration" means "government" — that is the exercise of sovereign authority[43]. A similar conclusion is reached by making comparative studies: the term "administration" had already been used in the declaration by the Supreme Council of the Allies on December 8, 1919 (the Curzon note). This Declaration acknowledged the Polish Government's right to "establish a regular administration" on the territories west of the line defined in the declaration — that is of the Curzon-line. Poland's sovereign authority over the territories was thus acknowledged by recognizing her competence to arrange for their "administration"[44].

If we enter on comparative studies on the history of international relations in order to find a precedent for determining the meaning

---

[42] Cf. A. Klafkowski, *Podstawy prawne*, p. 69. In spite of this, see revisionists: Nadolny, *op. cit.*, p. 105; Maurach, *op. cit.*, p. 118, *Ost-Handbuch* part 15, p. 21; Hoffmann, *op. cit.*, *passim*.

[43] A. Bramson in his paper on some legal aspects of the Oder-Neisse frontier (*Z zagadnień prawnych granicy nad Odrą i Nysą*) — published in a book dedicated to Julian Makowski on the 50th anniversary of his scientific work, Warszawa 1957, p. 107. A. Bramson used generally known English dictionaries: *The Shorter Oxford English Dictionary*, Oxford 1956, p. 24 and *Webster's New International Dictionary of the English Language*, London 1947, vol. I, p. 34. That dictionaries are admissible in interpreting agreements is confirmed by international awards. See L. Ehrlich, in his book on interpretation of treaties, (*Interpretacja traktatów*), Wyd. Prawnicze. Warszawa 1957, pp. 160—161.

[44] K. Grzybowski in his study on the constitution of contemporary Poland 1944—8 (*Ustrój Polski współczesnej 1944—1948*), Czytelnik, Kraków 1948, p. 47.

of "administration" we must conclude that this procedure was applied, in the case of the administration of Cyprus by Great Britain' in the years 1878—1914[45].

However, while in the case referred to the authority of the administering State was restricted in some respects[46], there are no indications of such restrictions in Section IX of the Potsdam Agreement. Consequently, in determining the essence of the term "administration" the practice of the States interested is decisive.

In the context of Section IX of the Potsdam Agreement, the term "administration" meant that the parties to the Agreement consented to the establishment of Polish administration on the Recovered Territories before the frontier on the Oder and Western Neisse had been formally affirmed in a peace treaty.

The permanent and sovereign character of Polish authority over the Recovered Territories is evidenced by the fact that the scope of Polish administration was subject to no restrictions[47].

As a rule, a State taking over a territory establishes its administration only after formal cession of the territory is effected in the treaty.

---

[45] We' may, owing to its peculiar character, ignore a second known instance of administration, viz., administration by the United States of the Panama Canal (since 1903).

[46] See annex to the convention between Gr. Britain and Turkey, June 4, 1878. L. Gelberg, in his work on International Law and diplomatic history (*Prawo międzynarodowe i historia dyplomatyczna. Wybór dokumentów*), Warszawa 1954, vol. I, pp. 128—129.

[47] The fact that the Potsdam Agreement imposed no restrictions on Polish administration is confirmed even by a revisionist author Nadolny, *op. cit.*, p. 91: "...sie (sc. victorious Powers) haben die ganzen deutschen Provinzen östlich der Oder und Lausitzer Neisse ...unter eine derartige polnische Verwaltung gestellt, als ob sie ein integraler Bestandteil Polens wären". Polish literature advanced the view that a cession of German territory was effected in favour of Poland in the Potsdam Agreement, with the Great Powers disposing of German territory in virtue of assumption of supreme authority and acting as a substitute for the cedent (Germany) temporarily in a state of incapacity for undertaking legal acts (A. Klafkowski, in an article on territorial cession and the peace treaty against the background of the Oder-Neisse frontier, "Cesja terytorialna a traktat pokoju na tle granicy Odra-Nysa Łużycka", *Przegląd Zachodni* 1957, No. 1, pp. 10—11, 27). Although this view may give rise to certain doubts owing to a want of clarity in the definition of the legal status of not only the cedent (Germany) but also the cessionary (Poland), it cannot be denied that the fundamental element of cession, viz., the passing of the Recovered Territories under Polish sovereign authority is applied in this case.

In this case, however, the Great Powers — giving effect to reiterated intentions — abandoned that rule.

This interpretation is further supported by the following items:

1) There was nothing to present of the Great Powers recognizing the Recovered Territories as a fifth zone of occupation, or of disposing of it in some other manner, which would indicate their connection with Germany. Quite to the contrary, however, the Great Powers emphasized the severance of these territories from Germany by introducing into the text the words "former German territories". If the Great Powers indeed intended to determine the final course of the post-war Polish-German frontier only in the peace settlement, they would not have placed on Poland the obligation of completely unrestricted administration of the territories. Arguments to the effect that they were acting under moral duress — allegedly in the face of accomplished facts[48] — changes nothing. Moral duress (even for example, in the case of the delegation of a vanquished state during peace negotiations) does not abrogate obligations assumed under such duress[49]. To maintain otherwise would be to challenge the validity of all peace treaties imposed on vanquished States. However, in the case of the Potsdam Agreement there can be no question of the Great Powers acting under any moral duress. The simple fact that these were victorious Powers exposes the irrelevance of such claims. Thus we are faced only with the incontestable fact of the Great Powers having consented to Poland's extending her exclusive and unrestricted authority to the Recovered Territories[50].

2) Approval of the territorial scope of the transfer of German population ordained by Section XIII of the Potsdam Agreement, applicable also to all the Recovered Territories[51], confirms the con-

---

[48] *Ost-Handbuch*, part 15, pp. 15, 46.

[49] J. Makowski, *Podręcznik*, p. 413; Oppenheim-Lauterpacht, *op. cit.*, vol. I, p. 803; Liszt-Fleischmann, *op. cit.*, p. 246.

[50] The exclusiveness of Polish administration on the Recovered Territories is emphasized also in the note of the Polish Military Mission to the American Occupation Authorities of June 3, 1946. *Zbiór Dokumentów* 1949, No. 10, pp. 670—680.

[51] This is recognized even by revisionists: Nadolny, *op. cit.*, p. 81; Hoffmann, *op. cit.*, p. 16; G. Rhode, "Die Deutschen im Osten 1945", *Zeitschrift für Ostforschung*, part 3, 1953, p. 353.

cept that by "administration" the Great Powers understood extension of Poland's sovereign authority to the Recovered Territories[52]. For if the Great Powers did not consider the Oder-Neisse frontier as finally settled, they would have opposed transfer of German population from the Recovered Territories. But it is a generally known fact that they themselves suggested the transfer linking it intimately with the problem of Polish post-war territorial accesions in the west, and, moreover, that after the Potsdam Conference, they actively co-operated in the transfer of Germans from the Recovered Territories. Thus, extension of the principle of transfer to the territories is incontestable evidence that "administration" was understood by the Great Powers to be tantamount to the *factual handing over to Poland of sovereign authority over the Recovered Territories*[53]. Formal confirmation of the Polish-German frontier could not be effected by the Potsdam Agreement, without the participation of a German Government. Participation of the latter became indispensable from the moment when the Great Powers decided to preserve a German State. However, a central German Government was to come into existence and accept the peace settlement only after the rebuilding of the political system — that is after democratization and denazification of Germany[54], which was bound to take some time. It is obvious, on the other hand, that territorial decisions had to be made immediately.

---

[52] Cf. M e i s t e r, *op. cit.*, p. 48.

[53] In his declaration of April 17, 1947, Polish Foreign Minister Modzelewski said: "I emphasize that the definition «under Polish administration» with reference to the western territories was formulated at the Potsdam Conference in this manner merely for formal reasons, since confirmation of frontiers lies within the competence of a peace conference. As regards the American Delegation, it was the second after the U.S.S.R. to accept the Polish frontier on the Oder and Neisse. When President Truman was reading the decision of the Big Three concerning Poland's frontier in the west, he deliberately emphasized that the formulation «under Polish administration» is merely a formal expression since the formulation «frontier» is a matter for the peace conference". *Zbiór Dokumentów* 1947, No. 5, p. 225; cf. also the declaration of December 29, 1945 by the then Prime Minister in the Polish National Council. *Records of the Proceedings of the Polish National Council*, Session IX, pp. 21—22.

[54] Cf. a different definition by A. K l a f k o w s k i, *Podstawy prawne*, p. 32, who reaches the same conclusion starting, however, from the doubtful premise that Germany had ceased to be a subject of International Law.

CHAPTER VI

THE QUESTION OF DELIMITATION OF THE POLISH--GERMAN FRONTIER

1. THE CONCEPT OF DELIMITATION IN THE THEORY AND PRACTICE OF INTERNATIONAL LAW

The procedure of delimitation is connected with legal problems involved in changes of State frontiers — strictly speaking, in the drawing of frontiers. Delimitation is a technical term but its exact meaning has still to be defined in both theory and international practice.

A view exists whereby four main stages in the process of settling State frontiers are distinguished:

1) Political decisions on the allocation of territory;

2) Delimitation of the boundary in a treaty or other official document, and the marking of such frontier on a map;

3) Demarcation of the boundary on the ground;

4) Administration of the boundary (settling of minor current frontier problems)[1].

When such a procedure is attempted in practice, it is found that the two first stages cannot always be strictly separated; the political decisions on the allocation not infrequently coincide with second stage — that is, with a more detailed definition of the course of the frontier and marking it on a map. This occurs when the general allocation of a territory is decided at a conference at which the peace

---

[1] S. B. Jones, *op. cit.*, p. 5.

treaty is prepared. The political decision is then not expressed in the peace treaty and relevant information may be obtained only from the records of the conference, if such are published. In the peace treaty appears only a description of the course of the frontier, possibly plotted on a map, usually an annex to, and integral part of, the treaty. In such instances, the second stage is already upon us.

Examples may be found in the 1919 Peace Conference which prepared the peace treaties with the Central Powers, and in the Paris Peace Conference after the Second World War at which were prepared the peace treaties, signed on February 10, 1947, with Italy, Finland, Hungary, Rumania and Bulgaria. At both conferences decisions were taken on the general allocation of the territories involved, but in the peace treaties are to be found, in most cases, detailed decisions describing more or less accurately the course of the new frontiers[2].

In the past, however, there have been agreements restricted merely to a general decision concerning certain territorial changes. We may take as an example the treaty between France and Sardinia, signed in 1860, providing for the cession to France of Savoy and the district of Nice. The treaty merely laid down in general terms that Savoy and the district of Nice were ceded to France, and left the settling of the frontier to a special mixed commission to be appointed[3]. Similarly, the peace treaty with Austria, signed at Saint Germain on September 10, 1919, comprised certain general territorial stipulations and left details of the frontiers to be settled at a later date[4]. In accordance with the fourstage scheme for the delimitation of a State frontier, the political decision does usually precede the detailed laying down of the frontier included in treaties — primarily

---

[2] For example see territorial stipulation in the peace treaties with Italy and Hungary (Feb. 10, 1947). *United Nations Treaty Series*, vols. 41, 49

[3] M. Fleischmann, *Völkerrechtsquellen*, Halle a/Saale, 1905, p. 62.

[4] For example Art. 59 of the Treaty of Saint Germain provided that: L'Autriche renonce en ce qui la concerne en faveur de la Roumanie, à tous droits et titres sur la partie de l'ancien duché de Bukovine comprise en deçà des frontières de la Roumanie, telles qu'elles seront ultérieurement fixée par les Principales Puissances alliées et associées". *Dziennik Ustaw* 1925, *item* 114.

peace treaties — effecting territorial changes. This second stage is precisely delimitation. The third stage — the demarcation of the frontier on the ground — must be preceded by the first two stages: by political decisions on the general allocation of the territory and drawing the frontier on a map. Delimitation of the frontier on the ground is referred to as demarcation and essentially concludes the process of the settling of State frontiers. The settling of current frontier problems is without constitutive consequence for the frontier. Relations between neighbouring States may be arranged in various ways: the more intimate they are, the broader will be the basis on which will be settled frontier problems such as exploitation and maintenance of frontier rivers, what is called small frontier traffic, tourist traffic in frontier zones, etc. The settling of such problems is within the scope of what is called frontier administration[5].

The division into four stages, as indicated above, of the process of frontier delimitation has not, however, been accepted by all writers. Specifically, there are differences of view as to the scope of the term delimitation. Some authors give to the notion of delimitation a very wide meaning, covering in addition to determination of the frontier in the treaty and drawing of it on a map, also the tracing of it on the ground (that is, demarcation)[6]; others restrict its meaning by identifying delimitation with demarcation and refer to the tracing of the frontier on the spot as delimitation[7]. Still others make a strict distinction between delimitation and demarcation as being two different legal functions[8].

---

[5] S. B. Jones, *op. cit.*, p. 5.

[6] J. Makowski, *Charakter prawny umów*, defined delimitation of frontiers as "detailed fixing of the frontier on a large scale map and marking it by poles set up in accordance with the map".

[7] L. Ehrlich, *Prawo narodów*, p. 428; Pradier-Fodéré *op. cit.*, vol. II, pp. 326—327; Oppenheim-Lauterpacht, *op. cit.*, vol. I, p. 483, footnote 4. Similarly, the two terms are used alternatively by G. Ireland, *op. cit.*, *passim.*

[8] Durdienievsky and Krylow, *op. cit.*; Lapradelle-Niboyet, *Repertoire de droit international*, Paris 1930, vol. VIII, p. 489; S. B. Jones, *op. cit.*, p. 57; N. Kercea, *Die Staatsgrenze in den Grenzflüssen* (Dissertation zur Erlangung der Doktorwürde, Friedrich-Wilhelm-Universität zu Berlin). Berlin 1916, pp. 24, 33—34.

Delimitation and demarcation are in the practice of States not, in fact, synonymous. When frontiers are changed, special international agreements are made on the fixing of State frontiers[9], and in all agreements modifying frontiers provisions are usually made for special mixed commissions to deal with the tracing of the frontier on the ground. The commissions are referred to by different terms: for example, in Art. 30 of the 1919 Treaty of Versailles, in the English text will be found, the term *Boundary Commission*, and in the French text, *Commission de délimitation*[10]. Similarly, in the peace treaties with the satellite States of the Axis, (February 10, 1947), English texts use the term Boundary Commission and French texts the term Commission de délimitation[11]. As regards Polish practice, the commission which fixed the Polish-Czechoslovak frontier in the district of Spisz in 1920 was referred to as a delimitation commission[12]. In more recent practice, the commission which traced the Polish-Soviet frontier in 1947 was officially termed the Polish--Soviet Mixed Commission for the Delimitation of State Boundaries between the Polish Republic and the Union of Soviet Socialist Republics[13]. On the other hand, the commission which traced the Soviet-Norwegian frontier in 1947 was termed the Mixed Soviet-Norwegian Commission for the Demarcation of the State Boundary between the Soviet Union and Norway[14]. Concerning earlier practice, it is relevant to mention Art. 10, point 4, of the Russian draft of a convention on compulsory arbitration, proposed

---

[9] G. Ireland, *op. cit., passim.*

[10] *Treaty of Peace between the Allied and Associated Powers and Germany and Protocol signed at Versailles, June 28, 1919,* p. 23; *Traité de Paix entre les Puissances Alliées et Associées et l'Allemagne et Protocole signés à Versailles le 28 Juin 1919,* p. 23.

[11] For example Art. 5 of the peace treaty with Italy, and Art. 1, point 4, of the peace treaty with Hungary (February 10, 1947). *United Nation Treaty Series,* vols. 41 and 49.

[12] In the advisory opinion of the Permanent Court of International Justice in the Polish-Czechoslovak dispute over Jaworzyna, *Publ. C. P. J. I.,* Series B, No. 8.

[13] *Dziennik Ustaw,* 1949, pos. 323.

[14] See final protocol (Dec. 18, 1947) of the Mixed Soviet-Norwegian Commission for the Demarcation of the State Boundary between the Soviet Union and Norway. *United Nations Treaty Series.* vol. 52.

to the 1899 Hague Conference, which refers to demarcation conventions (*Conventions de démarcation*) as being concerned with purely technical problems[15].

The above examples show that there is a considerable confusion as to the exact meaning of, and distinction between, delimitation and demarcation, both in theoretical literature and in the practice of States.

On the basis of the practice of States and the views of scholars, the following tabulation of the meanings given to the term delimitation may be deduced:

1) fixing of a frontier in a treaty and marking it on a map;

2) detailed description of the frontier and marking on the map, *as well as* tracing in on the spot;

3) description of the frontier in the treaty, marking it on the map and appointing a commission for tracing it on the spot;

4) the simple tracing of the frontier on the spot.

In actual fact, the entire question may be reduced to determining whether we are to understand by delimitation the fixing of a frontier in a peace treaty with or without marking it on the map, or the tracing of the frontier on the ground when it becomes a synonym for demarcation[16]. This differentiation is essential in determining the role of delimitation in the process of establishing State boundaries. Since if we are to understand delimitation to mean the definition of its course in the treaty and the marking of it on a map, it may have constitutive significance in determining the course of a State boundary, provided it is not preceded by a political decision relating to the general allocation of the territory in question, and that delimitation decisions represent in the particular case the only expression of the will of the parties, — that is, the *first* fundamental norm determining the course of the frontier in question.

If, however, delimitation is to mean simply the tracing of a frontier on the ground, — that is, if it is to be construed as a narrow

---

[15] *Conférence Internationale de la Paix*, La Haye, 18 Mai-29 Juillet 1899. Ministère des Affaires Étrangères (Dutch), La Haye 1907, Annexe 1 A.

[16] See S. B. Jones, *op. cit.*, p. 17: "...delimitation is employed both with the meaning above (that is, "...the choice of a boundary site and its definition in a treaty") and also as a synonym for demarcation".

synonym for demarcation, the giving of effect to it will be devoid of constitutive significance for the course of the given frontier. It will become merely a technical function obligatory in agreement with the norm laid down in the treaty and defining the course of the given frontier. This does not imply that the tracing of the frontier on the ground is devoid of political significance. On the contrary, like every act concluding the process of State boundary determination, it is in many instances of considerable political significance, since it constitutes an indispensable condition for normal relations between two neighbouring States.

The practice of States — as also a number of authors — tends to support the concept in which delimitation denotes nothing more than a technical function, — that is, the tracing on the spot of the course of a frontier fixed in the treaty. In common practice, the States concerned set up a mixed commission of their representatives[17] charged with tracing the frontier on the ground. When the commission has finished its work, it draws up a protocol stating that the tracing of the frontier on the ground has been completed. Small scale maps showing the boundary traced on the ground are usually added to the protocol, of which they constitute an integral part.

In the process of tracing the frontier on the ground, *participation of interested States is indispensable.* In practice, so far as may be ascertained, there have been no instances in which a State directly concerned has not been present when the frontier was traced on the ground.

2. THE CONCEPT OF DELIMITATION IN THE POTSDAM AGREEMENT

In the Section of the Potsdam Agreement headed "Poland" § B appears the following formulation:

---

[17] Exceptionally, such commissions include also representatives of third party States: for example, in agreement with the provisions of the peace treaty with Italy (Feb. 10, 1947), the commission charged with fixing the boundaries of the Free Territory of Trieste comprised, in addition to re-

"The three Heads of Government reaffirm their opinion that *the final delimitation of the western frontier* of Poland should *await the peace settlement* (my italics — B. W.)
The three Heads of Government agree that, pending the *final determination* (my italics — B. W.) of Poland's western frontier, the former German territories east of a line. . ."[18]

The formulation quoted from the Section of the Potsdam Agreement indicated above, "that the final delimitation of the western frontier of Poland should await the peace settlement", has in revisionist doctrine in the German Federal Republic become the subject of attacks. In West German literature, great importance is attached to the formulation, which is said to mean that the Heads of Government of the Great Powers thereby decided at the Potsdam Conference to leave open the problem of the Polish-German frontier until the signing of a peace treaty with Germany. Pending the signing of this treaty, German territory was to be defined by the 1937 frontiers[19]. An analogous standpoint is adopted by the Government of the German Federal Republic.

Let us now consider whether such conclusions are in fact warranted by the formulation quoted above.

The wording that "the final delimitation of the western frontier of Poland should await the peace settlement" means only the *western frontier* of Poland, leaving the delimitation of the Polish-Soviet frontier in East Prussia to be arranged as a separate question in accordance with Potsdam Agreement Sections headed "City of Königsberg and the adjacent area" and "Poland" — between Poland and the Soviet Union[20].

---

presentatives of Yugoslavia and Italy, representatives of the Great Powers. Similarly, Art. 48 of the 1919 Treaty of Versailles, envisaged participation of the representatives of other Powers in addition to those of France and Germany, in the commission set up to fix frontiers of the Saar Basin.

[18] *United Nations Documents*, p. 203.

[19] E. Kaufmann, *Deutschland's Rechtslage unter der Besatzung*, Stuttgart 1948, p. 23; Maurach, *op. cit.*, p. 113; Hoffmann, *op. cit., Ost-Handbuch*, part 15, p. 16; Sasse, *op. cit.*, p. 211; H. Kraus, *op. cit.*, p. 35, f. 80.

[20] The question of this frontier was settled in accordance with the Potsdam decisions by Polish-Soviet agreements concerning State Boundaries of August 16, 1945, (*Dziennik Ustaw* 1947, item 167), and March 5, 1957 (*Dziennik Ustaw* 1958, item 166).

What does the term *"final delimitation"* mean in the context of the Potsdam Agreement? The notion of delimitation is, as already agreed, not unambiguous; some authors construe it to defining a frontier in a treaty and marking it on a map[21] while others understand it to mean the detailed definition in a treaty, marking on a map, and also tracing on the ground[22]. In practice, for the most part, as well as in a considerable proportion of the doctrine, delimitation is understood to mean merely the tracing of the frontier on the ground, which cannot show any serious deviations from the frontier as defined in an agreement. Any such deviations may involve only minor boundary modifications, insignificant in relation to the fundamental course of the frontier[23].

In accordance with general principles applied in interpreting international agreements, the notion of "final delimitation" must by analysed in its context.

Here, attention is draw to the terminological differences between, on the one hand, the Section of the Potsdam Agreement headed "Conclusion of peace-treaties and admission to United Nations Organization" and on the other, Section headed "Council of Foreign Ministers" and "Poland". For, while in the case of Italy and the satellite States of the Axis the state of war was to be liquidated by the signing of peace treaties, in the case of Germany the agreement refers to a *"peace settlement"*, but not peace treaty. Whence the difference? It can only be surmised that as regards Germany — starting from the assumption that she was the State to undergo far-reaching transformation in order to prevent her from ever again threatening world peace — the Allied Powers did not intend to limit themselves merely to preparing and concluding a peace treaty, but construed their task as being much broader. The issues involved included the question of setting up a central Government of a united Germany, and also, most likely, the projecting of the conditions of a peace

[21] S. B. Jones, *op. cit.*, p. 5.
[22] J. Makowski, *Charakter prawny umów*, p. 22.
[23] This attitude has been adopted by Polish authors: A. Klafkowski, *Podstawy prawne*, pp. 31—32; J. Makowski, *Charakter prawny umów*, pp. 22—23. Analogical views are put forward by Meister, *op. cit.*, p. 48.

treaty in the interests of the United Nations. The Four Chief Allied Powers, in full appreciation of their responsibility for world peace, decided to deal with all questions involved in a liquidation of the state of war with Germany. The solution of all these problems was covered by the term "peace settlement", in which the peace treaty constitutes only one link in an entire chain of problems.

How then, in the light of the above considerations, are we to understand "final delimitation?" The Section headed "Poland" § B, makes the reservation that the "final delimitation" of Poland's western frontier should await the peace settlement. If this were to mean the settling of the substance of the frontier, it ought to be noted that the only legal act suitable for this purpose would be a peace treaty. But, since the Section of the Potsdam Agreement headed "Poland" § B fails to mention peace treaty and is referring merely to a "peace settlement", it is to be understood that the point in question involves only the tracing of the frontier on the ground, which must be considered among acts covered by the term "peace settlement" for reasons already referred to (implementation ot the conditions of a peace treaty). It is obvious that delimitation, thus conceived, could be effected only after the cession to Poland of the territories east of the Oder-Neisse line had been formally expressed in a peace treaty.

The above conclusion is supported by international practice referred to and by the bulk of the doctrine, both of which in principle identify delimitation with the tracing of the frontier on the ground. There is nothing in the Potsdam Agreement to indicate that the concept of delimitation was intended to have a broader significance, different from that accepted in general practice. On the contrary, it follows unequivocally from the context of the Potsdam Agreement, and especially from the transfer of German population from the Polish Recovered Territories, that "final delimitation" could have meant nothing but the formal technico-judicial function of tracing the frontier on the ground, feasible only after the state of war had been terminated. It follows that *the substance* of the Polish-German frontier was settled in the Potsdam Agreement.

How then is the postponement of "final delimitation"of this frontier till the "peace settlement" motivated? The point is that delimitation requires the participation of the States directly concerned. The States involved were Poland and Germany, but the latter was temporarily incapacitated from undertaking legal activities. Therefore, the Potsdam Conference had to postpone the "final delimitation" of the Polish-German frontier to a date when Germany would be able to participate — that is, when she would regain her capacity to undertake legal activities.

Some doubts may be occasioned by the formulation that "pending the final *determinations* of Poland's western frontier, the former German territories... shall be under the administration of the Polish State and for such purposes should not be considered as part of the Soviet Zone of occupation in Germany".

The term "final determination" is not adequately precise. It is used in Anglo-Saxon literature alternatively with the terms "demarcation" and "delimitation"[24]. In the context of the Potsdam Agreement, the term "determination" is used in manifest conjunction with such notions as "administration" and "former German territories", analysed in the preceding Chapters. These show, together with the decisions of the Section of the Potsdam Agreement headed "Orderly transfers of German populations"[25] that the territories east of the Oder-Neisse line were placed under Poland's sovereign authority

---

[24] For instance: G. Ireland, *op. cit.*, p. 33, refers to tracing of a frontier on the ground as *"physical determination"*. Also A. Klafkowski, *Podstawy prawne*, p. 31, states that the English terms *delimitation* and *determination* are used alternatively; H. Kraus, *Die Oder-Neisse-Linie . . . , op. cit.*, p. 35, f. 80, admits Klafkowski to be right, but says at the same time: "Unverständlich ist es anderseits, wenn er (i.e. Klafkowski) behauptet, aus den gebrauchten Wendungen folge, die endgültige Delimitierung im Friedensvertrage betreffe nur die Bestimmung der Grenze im einzelnen. Die Klausel, dass die endgültige Bestimmung der Westgrenze Polens der Friedenskonferenz vorbehalten bleiben solle, kann nur bedeuten, dass die Entscheidung darüber, welches Gebiet bei Deutschland verbleiben, welches an Polen fallen solle, der Friedenskonferenz obliege. Aber es kann nicht bedeuten, dass diese Konferenz nur noch technische Einzelheiten der Linienführung vorzunehmen habe. Derartige Spezialaufgaben sind nicht Sache einer Friedenskonferenz, sondern von Sonderkommissionen".

[25] See below Chapter VII.

without need to await final delimitation of the western frontiers which could not have meant anything but the delimitation on the ground of the boundary determined at the Potsdam Conference. The stipulations concerning "final delimitation" and "final determination" of the Polish-German frontier *do not concern the substance* of the problem but merely the *mode of procedure.*

West German revisionists have a predilection for recalling the controversy between American Secretary of State Marshall and Minister Molotov at the Moscow Session of the Council of Foreign Ministers in April 1947. Marshall declared that according to this interpretation of the Potsdam Agreement "final determination of the Polish-German frontier should await the peace settlement"[26]. Marshall suggested a departure from the Oder-Neisse frontier and giving to Germany certain areas of the Polish Recovered Territories.

The controversy between Marshall and Molotov did not concern the concept of delimitation. Neither of the parties defined their attitude in relation to that procedure, and both were in agreement that delimitation of the Polish-German frontier could be finalised only in the peace settlement. The controversy involved only the question as to whether the peace conference could modify the essential course of the frontier. The Soviet Foreign Minister declared that the Potsdam decisions settled the course of the Polish-German frontier and that "the resolution of the Potsdam Conference is final and not subject to revision"[27].

The viewpoint ascribing to delimitation a merely formal character was also accepted in the United States. A close collaborator of the American State Department stated with reference to the Potsdam formula relating to delimitation of the Polish-German frontier that the Soviet interpretation tended to construe it as a merely formal confirmation by the peace treaty of the Potsdam decisions without a resumption of discussions on the substance. "Their view" — concluded the American author — "seemed confirmed by subsequent

---

[26]   *Zbiór Dokumentów* 1947, No. 5, p. 213.
[27]   Molotov, *op. cit.*, pp. 429—430.

American approval of the transfer to Germany of the Germans in the area taken over by Poland"[28].

3. DELIMITATION OF THE POLISH-GERMAN FRONTIER IN THE BOUNDARY AGREEMENTS BETWEEN POLAND AND THE GERMAN DEMOCRATIC REPUBLIC

Difficulties in the preparation of the peace settlement for Germany created a new situation in that country. The Council of Foreign Ministers, to whom the Powers delegated in Potsdam the task of preparing the peace settlement, failed to bring about the establishment of a united German State with an all-German Government. Owing to divergencies of view as between the Great Powers, and a deadlock in negotiations, two German States came into being: the German Federal Republic and the German Democratic Republic.

This state of affairs produced important consequences in respect of International Law. Instead of a single all-German Government, there emerged two German Governments exercising sovereign authority over the territories of the German Federal Republic and the German Democratic Republic respectively.

Recognition by the Government of the German Democratic Republic of the Oder-Neisse frontier as a settled and existing Polish--German frontier became the basis of friendly relations between Poland and the German Democratic Republic. As a result of the recognition of the frontier, three agreements were signed concerning the boundary between Poland and Germany:

1) Declaration by the Governments of the Polish Republic and German Democratic Republic on delimitation of the settled and existing Polish-German Frontier on the Oder and Neisse, signed in Warsaw on June 6, 1950;

---

[28] J. C. Campbell, "The European Territorial Settlement" *Foreign Affairs* 1947, October, vol. 26, No. 1, p. 200.

2) Agreement between the Polish Republic and the German Democratic Republic on delimitation of the settled and existing Polish German State frontier signed at Zgorzelec on July 6, 1950;

3) Act concerning the effecting of delimitation on the ground of the frontier between Poland and Germany, signed at Frankfurt-on-Oder on January 27, 1951.

The Warsaw Declaration of June 6, 1950, was of particular importance since it recognized the Polish-German frontier as *settled and existing*. It expressed recognition by both parties of the decision of the Section of the Potsdam Agreement headed "Poland" as finally settling the Polish-German frontier. Furthermore, the Declaration provided for the signing within a month of an agreement concerning delimitation of the frontier. However, the Warsaw Declaration is not constitutive in character — that is, it does not create a new legal situation. It is a *declaratory* act in the sense that it recognizes as existing the legal situation established in the Potsdam Agreement[29]. The only new obligation imposed on the parties by the Warsaw Declaration is the so to speak "procedural" obligation to conclude within a month the agreements referred to in the Declaration.

In conformity with the Warsaw Declaration, the Polish Republic and the German Democratic Republic signed at Zgorzelec, on July 6, 1950, an agreement on the delimitation of the settled and existing Polish-German State frontier[30].

The Zgorzelec Agreement refers to the Potsdam Agreement as the agreement which *settled* the Oder and Western Neisse frontier (preamble, paragraph 4), and takes as its aim" establishment of immovable foundations for peaceful and good neighbourly co-existence between the two Nations" (preamble, paragraph 3).

In Art. 1 the two parties recognize as the State boundary between Poland and *Germany* (as a whole) the frontier defined in the Potsdam Agreement. The description of the frontier in Art. 1 fits the analogical description in the Potsdam Agreement.

---

[29] On declarations as agreements stating norms already in existence see L. Ehrlich's manual on International Law (*Prawo narodów*), p. 222.

[30] For text see *Zbiór Dokumentów* 1950, No. 8, pp. 704 ff.

Art 2 reads: "The Polish-German State frontier delimited in conformity with this agreement delimits also in a vertical plane the area of air, sea and the interior of the earth". This article defines the territorial scope of the authority of the two States, in conformity with generally accepted theory and practice of International Law[31].

Art. 3 provides for a Mixed Polish-German Commission of eight members, charged with delimiting the frontier on the ground. The eight member commission established was a parity commission frequently met with in international practice — that is, it functioned without a chairman and consisted of members delegated in equal numbers by the two parties.

Art. 5 commits the parties to concluding a special act, usual in international practice[32], concerning the carrying out of the delimitation on the spot of the frontier between Poland and *Germany*.

Evaluating the judical significance of the Zgorzelec Agreement, its *executive character* should be emphasized as regards both the Potsdam Agreement and the Warsaw Declaration. Both are manifestly referred to in the preamble. As regards the legal status of the Polish-German frontier, the Agreement, much like the Warsaw Declaration, is self-evidently *declaratory* in character. The course of the western frontier of Poland defined in Art. 1, is in conformity with the description of the frontier in the Potsdam Agreement. The Article omits only East Prussia a part of which was accorded to Poland under the Section of the Potsdam Agreement headed "Poland" since on this territory now runs the Soviet-Polish frontier which could not be the subject of an agreement between Poland and the German Democratic Republic.

The Zgorzelec Agreement was another step towards the formal stabilization of the Polish-German frontier.

The Act recording the effecting of delimitation on the ground of the Polish-German frontier, envisaged in Art. 5 of the Zgorzelec

[31] Durdienievsky and Krylow, *op. cit.*, K. Strupp, *Wörterbuch des Völkerrechts*, vol. II, p. 615; Liszt-Fleischmann, *op. cit.*, pp. 136, 140 ff; Guggenheim, *op. cit.*, vol. I, pp. 337—340; J. Makowski, *Podręcznik*, p. 100, Oppenheim-Lauterpacht, *op. cit.*, vol. I, p. 417.
[32] Durdienievsky and Krylow, *op. cit.*; K. Strupp, *op. cit,.* vol. II, p. 616; *Dictionnaire Diplomatique*, vol. I, p. 940.

Agreement, was signed on January 27, 1951, at Frankfurt-on-Oder[33]. The text of the Act is preceded by a brief preamble in which the parties declare themselves desirous of peace and friendship between the two Nations. The Act consists of two Articles, and the annexes comprise a specification of documents and a map. The annexes, as also the documents mentioned therein, are an integral part of the Act. Article 1 of the Act reads as follows:

"In fulfilment of Art. 5 of the Agreement signed at Zgorzelec on July 6, 1950, between the Polish Republic and the German Democratic Republic concerning the delimitation of the settled and existing Polish-German State frontier, the two parties declare that the State frontier between Poland and Germany[34] referred to in Art. 1 of the Agreement, has been delimited on the spot by a mixed Polish-German Commission appointed under Art. 3 of the above Agreement".

Analogically to the relevant provisions of the Warsaw Declaration and the Zgorzelec Agreement, Article 3 also emphasizes the Polish-German frontier as "settled and existing".

The Frankfurt Act is an act announcing the termination of the work of the Mixed Commission charged with effecting the delimitation on the ground of the Polish-German State frontier.

The agreements so far discussed did not create a new legal situation — as regards the Polish-German frontier — and they can therefore be described as declaratory. The recognition of the Oder-Neisse frontier as legally settled and existing, not only emphasized the fact that the agreements referred to the frontier between Poland and Germany as a whole, but followed from the Potsdam Agreement accepted by the parties as the only legal basis for Germany's territorial pattern. The agreements introduce an additional element, indispensable for the delimitation on the ground of the Polish-German frontier, namely the agreement of the German State neighbouring with Poland. Since the victorious Powers repudiated the concept of Germany's *debellatio*, it became necessary to supplement the

---

[33] For text see *Dziennik Ustaw* 1952, item 346, later referred to as the Frankfurt Act.
[34] The title of the Act also refers to the frontier between Poland and Germany.

Potsdam decisions on the Polish-German frontier with a signature of the German Government. As regard the delimitation on the ground of this frontier consent of the German Government was expressed in the agreements on delimitation of the Polish-German frontier.

Faced with the problem of classification of the boundary agreements referred to above, it is a matter of consideration as to which of them ought to be referred to as the delimitation agreement. Attention has already been drawn to the ambiguous character of the term delimitation. However, whether the scope of the term be restricted (by identifying it with demarcation—that is with tracing of the frontier on the ground or extended (to cover the laying down of the course of the frontier in an international agreement and marking it on a map), the agreements between Poland and the German Democratic Republic effect delimitation in either sense.

The interests of the Polish and German Nations required final stabilization of the Polish-German frontier. The boundary agreements between Poland and the German Democratic Republic have become an indispensable legal instrument in the process of final settlement of Poland's western frontier: they effected delimitation of the frontier on the basis of the Potsdam Agreement. *The boundary agreements between Poland and the German Democratic Republic constitute an indispensable link of the peace settlement, terminating the process of settling the Polish-German frontier by delimitating it on the ground.*

CHAPTER VII

THE LEGAL BASIS OF THE TRANSFER OF GERMAN POPULATION FROM THE POLISH RECOVERED TERRITORIES

1. CAUSES AND AIMS OF THE TRANSFER

Transfer of population as a means of solving conflicts between nationalities is not an innovation introduced by the Great Powers, parties to the Potsdam Agreement. The best known example in the history of 20th Century international relations is the compulsory transfer of Greek population from Turkey in the years 1922—1926[1]. The transfer was given great publicity at that time and evoked conflicting comments. Nevertheless, it was again employed in 1937, when Arab and Jewish populations were exchanged in Palestine with a view to solving the Arab-Jewish conflict[2].

During the Second World War, large-scale transfers of population were undertaken by the Nazi Reich, by virtue of several agreements concluded in the years 1939 to 1941 and involving transfer of German

---

[1] In 1922, Greece went to war with Turkey in an attempt to extend her territory by taking advantage of what was thought to be Turkish weakness after the First World War. When the Greek armies had been defeated and were withdrawing in confusion from Asia Minor, the very numerous Greek population, inhabiting largely Thrace and the coast-line of Asia Minor, took to flight. In this way, more than one million Greeks left Turkish territory. On January 30, 1923, under the aegis of the Peace Conference sitting at Lausanne, an agreement was concluded legalizing the situation thus created. As a result of the agreement, a compulsory exchange of Greek and Turkish populations from Turkey and Greece respectively, was effected. Thus, 1,250,000 Greeks (not including those who had fled earlier of their own volition) left Turkey, and 350,000 Turks evacuated Greece. J. B. Schechtman, *op. cit.*, pp. 16 ff; cf. K. Strupp, *Wörterbuch des Völkerrechts*, vol. I, p. 819.

[2] J. B. Schechtman, *op. cit.*, p. 22.

minorities from the Baltic States, the Union of Soviet Socialist Republics, Rumania and Italy[3]. As a result, roughly 500,000 Germans were transferred to Germany[4]. The Nazi authorities needed this population for their attempt to Germanize "the eastern territories incorporated into the Reich". With the same object, the German authorities expelled from this area roughly 1,600,000 Poles and Jews[5] who were transferred to the so-called *General Gouvernement*, and settled in their stead the German population transferred from Eastern Europe[6]. Further changes in the national structure of Polish lands were effected by various forms of the German national list (*Volksliste*) which established the group of what were called *Volksdeutsche*[7]. Finally, there was a considerable influx into Polish territories of officials and functionaries with their families from Germany (*Reichsdeutsche*)[8].

---

[3] Agreements concluded by Germany: October 15, 1939, with Estonia; October 21, 1939, with Italy; October 30, 1939, with Latvia; November 3, 1939, and September 5, 1940, with the Soviet Union; October 23, 1940 with Rumania; and January 10, 1941, a third time with the Soviet Union; *ibid.*, pp. 39-40.

[4] See Tables, E. Kulischer, *The Displacement of Population in Europe*, Montreal 1943, p. 170.

[5] After Kulischer, *op. cit.*, p. 54; on the other hand, J. B. Schechtman, *op. cit.*, p. 271, puts the number of Poles and Jews expelled at roughly 1,300,000, but from the *Wartheland* only. He emphasizes that it is necessary to add the number, unknown to him, of those expelled from Upper Silesia and the *Gau Danzig-Westpreussen.* Cf. interesting data relating to transfers from the so-called *Wartheland* and based on Nazi sources, published in an article by St. Waszak on the assessment of Greiser's national campaign "Bilans walki narodowościowej Greisera" *Przegląd Zachodni* 1946, No. 6.

[6] Hitler's displacement of the Polish population from the Poznań region, Pomerania and other "territories incorporated into the Reich" is like most of the other acts during the German occupation of Poland to be seen as illegal. See Art. 6, point *b* of the Statutes of the International Military Tribunal — T. Cyprian and J. Sawicki, *Materiały Norymberskie*, Warszawa 1948; cf. also A. Klafkowski's work on German occupation from the standpoint of the Law of Nations, *Okupacja niemiecka w świetle prawa narodów*, Poznań 1946, and K. M. Pospieszalski's on Poland under German law 1939—1945 (Western Territories), *Polska pod niemieckim prawem 1939—1945 (Ziemie Zachodnie)*, Poznań 1946, p. 251.

[7] The German national list is dealt with in detail by K. M. Pospieszalski, *op. cit.*, p. 41.

[8] E. Kulischer, *op. cit.*, pp. 36—37, quotes after German sources that over 400,000 *Reichsdeutsche* went to the "Warthegau" alone; he puts the number of such Germans (in 1943) on the "territories incorporated into the Reich" at least 500,000, and for the whole of Poland (inclusive of the *General Gouvernement*) at roughly 800,000; cf. tables given by the same author on p. 170, and the data for 1941 quoted by St. Waszak, *op. cit.*

This German national mosaic existed on Polish territories until the beginning of the Soviet Army's victorious offensive, which liberated Poland—that is until January 1945. Before the advancing Soviet offensive, the entire immigrant German population, together with the *Volksdeutsche*, left Polish territories in confusion, partly voluntarily and partly owing to compulsory evacuation affecting not only the German population in the *General Gouvernement* and the "territories incorporated into the Reich," but also the areas granted later to Poland by virtue of the Potsdam Agreement.

According to West German sources, roughly half the German population formerly inhabiting the territories east of the Oder and Western Neisse arrived on German territory in wholesale flight and evacuation ordered by the Nazi authorities[9]. No doubt, the figure would have been still higher, were it not for the rapid advance of the Soviet Army, which frequently overtook columns in flight and sent them back to where they had been living[10]. These facts support the contention of the Soviet Delegation at the Yalta and Potsdam Conferences that the German population was spontaneously leaving the territories east of the Oder and Western Neisse[11].

The transfer of the German population from Polish post-war territories was part and parcel of a general settlement of the question of national minorities agreed upon by the Allies towards the close of the Second World War.

The system of protecting national minorities initiated and operated by the League of Nations was a complete failure. The decline of the League's system was rooted in the following facts: 1) minority treaties were forced only on certain small nations, whereas the Great Powers were free from any such obligations (discrimination); 2) States with populations ethically related to the minorities interceded on behalf of

---

[9] *Die Vertreibung der deutschen Bevölkerung aus den Gebieten östlich der Oder-Neisse*, Verl. Bundesministerium für Vertriebene, vol. I/1, p. 23 E.

[10] *Ibid., passim.*

[11] W a g n e r, *Die Entstehung der Oder-Neisse Linie*, Stuttgart 1953, p. 153. After the Yalta Conference, Foreign Secretary Eden declared that the decision involving a change in Poland's western frontier was based on the assumption that the German population was to be removed. He said that in many instances it was in fact no longer there. (W a g n e r, *op. cit.,* p. 135).

the latter and used these as a pretext for interfering in the internal affairs of other States (intervention); 3) certain national minorities abused for provocative purposes the rights granted to them by minority treaties (irredentism), 4) the policies of ethnically compound nations were not properly liberal towards minorities (oppression). Another failure resulted from attempting to solve the minorities problem on an international basis: "...the kin-states persisted in regarding the oppression of the co-nationals as an affront to themselves, rather than to the international community, and in attempting with frequent success to inject into the procedure just those elements of bilateral conflict which the League system had been intended to exclude"[12]. The Germans in particular discredited the idea of minorities protection. The American author Claude thus defines the role played by Germany in minority problems: "...notably the Germans of the various minority states... strove relentlessly to embarass and undermine their host-states"[13] and further—"Germany and the other champions of particular minorities were not at all symphathetic with the aims of the League system or its basic principles. They were influenced in the first place by the deterministic implications of the principle of nationality"[14].

As events preceding the Second World War proved, German minorities in Poland and Czechoslovakia acted to a considerable degree as Hitler's "fifth column" which, when the word was given, began diversive action against their host-States. Advancing claims impossible of acceptance by any sovereign State, they created by provocative behaviour the pretext required for aggression. For instance, the demands Henlein made as the leader of the Nazi Sudeten-German Party at the Congress at Carlsbad in November 1938, and especially point 8 of the demands—"Full freedom to profess German nationality and the German *Weltanschauung*"—can be described only as concealed or open war against political liberty and democracy, and in favour of the German domination in Central and Eastern Europe by direct or indirect means[15]. The loyalty of most of the German minority in

---

12 Claude, *op. cit.*, p. 45.
13 *Ibid.*, p. 44.
14 *Ibid.*, p. 45.
15 E. Wiskemann, *op. cit.*, p. 50.

Poland also gave to legitimate doubts. The German organizations frequently cloaked their political aims under the camouflage of cultural work. In Gdańsk, even at a time when Polish-German controversies were least acute, i.e. after the nonaggression pact of 1934[16], German activities were still of a provocative character. Polish misgivings were confirmed in the autumn of 1938, when the Nazi *Jungdeutsche Partei* followed the example of the Sudeten Germans and claimed what they called *Volksgruppenrecht*[17]. Thenceforth, among most of the German minority, unrest began to grow, and there was much talk of an impending "liberation" by Hitler. This was undoubtedly equivalent to a declaration of disloyalty to Poland[18].

By the end of March, 1939, the Nazi press unleashed a systematic campaign against alleged Polish cruelties against the German minority.

---

[16] *Ibid.*, p. 35.

[17] The *Volksgruppenrecht* — that is, the rights of national groups, was a product of the Nazi political doctrine. The Nazis demanded extensive autonomy for German minorities, inclusive of the right to set up a separate State organization of their own, within the host-State. The right of national groups was based on the principle declared by Hitler in 1938 and professing "co-national intervention" — that is, intervention of the Reich on behalf of the German population in other States, in opposition to the State in which the population was living and to which it owed allegiance. During the Second World War, the "rights of national groups" for German minorities were extorted by Hitler from Slovakia, Hungary, Rumania, Bulgaria and Croatia. The scope of the privileges granted to the German minorities varied in the various countries. Further to this subject, see K. M. Pospieszalski, *op. cit.*, pp. 233 ff.

The *Volksgruppenrecht* claim was put forward in Poland in November 1938 by the *Jungdeutsche Partei*. Their leader, Wiesner, declared: "...owing to State laws (Polish), the national group can never defend an individual, since it has no juristic personality and because the State (Poland) — in spite of continual demands made by the group — has to this day refused to this group the right to act on behalf of all their co-nationals and to see that treaties are respected". In this connection, Wiesner demanded: "This individual status and exclusive defence of the individual must be done away with. Instead, the entire national minority policies, of both the national group and the State, must be based on the conception of the right of the national group". Explaining his demand in greater detail, Wiesner claimed such conditions as "would grant particular representatives of the national group the right to speak and act on behalf of the entire group, to conclude agreements and treaties, to take over protection of the individual — in brief: to do all that has hitherto been reserved to the individual on the strength of national minority treaties". J. Winiewicz, in his book on mobilization of German potential in Poland — *Mobilizacja sił niemieckich w Polsce*, Warszawa 1939, pp. 198—199.

[18] This is E. Wiskemann's evaluation, *op. cit.*, p. 42.

The slanderous character of this campaign was exposed by the fact
that even the Nazi authorities refrained from lodging diplomatic protests. The activities of the bulk of the German minority in Poland in the
period immediately preceding the outbreak of the Second World
War—that is in August 1939—has been defined in English studies
in the following sentence: "The minority (German—B.W.) was by
now in fill operation as Hitler's fifth column"[19].

The American author Claude says about it:

"Germany gave active support to associations of Germans who lived
in the minority states, ostensibly to aid them in their legitimate efforts to
develop their cultural life and to press their demands for effective protection
against oppression. Those organizations became centres of German irredentist
propaganda, and, after the advent of the Nazi regime in Germany, they clearly
served as instruments of the foreign policy of the German state. Germans in
the minority states were impregnated with the ultra-nationalist doctrines of
Nazism, and were induced to repudiate the ideal of the League system — that
they should become loyal minorities sharing with tolerant majorities in the
building of a stable European order along the lines laid down at Paris — in
favor of the ideal of union with their co-nationals in a Greater German State.
The Hitlerian regime did not succeed in winning over all the *Auslandsdeutsche*
to its cause, but it did weld large numbers of them into charges of «human
dynamite», ready to be detonated at the command of the *Führer*. Long before
Hitler brought German minority groups into active service as units of a wartime «fifth column», Germany had discredited the League system for minority
protection by encouraging and underwriting disloyal activities among its
beneficiaries[20]".

By and large, the German minorities, especially in Czechoslovakia
and Poland, may be said to have played the part of *agents provocateurs*
for German aggression, and responsibility for their aggressive attitude
lies not only with Hitlerian inspiration. Wiskemann, for instance,
reports that anti-Hitlerite group of the Sudeten Germans (Social
Democrats) sought, while in exile in London, during the war, to enter
into negotiations with the Czechoslovak government in exile—on terms

---

[19] Wiskemann, *op. cit.*, p. 43. For activities of Germans abroad on
the eve of the Second World War and during the war, see the official United
States publication: *National Socialism, Basic Principles, their application by
the Nazi Party's Foreign Organizations, and the use of Germans Abroad for
Nazi Aims*, by R. E. Murphy, F. B. Stevens, H. Trivers, and J. M.
Roland, Washington 1943.

of relations between equal States—claiming from post-war Czechoslovakia the right to elect their own German parliament, government and head of State[21]. This meant in fact the acceptance of the Hitlerite principle of the right of national groups (*Volksgruppenrecht*).

These facts amply justified eliminating after the war the hotbed of international conflicts which German national minorities had proved themselves.

During the Second World War, three fundamental solutions of the minority problem were discussed by the Allies: 1) international protection of minorities, which meant a return to the League of Nations system; 2) radical solution of the problem by transfer of population; and 3) protection of minorities within the framework of general protection of human rights[22]. However, the conception involving transfer of population prevailed. "The idea of the transfer of population was the dominant element in wartime thought regarding approaches to a solution of the minority problem"[23].

By way of justification, it was emphasized that transfer of populations would be in agreement with the interests of the minorities as well as those of host-States, would constitute a just punishment for aggressors, and would serve international interests (elimination of sources of conflict)[24]. The principle of transfer was championed especially by the Czechoslovak Government with reference to the Sudeten Germans, even in September 1941[25]. In August 1942, the project was approved by the British Government, and in June 1943, by the United States and the Soviet Union. The memoirs of the former President Beneš reveal that during talks with him, on June 7, 1943, President Roosevelt expressed agreement to the transfer of national minorities from East Prussia, Transylvania and Czechoslovakia.

Although the idea was conceived by the Czechoslovak Government, the principle was applied to post-war Poland on the initiative of

[20] Claude, *op. cit.*, pp. 46—47.
[21] Wiskemann, *op. cit.*, p. 64; E. Beneš, *Memoirs*, Boston, p. 315.
[22] Claude, *op. cit.*, Chapter II, *passim*.
[23] *Ibid.*, p. 93.
[24] *Ibid.*, pp. 99—100.
[25] Wiskemann, *op. cit.*, p. 62, mentions that such an operation was contemplated by the Czechoslovak Government even in 1938, in anticipation of a war with Germany.

the Western Powers. The Soviet Union, not an initiator of the transfer, expressed its agreement.

The attitude of the Western Powers with regard to the transfer was expressed in the declarations of the American and British Governments before, during and after the Yalta and Potsdam Conferences.

It was the subject of discussions in March 1943, during Foreign Secretary Eden's visit to Washington. On March 14, 1943, President Roosevelt and Foreign Secretary Eden agreed that East Prussia should be given to Poland after the war[26]. On that occasion, the necessity of transferring the German population from these territories was raised for the first time. The point was raised by President Roosevelt, who said that "...in any circumstances the Prussians cannot be trusted". President Roosevelt thought transfer of the German population to be the only safeguard of peace, and recalled on that occasion the example of the transfer of the Greek population from Turkey after the First World War[27]. Two days later, i.e. on March 16, 1943, the Soviet Ambassador in Washington communicated his Governments' agreement to the granting of East Prussia to Poland after the war[28]. In the summer of 1943, the same problem—the granting to Poland of East Prussia and the transfer of German population inhabiting it—was referred to again in a talk between President Roosevelt, the Ambassador of the Polish London Government Ciechanowski, and an envoy of the same Government, Karski. President Roosevelt said during the talk that the "Pomeranian Corridor" must be abolished by giving East Prussia and

---

[26] Sherwood, *op. cit.*, vol. II, p. 707.

[27] A note by Harry L. Hopkins, who took part in the talks and was a close adviser of President Roosevelt, reads as follows: "The President said he thought we should make some arrangement to move the Prussians out of East Prussia the same way the Greeks were moved out of Turkey after the last war; while this is a harsh procedure, it is the only way to maintain peace and that in any circumstances, the Prussians cannot be trusted". Sherwood, *op. cit.*, vol. II, p. 708. Wagner, *op. cit.*, p. 29, footnote 2, comments upon the declaration made by Roosevelt and suggests that in making it the President of the United States was under the influence of Polish circles who were at that time discussing the transfer of Germans from the territories Poland was to receive after the war. Wagner quotes the programme of the Polish resistance movement, published in New York in 1943, in which the demand was made for a transfer of the German population settled on Polish territories for purposes of Germanization, together with the *Volksdeutsche*.

[28] *Quellen*, p. 52.

Gdańsk to Poland[29]. In the Autumn of 1943, the plan was, during British-Soviet talks in London, approved on behalf of the Soviet Government by Ambassador Maiski[30].

The fact that the transfer of Germans and the contemplated moving of the Polish-German frontier were being treated as one closely interconnected problem, was emphasized by Prime Minister Winston Churchill in his talks with the Polish London Government in January 1944[31].

Churchill's proposals were supported by the Government of the United States[32]. Churchill's agreement to base the Polish frontier on the River Oder is clear also from the report he made on January 14, 1944, to the House of Commons on British Government plans with regard to Germany, and from his speech of December 15, 1944[33]. A comparison of Churchill's proposal (January 1944) with Roosevelt's plans (March 1943), shows that the transfer of the German population as a means of securing future peace was conceived by the Western Powers—maybe under the influence of the plans of the Czechoslovak Government.

The American point of view with regard to the question of transfers is defined in a document by the Post-War Planning Committee of the Department of State (November 22, 1944).

"The United States Government should not favor any general transfer of minorities. . . The objections to a general transfer of minorities do not necessarily apply to transfers of specially selected groups. However, the United States Government should admit such transfers only where it is convinced that they will improve relations between the countries concerned and contribute to greater stability in Europe. To achieve these ends, transfers should be carried out in orderly manner over a period of time, with provision for resettlement, and under international auspices"[34].

Immediately before the Yalta Conference, the Foreign Ministers of Great Britain and the United States met in Malta and discussed

---

[29] *Ibid.*, pp. 54—55.
[30] *Ibid.*, p. 57.
[31] Cordell Hull, *op. cit.*, vol. II, p. 1436; *Ost-Handbuch*, part 6, p. 33; *Oder-Neisse*, p. 64; *Pierepiska*, vol. I, p. 204.
[32] Cordell Hull, *op. cit.*, vol. II, p. 1438.
[33] *Parliamentary Debates, Official Report*, vol. 406, No. 1, p. 1483.
[34] Claude, *op. cit.*, p. 230, footnote 26.

various possible variants of the Polish-German frontier. The results
of this analysis were communicated by Secretary Eden to Prime
Minister Churchill, in writing, on February 1, 1945. In point 8 it says:

"The cessions upon which we and the Americans are agreed would
involve the transfer of some 2 ¼ million Germans. The Oder frontier, without Breslau and Stettin, would involve a further 2 ¼ million. The Western
Neisse frontier with Breslau and Stettin would involve an additional 3 ¼
million, making 8 million in all"[35].

This again confirms the fact that modifications of the Polish-German
frontier and a transfer of population were seen as a single question. After
the Yalta Conference, Prime Minister Winston Churchill declared in his
speech on February 27, 1945, already referred to, that the Great Allied
Powers intended to take measures more effective than those after the First
World War, in order to prevent another German aggression. It is evident
that Churchill included in these measures the transfer of population.

The Soviet Union's positive attitude to the procedure of transfer
of national minorities as a means for settling existing and potential
international conflicts, is manifest in its acceptance of Czechoslovak
plans, consent to the transfer of Germans from Poland, and also in
later declarations by Molotov and Vyshinski. Foreign Minister Vyshinski made it plain that:

"The Soviet Government believes that one of the practicable ways
of solving ethnic problems when a conflict of national interest is involved,
is to free one country from persons allied by descent with another country
and to settle these persons in favourable conditions in their fatherland"[36].

2. TRANSFERS IN THE POTSDAM AGREEMENT

The Potsdam Agreement, which fixed the post-war Polish-German
frontier on the Oder and Western Neisse provided, in Section XIII
headed "Orderly transfers of German populations":

---

[35] Quoted after Wiskemann, *op. cit.*, p. 83.
[36] A. J. Vyshinski, *Voprosy Miezhdunarodnovo Prava i Miezhdunarodnoi Politiki*, Moskva 1949, p. 60.

"The conference reached the following agreement on the removal of Germans from Poland, Czechoslovakia and Hungary:

"The three Governments, having considered the question in all its aspects, recognize that the transfer to Germany of German populations, or elements thereof, remaining in Poland, Czechoslovakia and Hungary will have to be undertaken. They agree that any transfers that take place should be effected in an orderly and humane manner.

"Since the influx of a large number of Germans into Germany would increase the burden already resting on the occupying anthorities, they consider that the Allied Control Council in Germany should in the first instance examine the problem with special regard to the question of the equitable distribution of these Germans among the several zones of occupation. They are accordingly instructing their respective representatives on the Control Council to report to their Governments as soon as possible the extent to which such persons have already entered Germany from Poland, Czechoslovakia and Hungary, and to submit an estimate of the time and rate at which further transfers could be carried out, having regard to the present situation in Germany.

"The Czechoslovak Government, the Polish Provisional Government, and the Control Council in Hungary are at the same time being informed of the above, and are being requested meanwhile to suspend further expulsions pending the examination by the Governments concerned of the report from their representatives on the Control Council"[37].

In these decisions, attention is directed to the terminology, which clearly shows that the Powers reached *agreement* after they had considered the question in all its aspects[38].

Furthermore, the statements made indicate that the parties to the Potsdam Agreement analysed all possible controversial points concerning the question of the transfer of the German populations and, therefore, their further actions expressed the decisions taken at the Conference.

It should be emphasized that the decisions in Sections XIII and IX of the Potsdam Agreement constitute an organic entity and, conse-

---

[37] *United Nations Documents*, pp. 205, 206.
[38] Cf. interpretation by A. Klafkowski, *Podstawy prawne*, pp. 79 ff. and in his article on legal bases of the transfer of German population, "Podstawy prawne wysiedlenia ludności niemieckiej" *Administracja i Samorząd na Ziemiach Odzyskanych*, 1947, Series A, fascicle 7—8.

quently, should be treated as such. It is of considerable importance that the role of Poland was in the light of the decisions made in Section XIII, very limited. Polish literature stresses that Poland was ordered to remove Germans from her post-war territory[39].

This follows from an interpretation of Section XIII of the Agreement: the formulation "The three Governments, ...recognize that the transfer to Germany of German populations or elements thereof, ...*will have* to be undertaken", implies in fact an order given to Poland, Czechoslovakia and Hungary.

Furthermore, it follows from the text of Section XIII of the Potsdam Agreement that:

1) The Allied Control Council was to be in charge of resettlement on German territory. The Council was to investigate the question of fair distribution, as between particular zones of occupation, of the population transferred. Representatives of the Powers in the Council were to report to their Governments on the extent to which the return to Germany of German populations from Poland, Czechoslovakia and Hungary had already taken place, and, furthermore, they were to define the time, limit and rate of further transfers.

2) The transfers were to be carried out by the Polish and Czechoslovak Governments and in Hungary by the Allied Control Council. The fact that responsibility for transfers from Hungary was placed with the Allied Control Council—that is with an organ of the Allies—constitutes further evidence that the Three Great Powers actually ordered the transfers.

3) There was an obligation to integrate the German population transferred. The obligation is not implicitly formulated in the decisions of the Potsdam Agreement, but it was a logical and obvious consequence of the transfer of population who, after all, had to find new opportunities for life. The responsibility for seeing that integration was effected devolved upon the Allied Control Council, or, in fact, on the authorities over particular zones of occupation; the actual integration was to be effected by the German administration envisaged in the Potsdam Agreement.

---

[39] A. K l a f k o w s k i, *Podstawy prawne*, 1947, p. 84.

Section XIII of the Potsdam Agreement constitutes a fundamental argument in favour of the definite and unchangeable character of the Potsdam decisions with regard to the Polish frontier. This was twice stated by Foreign Minister Molotov. In reply to the speech made by Secretary of State Byrnes at Stuttgart on October 6, 1946, which queried the definitive character of the Polish frontier, Molotov gave an interview to a correspondent of the Polish Press Agency (PAP) in which he declared:

"... Who could suppose that this transfer of the Germans has been undertaken merely as some sort of temporary experiment? Those who have made the decision to transfer the Germans from these territories, in order to enable Poles from other districts of Poland to settle there immediately, cannot propose after a lapse of time precisely opposite decisions. The very idea of such experiments with millions of people, let alone the cruelty of such steps with regard to Poles as well as the Germans themselves, is inconceivable"[40].

The next statment came at the Moscow session of the Council of Foreign Ministers on April 9, 1947, when Molotov pointed out that the territories granted to Poland under the Potsdam Agreement were already settled by Poles, and declared:

"All this proves that the resolution of the Potsdam Agreement concerning Poland's western frontier was considered by our Governments as final. Accordingly, over the period, measures have been taken to populate these territories with Poles"[41].

It was not only Molotov who emphasized that the transfer of Germans and a definite settling of Poland's western boundary were one and the same question. It is worth while to mention also President Truman's statement on the Potsdam Conference, broadcast on August 9, 1945, in which he declared:

"The territory the Poles are to administer will enable Poland better to support its population. It will provide a short and more easily defensible *frontier* (my italics — B. W.) between Poland and Germany. Settled by Poles, it will provide a more homogeneous nation"[42].

---

[40] W. M. Molotov, *Voprosy Vnieshniey Politiki*, Moskva 1948, p. 244.
[41] *Ibid.*, p. 429.
[42] *Zbiór Dokumentów* 1946, No. 9, p. 268.

m

Furthermore, it follows from the statement that in President Truman's view, the settling of the frontier is intimately correlated with the transfer of the German population from the territories granted to Poland and with settling them with Polish population.

The statements by Minister Molotov and President Truman have the character of authentic interpretation.

The Potsdam Agreement, which ordered transfers of the German populations from Poland, Czechoslovakia and Hungary, simultaneously made it an obligation on the Allied Control Council in Germany to prepare suitable conditions and plans for the transfers. On November 20, 1945, the Allied Control Council passed at the twelfth meeting executive acts to Section XIII of the Potsdam Agreement. The Council not only prepared detailed plans for the transfer of German population from Poland, Czechoslovakia and Hungary, but extended the decisions to cover Austria as well.

Detailed plans for transfer made the following provisions:

1) the entire German population to be moved from Poland will be admitted to the Soviet and the British zones of occupation in Germany (2 and 1.5 million respectively);

2) the entire German population to be moved from Czechoslovakia will be admitted to the Soviet and American zones of occupation in Germany (750 thousand and 1,750 thousand respectively);

3) the entire German population to be moved from Hungary will be channelled into the American zone of occupation in Germany (500 thousand),

4) the entire German population to be moved from Austria will be admitted in the French zone of occupation in Germany (150 thousand)[43].

To carry this plan into effect, the Combined Repatriation Executive was set up. Col. Carroll and Comm. Konarski, representing Great Britain and Poland, made on February 14, 1946, an agreement concerning the manner of transfer, transport facilities and routes[44].

[43] *Parliamentary Debates, House of Commons*, vol. 417, No. 63, p. 1474.
[44] Meister, *op. cit.*, pp. 71—72.

3. INTEGRATION OF REPATRIATED GERMANS

In addition to preparing transfer plans and carrying them into effect, the Allied Control Council was also responsible for ensuring that the population transferred into Germany should be integrated as rapidly as possible with the local population. This responsibility obviously devolved upon those placed in authority over the particular zones of occupation. This obligation has never been queried, but has rather been clearly confirmed in several acts. For instance, the Instruction given to General Clay, Commander-in-Chief of American occupation authorities in Germany, by the Departments of State, War and Navy of the United States, made the General responsible for making certain that German repatriates be given the same rights as existing residents; furthermore, he was to assist German authorities in carrying out the programme of settlement[45]. On February 19, 1947, the American authorities in Germany issued a law concerning the reception and absorption of German repatriates[46]. Similary, the British note of Febuary 2, 1949, to the Polish Embassy, confirms the obligation to integrate repatriates [47]. This obligation also follows from the fact that the German repatriates were left outside the scope of the International Refugee Organization[48].

Integration involved, in actual fact, 11,602,000 repatriates[49]. This is the total figure of German repatriates in West Germany and in the German Democratic Republic. It embraces also those who left their homes spontaneously (not as a result of transfers) before the approaching Red Army. It is a significant fact that the Ger-

---

[45] Leo W. Schwarz, *Refugees in Germany Today*, New York 1957, pp. 51, 128 point 3.

[46] W. Jänicke, "Refugees: Bavaria 1947", *The Annals of the American Academy of Political and Social Science*, November 1948, p. 109.

[47] *Zbiór Dokumentów* 1949, No. 2, pp. 163—164.

[48] *The Refugee in the Post-War World*, Preliminary Report of a Survey of the Refugee Problem, Geneva 1951, Part II, Appendix to the constitution of IRO.

[49] Data quoted from statistics given by E. Osmańczyk, *Niemcy 1945—1950*, Warszawa 1951, confirmed also by W. Pieck in a speech published by *Neues Deutschland*, August 13, 1949, No. 188.

man press and scientific publications quote grossly exaggerated figures of German repatriates, ranging between 12 and 16 million[50]. The idea, of course, is to show that Germany, within the frontiers of 1945, is incapable of absorbing such a mass of people.

Such a contention is plainly disproved by facts[51]. In restricting ourselves to the problem of integration of repatriated persons in Germany, as considered from the political viewpoint alone, we have to deal separately with the German Democratic Republic on the one hand, and the German Federal Republic on the other.

In the German Democratic Republic, the problem can hardly be said to exist now; it has already been solved. In spite of the fact that the German Democratic Republic was, by comparison with other parts of Germany, faced with the greatest difficulties in this respect, since it had to absorb 4,300,000 German repatriates [52], it has dealt with the problem effectively.

Prime Minister Grotewohl declared:

"In the German Democratic Republic, all arriving repatriates have since 1945 been treated on a basis of equal civic rights. This is best shown by the fact of their being absorbed in production processes, having equal housing rights, taking a share in the benefits of the land reform, engaging on a considerable scale in handicrafts and trade, receiving — that is those unfit for work, the aged, and repatriates' small children — special social care"[53].

---

[50] See e.g. *Die Stimme der Vertriebenen*, November 1949 and *Neue Heimat*, February 18, 1950; cf. R. L a u n, *op. cit.*, p. 12, 7. E. W. M e y e r, in *Die Grundlagen für den Frieden mit Deutschland*, Wiesbaden, puts the number of German repatriates at 16 million.

[51] A demographic analysis of this problem was given by St. W a s z a k in the article on the overpopulated Germany and the Germany that is dying out — "Zagadnienie Niemiec przeludnionych i Niemiec wymierających", *Państwo i Prawo*, 1949, No. 1; cf. also H. S a u e r m a n, "Demographic Changes in Post-War Germany", *The Annals of the American Academy of Political and Social Science*, November 1948.

[52] To the British zone there arrived 3,800,000 German repatriates, to the American zone 3,300,000, to the French zone only 150,000. Data quoted after a speech by W. P i e c k, published in *Neues Deutschland*, August 13, 1949, No. 188.

[53] See Prime Minister Grotewohl's interview with *Trybuna Ludu*, March 2, 1951, No. 60. In that interview, Prime Minister Grotewohl added: "Within the general framework of plans for employment, repatriates are treated on an equal footing with all others. Almost 1½ million repatriates are active professionally, including 150,000 in public administration. Roughly

Even on October 7, 1949, the Manifesto of the National Front of Democratic Germany, included as its chief goals "to ensure to repatriates accommodation and work in all areas"[54]. This intention is also reflected in the legal provisions of the Constitution of the German Democratic Republic[55].

Still more important is that the integration intended has in fact been achieved. The process obviously involved difficulties[56], but they have been overcome. The literature of the German Democratic Republic insists that with the change of situation, the last traces of differences between the former inhabitants and repatriates have been forgotten[57].

In the German Federal Republic there are now roughly 7,800 thousand German repatriates[58]. The process of integration did not

---

450,000 young people are in schools or engaged in production. Young people in the German Democratic Republic know nothing of unemployment. Repatriates received 35 per cent of the land made available by the land reform, were given more than 90,000 new peasant-type farms. Thereby, 400,000 repatriates have become settlers again. Numerous repatriated persons have found secure existence in handicrafts and the high skill many of them possessed has proved a valuable contribution to the development of our crafts. Conversion of old savings was very liberally treated in the case of repatriates, in spite of the fact that in many cases certain documents were missing. Repatriates with no means of livelihood or unfit for work, are supported in accordance with effective regulations. The economic situation of repatriates was further improved by the Act passed on September 8, 1950 which made available to them credits for the purchase of household equipment. In recent years we have in fact succeeded in creating for the repatriates a new homeland in the German Democratic Republic, and today those who experienced particularly sharply the results of Hitler's barbarism are engaged on equal terms as citizens in the peaceful reconstruction of our economy".

[54] *Zbiór Dokumentów* 1949, No. 10, p. 861.

[55] See Art. 26, par. 2 of the Constitution of the German Democratic Republic.

[56] Referred to by President W. Pieck in addressing repatriates: "Dass aber den Umsiedlern in ihrer Not geholfen werden kann, das haben wir in der sowjetischen Besatzungszone bewiesen. Natürlich sind dabei grosse Schwierigkeiten zu überwinden, da ja auch die Lage der übrigen Bevölkerung noch sehr viel zu wünschen übrig lässt und noch sehr viel getan werden muss, um sie ausreichend mit Nahrung, Kleider und Wohnung zu versehen". *Neues Deutschland*, August 13, 1949, No. 188.

[57] Meister, *op. cit.*, p. 36.

[58] *Weissbuch über die amerikanisch-englische Interventionspolitik in Westdeutschland und das Wiedererstehen des deutschen Imperialismus*, Leipzig 1951, states that this figure is 600,000 higher than the number of people who actually inhabited the former German territories in the east.

run an even, unobstructed course. In the first post-war years the economic situation of the repatriates was very difficult[59]; later on, it improved with the general economic situation in the Federal Republic. In some quarters, it is claimed that it is precisely the repatriates who have markedly contributed to the economic development of the Republic and have played a notable part in the industrialization of certain traditionally agricultural districts of western Germany[60]. The high relative standard of living in the German Federal Republic refutes former revisionist claims that the German repatriates could not be absorbed since that would threaten the German economy with utter disaster.

German repatriates from Central and Eastern Europe have become a centre of special interest for resurgent revanchist tendencies. In a persistent effort to restore German domination in Europe despite the catastrophe of the war, post-war German revisionism seeks justification among the repatriates. Inherently, and in its aims it is not different from Hitlerism; the only difference lies in the methods employed in advocating its expansionist policies.

In the present work we are concerned only with certain aspects of German revisionism — those having a direct bearing on our subject. These aspects include exploiting German repatriates for revisionist aims.

The first symptoms of revisionism awakening in West Germany became noticeable even in the very first years after the war.

The first associations of repatriates were indeed disbanded in 1946 by occupation authorities as incompatible with the aims of the Potsdam Agreement; the liquidation, however, was spurious and they in fact continued to exist under different guises. The absence of uniformity in regulations in this respect in the different zones of occupation gave rise to various associations of repatriates, disguised as a rule as "partner-ships of interest" (*Interessengemein-*

---

[59] The West German press frequently gave examples of the hardships suffered by repatriates up to 1950. See e.g., *Niedersächsische Volksstimme* August 11, 1949, *Westfalenpost* February 8, 1949, *Nordwest Zeitung* July 2, 1949, *Hessische Nachrichten* June 28, 1949, *Die Stimme der Vertriebenen* October 30, 1949 and September 17, 1950.

[60] Wiskemann, *op. cit.*, p. 202.

schaften)[61]. Under the cloak of social and economic work, they in fact carried on revisionist political activities.

The stimulus for the first open revisionist manifestations was provided by utterances of British and American statesmen. The first of these was Churchill's speech in the House of Commons, as early as August 16, 1945[62], and subsequently at Fulton in 1946, where he deplored the lot of "expelled" Germans[63]. On November 6, 1946, Secretary of State Byrnes denied in his widely known Stuttgart speech that the Potsdam Agreement finally settled the Polish western frontier[64].

These speeches provided a stimulus to revisionism and revanchism among nationalist elements in Germany. Invigorated by the declarations, revisionist propaganda sprang up and developed, clamouring for abolition of the boundary on the Oder and Western Neisse. In a short time it involved also certain centres outside Germany. The New York "Committee against mass transfers", set up in 1947, addressed a memorandum to the United States Government in which it challenged Poland's rights to the territories east of the river Oder[65]. German revisionist propaganda did not fail to involve German clergy, who received a powerful stimulus in the pastoral letter issued by Pius XII for Christmas 1947.

The intensity of the revisionist propaganda which took advantage of the mood of German repatriates in the western zones of oc-

---

[61] A. Liczbańska, in an article on organizations of German repatriates, "Organizacje przesiedleńców niemieckich", *Przegląd Zachodni* 1957, No. 1, p. 103.

[62] *The War Speeches of the Rt Hon. Winston Churchill*, compiled by Ch. Eade, Cassel & Co., London, p. 518.

[63] *Zbiór Dokumentów* 1946, No. 10—11, p. 305.

[64] The reaction to Secretary Byrnes's Stuttgart speech of November 6, 1946, may be seen from an article by P. Loebe. "Ein erster Lichtblick", published in *Telegraf*, September 8, 1946: "Die ebenso freimütigen wie weitblickenden und menschenfreundlichen Worte, die der amerikanische Aussenminister am 6 September in Stuttgart gefunden hat, haben für das deutsche Volk ein erstes Aufatmen gebracht... Besonders aufatmen aber werden die Millionen von Deutschen aus den Ostgebieten, die in Gefahr standen, nicht nur ihre ganze Habe, sondern auch ihre Heimat für immer zu verlieren... Nun, da diese tapferen Worte vor der ganzen Welt gefallen sind, dürfen auch wir im Namen der Bedrängten unsere Stimme wieder erheben...".

[65] Text of the memorandum published in *Die wirtschaftliche und soziale Struktur Deutschlands*, Anl. V zu Reparationen, Sozialprodukt, Lebensstandard. "Versuch einer Wirtschaftsbilanz", Bremen 1949, pp. 11—12.

cupation, may be gauged from a number of notes from the Polish
Military Mission in Berlin presented to British, American and French
authorities, and to the Allied Control Council, requiring that steps
be taken to counteract this propaganda[66]. Reassured by the pas-
sive attitude of Allied authorities in the western zones of occupation, German revisionists became, at meetings and rallies of repatriates, more and more outspoken and, not satisfied with claims for
a revision of the Potsdam Agreement, began to talk of "German
territories between the Oder and the Vistula"[67], of the need for
organizing a "black Reichswehr" in order to solve the eastern problem by force[68], and of the Vistula as the "German river of destiny[69]."
Revisionists also opposed the grant of equal rights to German repatriates, since such would put a brake on the campaign for a return to the "German eastern territories"[70].

This entire campaign was unquestionably incompatible with the
decisions of the Potsdam Agreement and with the acts issued by
the Allied Control Council. Section III of the Potsdam Agreement
provides for the taking of "measures necessary to assure that Germany never again will threaten her neighbours or the peace of the
world". Directive No. 40, dated October 12, 1946, issued by the
Allied Control Council, made it an offence to propagate nationalistic
and militarist ideas (point 2 a) calculated to evoke a hostile attitude
to the occupying Powers (point 2 b), or to criticize the decisions
of the Allies (point 2 d)[71].

As the conception of a seperatist German Federal Republic more
and more clearly took shape, there appeared numerous unions of
repatriates, the *Landsmannschaften*, which enrolled repatriates ac-

---

[66] The notes cover the years 1946—1948, and are published in *Zbiór
Dokumentów* 1948, No. 10.

[67] Note from the Polish Military Mission to the Allied Control Council,
Berlin, December 6, 1946, *ibid.*, p. 691.

[68] Note from the Polish Military Mission to the Allied Control Council,
Berlin, October 18, 1946, *ibid.*, pp. 687—688.

[69] Note from the Polish Military Mission to the Allied Control Council,
Berlin, May 13, 1947, *ibid.*, pp. 696—697.

[70] Note from the Polish Military Mission to the Allied Control Council,
Berlin, October 23, 1947, *ibid.*, p. 704.

[71] *Official Gazette of the Control Council for Germany*, No. 11, October
31, 1946, p. 212.

cording to the districts they formely inhabited[72]. After the advent
of the German Federal Republic, a separate repatriate's political
party was set up under the name of *Bund der Heimatvertriebenen
und Entrechteten*, abbr. *B.H.E.* (The Union of those Expelled from
the Homeland and Outlawed). The aims pursued by the party in
international politics are thus set out in its programme:

"Recovery of the unlawfully alienated eastern territories. We do not
believe, however, that it will suffice to raise a claim for them to be restored.
We hold it to be our duty to be prepared to resettle these territories. To human wrecks forced to live idle in temporary accommodation, this will not
be possible. . ."[73]

Therefore, as regards internal politicy, the *B.H.E.* party demanded complete integration of repatriates in the social and economic life of the German Federal Republic. However, the foreign
programme of the *B.H.E.* party — revisionism — and its home

---

[72] The number of organizations of repatriates is enormous. I shall
mention merely the *Landsmannschaften*: *Bund der Danziger, Deutsch-Baltische
Landsmannschaft, Gemeinschaft der deutschen Umsiedler aus Bessarabien,
Karpatendeutsche Landsmannschaft Slowakei, Landsmannschaft der Banater
Schwaben aus Rumänien, Landsmannschaft Berlin — Mark Brandenburg,
Landsmannschaft der Buchenlanddeutschen, Landsmannschaft der Deutschen
aus Jugoslavien, Landsmannschaft der Deutschen aus Russland, Landsmann-
schaft der Deutschen aus Ungarn, Landsmannschaft der Dobrudscha- und
Bulgariendeutschen, Landsmannschaft der Litauendeutschen, Landsmannschaft
der Oberschlesier, Landsmannschaft Ostpreussen, Landsmannschaft Schlesien
(Ober- und Niederschlesien), Landsmannschaft der Siebenbürger Sachsen,
Landsmannschaft Weichsel-Warthe, Landsmannschaft Westpreussen, Pommer-
sche Landsmannschaft, Sudetendeutsche Landsmannschaft*. In addition there
are scores of larger and smaller organizations of repatriates from either
particular areas (e.g. *Heimatgruppe Breslau in Köln*) or certain professions
(e.g. *Notverband vertriebener Hochschullehrer*), or from some larger territorial
units (e.g. *Landsverband Oder-Neisse*), The *Landsmannschaften* have a union
of their own, the *Verband für Landsmannschaften*. The entire mosaic of
organizations, almost invariably revisionist in character, calls for a separate
study. The purpose of the organizations was defined by Thedieck, Secretary
of the State in the Government of the German Federal Republic as follows:
"Grundfalsch wäre es, die Landsmannschaften als eine Art von Heimat-
ersatz der vertriebenen Ostdeutschen zu werten. Die wesentliche Aufgabe
der Landsmannschaften und den tiefsten Sinn im Zusammenwirken mit
allen Stämmen und Gliedern unseres Volkes sehen wir in der Wiedergewin-
nung des deutschen Ostens". — *Bulletin des Presse- und Informationsamtes
der Bundesregierung*, September 23, 1953.

[73] *Die Welt*, July 12, 1950.

policy — integration — came into serious conflict. A probe of public opinion in the German Federal Republic[74] showed that integration tended to take the edge off revisionism, whereas the *Landsmann-schaften* not only strove to retrieve the frontiers of 1937, but, as Wiskemann says, "a demand for those of 1914, which history condemned long ago, is implicit in all the utterances of that near-Nazi world"[75].

Therefore, Wiskemann very aptly describes the policies of the Government of the German Federal Republic in relation to the question of repatriates when she says:

"Thus official German policy with regard to the Eastern and Sudeten Germans and the frontiers across which they were expelled is a strange amalgam. . . His (Adenauer's — B. W.) budding Foreign Office pursues an opportunist policy which makes the most of ancient racial antipathies and of anti-Communist feeling, especially in the United States. The Minister for Refugees is pledged to push through the integration of the German immigrants in the West German Republic. They all repudiate the Oder--Neisse line although they know that the success of integration is bound to undermine both the desire and the need to revise it. It would seem to be

---

[74] Wiskemann, *op. cit.*, p. 204, footnote 2, quotes the results of a Gallup poll in West Germany in 1953. To a question asking repatriates whether they would return to the east if these lands were restored to Germany, only 55% of the replies were unequivocally affirmative. The British authoress believes that the number of those who would refuse to return has since increased, and even so, many replied in the affirmative merely under the pressure of revisionist propaganda. It is worth while to note that in the German Federal Republic an effort is made, merely for political purposes, to preserve the category of repatriates by artificial means. In this category are reckoned the children of repatriates of age groups 1—14. These age groups include children born in the Federal Republic, to an estimated total of 669,000. See: Fr. Szymiczek's review on the "Statistisches Taschenbuch über die Heimatvertriebenen in der Bundesrepublik Deutschland und in West-Berlin, Wiesbaden 1953", *Przegląd Zachodni* 1956, No. 7/8, p. 381; Wiskemann, *op. cit.*, writes p. 162 footnote 3: "A child counts as a refugee if its father was a refugee, and as "native" if its father was "native".

[75] Wiskemann, *op. cit.*, p. 293; Meister, *op. cit.*, p. 9, quotes Seebohm, Minister in the Federal Government, who said in December 1951: "Ich habe mich bei der Betrachtung der deutschen Ostprobleme dagegen ausgesprochen, dass man jetzt so viel von Grenzen von 1937 spricht. Es ist selbstverständlich, dass damit nur die Ostgebiete gemeint sein konnten. Ich habe darauf hingewiesen, dass diese aufgehoben werden müssen, damit wirtschaftliche Räume entstehen, die gross genug sind, um die Lebensgrundlage für unser Volk und für die europäische Nation zu sichern".

contradictory for an Oberländer[76] to support an Adenauer: perhaps the formula is "let us grow strong first with Adenauer as our shield. At present we can discuss unimportant frontier adjustments and agree that East Prussia is permanently lost. Later, when strength is achieved, it will not matter if the immigrants have settled down; with an army of our own we can exploit a new situation to get back something like the frontiers of 1914 either in the name of Germany or of Europe"[77].

4. REVISIONISTS' JURISTIC ARGUMENTS

In the revisionists' juristic arguments, great importance is attached to the question of transfer of population, which they claim to be incompatible with International Law. Precisely because the transfers constitute the decisive argument proving the final and irreversible character of the Potsdam decisions on the post-war Polish-German frontier, this question is fundamental to revisionist juristic constructions designed to undermine the legal foundations of the Oder-Neisse line.

The argument is doubly significant since it has a bearing on the formal aspects of the question as well as on its essence. Formally speaking, the decisions of Section XIII of the Potsdam Agreement are evidence of the will of the parties to transfer definitively to Poland the lands east of the Oder and Western Neisse. For it is alien to judicial logic to make a *temporary* decision to transfer the lands east of the Oder under Polish administration while agreeing to transfer the German population and to settle the lands with Poles. As to the essence of the matter, the decisions of section XIII of the Potsdam Agreement completely changed the national status of the territories making them — in recognition of Poland's rightful claims — to all practical purposes *Polish*. Any *restitutio in integrum* would inevitably once more involve the migration of millions of people, which is practically unthinkable.

---

[76] Oberländer — Minister for Refugees in the Federal Republic.
[77] Wiskemann, *op. cit.*, pp. 208—209.

Revisionist arguments aimed at the legal foundations of the transfer of German populations can be reduced to the following:

1) transfers of German populations are incompatible with the right to self-determination since the people concerned had not been asked to express consent;

2) transfers of German populations are incompatible with human rights especially with what they call *Recht auf die Heimat* (the right to a homeland);

3) transfers of German population have been unlawfully extended to cover territories east of the Oder and Western Neisse, whereas in accordance with the Potsdam Agreement they should have been effective only on pre-war Polish territories[78].

As to the first point, most frequently invoked is the Atlantic Charter[79]. In the eyes of revisionists, the right to self-determination boils down to the right to a plebiscite[80]. As has already been pointed out, the Great Powers *deliberately* refused to contemplate plebiscites with regard to territorial changes affecting Germany, and preserved Germany's right to self-determination only as concerning the right to State-hood, and even then under certain definite safeguards (democratization, demilitarization, denazification, etc.). Also post-war practice has shown that transfers have frequently been resorted to as a means for solving international conflicts. Transfers effected in the years 1945—1947 (Japanese minorities from the countries of the Far East, exchange of Hindus and Muslims in India, exchange of Hungarians and Slovaks by virtue of the 1947 Agreement), and even in the years 1950—1951 (transfer of 150,000 Turks from Bulgaria) have been tacitly approved by the United Nations[81]. These

---

[78] The revisionists also demagogically claim that transfer involved the crime of genocide (C. Reece, *On German Provinces East of Oder-Neisse Line, and Economic, Historical, Legal, and Political Aspects Involved*, Washington 1957, p. 4; cf. G. Decker, *Das Selbstbestimmungsrecht der Nationen*, Göttingen 1955, p. 229). The irrelevance of this argument was formally proved in a U.N. discussion on the draft for a convention on genocide when the Secretariat of the United Nations officially declared that transfer cannot be embraced by the definition of genocide. (Claude, *op. cit.*, p. 155).

[79] Hoffmann, *op. cit.*; Kraus, *op. cit.*, p. 27 and others.

[80] Laun, *op. cit.*, pp. 32—35.

[81] Claude, *op. cit.*, p. 191.

fact have led the American author Claude to believe that "the idea of transfer has become a dominant element in current thinking about the minority problem"[82].

As to the second point, revisionists invoke the Declaration of Human Rights, passed by the United Nations General Assembly on December 10, 1948, and especially Articles 2, 9 and 13 of the Declaration. Article 2 provides in point 1 that all people, irrespective of age, sex, religion or social origin may claim the freedoms and rights set forth in the Declaration. Furthermore, point 2 of the Article provides that no discrimination shall be made irrespective of whether the country to which a person belongs is independent or whether its sovereignty is in any way limited. Article 9 provides that nobody shall be arbitrarily arrested, detained or exiled. Article 13, point 1 reads: "Everyone has the right to freedom of movement and residence within the borders of each state", and point 2 of the Article: "Everyone has the right to leave any country, including his own, and to return to his country". Revisionists construe point 2 of Article 13 as the formulation of what they call the *Recht auf die Heimat* (the right to a homeland). They interpret Articles 9 and 13 in conjunction with Article 2, and claim that not only the *Recht auf die Heimat* but simply all human rights proclaimed in the Declaration have been violated as regards the German repatriates[83].

From the formal point of view, we might limit ourselves to observing that the Declaration of Human Rights adopted by the United Nations General Assembly has not the legal standing of an international agreement[84]. Furthermore, its stipulations cannot be invoked retrospectively. However, even an analysis of the substance of the claim — irrespective of strictly formal aspect — leads us to conclude that the revisionist arguments are irrelevant because:

1) the German population was not transferred arbitrarily but on the basis of international legal standards laid down in an interna-

---

[82] *Ibid.*, p. 210.

[83] Hoffmann, *op. cit.*, p. 29.

[84] R. Laun, *op. cit.*, p. 36; H. Guradze, *Der Stand der Menschenrechte im Völkerrecht*, Göttingen 1956, p. 127, and the literature quoted therein.

tional agreement concluded by the Great Powers who — following
the unconditional surrender — acquired complete authority to determine Germany's future;

2) Article 13 of the Declaration of Human Rights cannot abol-
ish the right of a State — existing and respected everywhere — to
refuse to accept the presence on its territory of persons who are not
subjects of that State and who have even demonstrated their hostility
towards it. It is worth while to quote a British source on pre-war
activities of the German minorities in Poland and Czechoslovakia:
"No sovereign State could accept the claims of a community which
was vowed to its destruction to exist within it"[85].

The conception of Human Rights cannot extend to interference
with the internal problems of States. Even during the Second World
War, there were declarations by British statesmen, clearly pro-
nouncing that protection of human rights does not imply interference
with the internal affairs of other States[86].

Consequently, it may be taken that in Poland and Czechoslovakia
the procedure of xenelasy[87] has been applied as a special kind of reprisal against Germans for the crimes committed during the occupation and for the hostile activities of German minorities in these
States before the Second World War.

The West German scholar, Professor Laun, takes his stand on
the *Recht auf die Heimat* and erects the following juristic structure:
there is a universally respected International Law within which
sovereignty of the State, conceived in the absolute sense of the word
(that is, unrestricted legal omnipotence of the State), clashes
with the human rights which restrict such omnipotence [88]. Laun
maintains that there are only two ways of eliminating the contradiction in International Law: either the sovereignty of the State is
superior to human rights, or *vice versa*[89]. By referring to human

---

[85] Wiskemann, *op. cit.*, p. 50.
[86] Claude, *op. cit.*, p. 77.
[87] Xenelasy — general banishment of aliens from a State. Applied
as a form of reprisal. J. Makowski, in his textbook on International Law,
p. 45.
[88] Laun, *op. cit.*, p. 27.
[89] *Ibid.*, p. 29.

rights, Laun has in mind the rights of all men in relation to all men — that is also the rights of all men in relation to the State. Human rights thus come in conflict with the legal omnipotence of the State — that is, with its sovereignty. On this foundation, Laun erects the thesis that both the Polish and Czechoslovak Governments have transgressed their rights derived from State sovereignty[90].

This reasoning evokes the following critical remarks:

a) It is an error to treat the sovereignty of the State and human rights as alternatives. Sovereignty of the State is by no means equivalent to omnipotence, and human rights can be perfectly well dovetailed with State sovereignty. Professor Laun's error consists in construing State sovereignty as State *omnipotence*, whereas the essence of sovereignty is not omnipotence — that is completely unrestrained freedom of action — but complete independence and autonomy in internal as well as foreign relations. In foreign relations, State sovereignty is restricted by the sovereign rights of other nations. In relations to the State's own citizens and territory, State sovereignty

---

[90] With regard to the Sudeten Germans, Professor Laun formulates the following thesis: the treaty of St. Germain (1919) was defective from the point of view of universally prevailing International Law, since it violated the right to self-determination by subjecting to Czechoslovak authority the German population without asking for their consent. He also believes the Munich Agreement of 1938 to be defective, since it compelled the Czechoslovak Government by the threat of force to relinquish the Sudeten. However, he believes the act to be in agreement with the right to self-determination. All States, according to his opinion in the period 1939—1945 recognized Sudeten to be German territory. Thus there arises the dilemma: we have to assume the annexation of Sudetenland either as entirely devoid of legal consequences, or as having had some such consequemces. In the first case, Czechoslovakia expelled 2½ or 3 million of her own citizens against their will—that is illegally, in the second, she expelled the same number of German citizens.

Professor Laun's thesis is based on entirely erroneous legal premises: 1) he ignores the Nüremberg verdict which clearly exposed the criminal character of the seizure of first Sudetenland and, then, Czechoslovakia; 2) he ignores the record of the German minority in Czechoslovakia, who most certainly indulged in diversionary activities aimed against the independent existence of the Czechoslovak State; 3) he justifies initiation of aggression on the grounds of giving support to subversive activities of German minorities inspired by Hitler; 4) he denies Czechoslovakia the right to self-defence; 5) he ignores the decisions made by the Great Powers at Potsdam with regard to transfers of German populations; 6) he ignores the fact that the British Parliament annulled the Munich Agreement even in 1942. It is not difficult to see that Laun follows the Hitlerite line of thought.

can indeed not be seen as subject to any restrictions, but this does not confer arbitrary power on the State. Relations between State authorities and citizens are regulated by internal law and within every law-abiding State the authorities are restrained by the provisions of the internal law which protects the interests of individual citizens against abuses which might be attempted by State authorities. On the other hand, the internal law must protect the interests of the State against arbitrary action by individual citizens or groups of citizens. Thus, State sovereignty can perfectly well run in harness with human rights, provided it is a law-abiding State which is involved and provided the citizens do not abuse their rights to the prejudice of the State.

b) The direction of post-war tendencies as regards protection of human rights and application of such protection to national minorities has in general been

"to subsume the problem of national minorities under the broader problem of ensuring basic individual rights to all human beings, without reference to membership in ethnic groups. The leading assumption has been that members of national minorities do not need, are not entitled to, or cannot be granted, rights of a special character. The doctrine of human rights has been put forward as a substitute for the concept of minority rights, with the strong implication that minorities whose members enjoy individual equality of treatment cannot legitimately demand facilities for the maintenance of their ethnic particularism. Thus, the human rights movement has been spiritually allied with the idea that the collective identity of national minorities may quite properly be broken down by a process of assimilation"[91].

c) The concept *Recht auf die Heimat* is juristically undefined. In official declarations by the Government of the German Federal Republic it is described as *politisches Ordnungsprinzip* (principle of political order) the elements of which are claimed to be rooted in the Atlantic Charter, the Charter of the United Nations, the Declaration of Human Rights, and the European Convention on the protection of human rights and fundamental freedoms (November 4, 1950) in conjunction with the supplementary protocol (May 20, 1952);

---

[91] Claude, *op. cit.*, p. 211.

furthermore, the concept is associated with the right to self-determination and human rights[92]. G. Decker defines the *Recht auf die Heimat* as simply the right of the repatriates to return to the territories from which they were transferred, but he makes no reference to the question of State authority[93]. Laun, confining himself merely to an analysis of Article 13, point 2 of the Declaration of Human Rights, concludes that the Article permits the new Slav settlers on the territories from which the German population has been transferred, to assume that this is now their homeland[94]. The British scholar Wiskemann ironically asks whether it was a violation of the *Recht auf die Heimet* when inhabitants of the lands east of the Oder and Western Neisse left these lands and moved to West Germany for economic reasons? Furthermore, how long could the *Recht auf die Heimat* be maintained — through how many generations?[95] Recently, among West German jurists, the view has been advanced that gradually "a certain Polish *Recht auf die Heimat*" has also developed[96].

In the light of pre-war and post-war practice, the entire revisionists' argument, based on the *Recht auf die Heimat*, clearly shows what Germans understand by this *Recht*: the *Recht auf die Heimat*

---

[92] Statement by Hallstein, Federal Secretary of State, at the 161st meeting of the Bundestag (September 28, 1956). *Internationales Recht und Diplomatie*, fascicle 3/4 (1956), p. 276.

[93] G. Decker, *Das Selbstbestimmungsrecht der Nationen*, Göttingen 1955, p. 229.

[94] R. Laun, *op. cit.*, p. 36, The daily *Westfälische Rundschau* (May 26, 1956) wrote: "During the meetings of Germans from the Sudeten and Pomerania there have been numerous references to the *Recht auf die Heimat* which, from the judicial viewpoint, represents no settled standard. If it is intended to admit the *Recht auf die Heimat* as a general human law, then it may merely mean, like that law, that the right to return to the country of birth, or parish of origin, is the privilege of every man wishing to avail himself of such right. Consequently, it cannot be equivalent to a State's legal claim to this or that territory".

[95] Wiskemann, *op. cit.*, p. 183, here refers to a well known phenomenon occurring in the 19th and 20th centuries on the onetime German eastern provinces, viz., the *Ostflucht* (the flight of Germans from the eastern German lands to the west; roughly 4,600,000 people emigrated from the eastern provinces in the years 1840—1939. Simply from the territories recovered by Poland in 1945, close on 2½ million had emigrated over a period of 70 years).

[96] The view expressed by Professor Ulrich Scheuner during a discussion on the declaration made by Professor Carlo Schmidt at Bad Neuenahr (July 5, 1956) concerning the Oder-Neisse frontier.

means to the revisionists at least what the *Volksgruppenrecht* meant
to the Nazis — that is the right of German minorities to set up their
own and separate State organization within the host-State[97] or even
to incorporate the lands east of the Oder and Western Neisse, as
well as the Sudeten into Germany.

As regards the third point, the facts themselves contradict the
claim that the decisions of the Potsdam Agreement involve only the
German population *of pre-war Poland* (or of Polish territories before
1937), *but not of the Recovered Territories* — said by West German
authors to be merely administered by, but not permanently granted
to, Poland[98]. Even the Yalta Agreement envisaged "substantial accessions of territory in the North and West" for Poland, at the expense of Germany. The intendent extension of Polish territory was
confirmed in numerous official pronouncements by American and
British statesmen (for example, Byrnes challenged in his Stuttgart
speech only the finality of the Potsdam decisions, but he confirmed
the principle of Poland's territorial accessions at the expense of
Germany. So did Marshall in April 1947 at the Moscow Meeting
of the Council of Foreign Ministers[99]. Section XIII of the Potsdam Agreement did not restrict transfers of German populations to
pre-war Polish territories (before September, 1939), but covered
also the territories granted to Poland after the war. The idea of
transferring Germans from the territories to be granted to Poland
was conceived by the Western Powers as early as 1943, and was
subsequently confirmed by official representatives in numerous pronouncements. Furthermore, the question was associated with that of
settling the Polish population transferred from the territories ceded
by Poland to the Soviet Union. This population was to settle the
territories east of the Oder, and the Allies excluded *a priori* a possible
mixing of the Polish and German populations (cf. the speeches by
Churchill [December 15, 1944] and Truman [August 9, 1945] already
referred to).

---

[97] See discussion in *Der Europäische Osten* in the years 1955—1957.
[98] Hoffmann, *op. cit.*, p. 13; Maurach, *op. cit.*, p. 108; B. Meissner,
op. cit., p. 65.
[99] *Zbiór Dokumentów* 1947, No. 5, p. 217.

5. THE ATTITUDE OF THE OCCUPYING POWERS
TOWARDS THE TRANSFER

It clearly follows from the bulk of the preliminary materials illustrating the attitude of the Western Powers with regard to the problem of the transfers of the German populations, that the United States and Great Britain believed this matter to be inseparable from territorial changes made for the benefit of Poland. This is especially striking in Foreign Secretary Eden's report to Prime Minister Churchill, of February 1, 1945, already referred to.

This was shown still earlier in certain utterances by Prime Minister Churchill, especially his speech — already referred to — of December 15, 1944.

All this goes to show that the transfer of the German population from Poland, envisaged by the Potsdam Agreement, was to involve not only pre-war Polish territories, but also the territories to be granted to her after the war. This is particularly supported by the fact that the Occupying Powers, inclusive of the Western Powers, actively co-operated in the transfers and took it for granted that the transfers involved first above all the territories accorded to Poland at Potsdam.

Revisionist authors in the German Federal Republic claim that as early as August 1945 Churchill dissociated himself from the scope and manner in which the transfers were effected, but Churchill was at that time leader of the opposition and not a Head of Government, and, therefore, his words did not have the character of an official Government declaration. If on the other hand, we recall the official declaration he made earlier, when he was still Prime Minister, especially his speech of December 15, 1944, when he referred to a "clean sweep", we must ignore his opinion of August 1945 since it is obviously tainted with considerations of political expediency[100].

---

[100] *The New Statesman and Nation* (March 30, 1946) wrote: "Mr. Churchill is one of the most ingenious, as well as unscrupulous politicians. So I suppose he will find something to say when he is reminded in the House of Commons that he was himself one of the authors of the settlement of Eastern Europe which he now so eloquently attacks".

It should be borne in mind that during the Yalta and Potsdam negotiations, Churchill and the American Delegation raised certain objections to what they thought an excessive expansion of Polish territory in the west for the very reason that this would involve more extensive transfers of the German population. Revisionists furthermore quote an official declaration by Bevin (October 10, 1945), to the effect that the policy of the Polish administration of that time would decide the British attitude towards the final territorial settlement of Polish frontiers[101]. This they construe as a warning to Poland with reference to the scope of transfers and the manner of effecting them. The statement affords no basis for such conclusions. The sentence may mean that the British Government reserved final judgement on the Oder-Neisse frontier until satisfied that: 1) Polish Government policies are more congenial to the wishes of the British Government, or 2) Poland is capable of settling and managing the economy of the territories she acquired by virtue of the Potsdam Agreement. The latter seems the more plausible interpretation, especially when confronted with another pronouncement by Bevin (August 20, 1945) in which he said: "The question where the final delimitation of the frontiers will rest depends to a very large extent on what population returns to Poland"[102]. On October 22, 1946, Foreign Secretary Bevin declared that the British Government did not see why they should indeed ratify the cession of these large territories to Poland, until they were satisfied that the assurances given to them had been fully implemented. The Government — as he maintained — did not wish a desert to be created from which Germans had been excluded, and which the Poles were unable to populate[103].

Hence, the British Government — having a peculiar interest in transfers from Poland since the Allied Control Council's plans (November 20, 1945) provided for the Germans from the Recovered Territories to be transferred to the British zone of occupation — by no means challenged the scope of transfers, and merely recorded the fact the Potsdam German-Polish frontier was dependent upon

---

[101] Hoffmann, *op. cit.*, pp. 15—16.
[102] *Zbiór Dokumentów* 1947, No. 4, p. 207.
[103] Hoffmann, *op. cit.*, pp. 17—18.

Poland's ability to settle and to manage the territories east of the Oder and Western Neisse. The irrelevance of revisionist conclusions is best revealed by the fact that Foreign Secretary Bevin's declarations brought about no change in the work of British authorities in Germany (agreement between British and Polish representatives in the Combined Repatriation Executive, February 14, 1946) which actively cooperated in the transfers and approved thereby endorsed both the extent and the territorial scope of this action[104].

Reference should also be made to the official position of the British Government with regard to transfers of the German population, defined in the debate in the House of Lords (January 30, 1946). In replying to a question by the Bishop of Chichester, Lord-Chancellor Jowitt stated that the British Government, though in sympathy with those affected, believe that the "future peace is best served by removing the German population, which has proved not digestible or assimilable, back from those countries to Germany"[105].

As regards to the legal foundations of the transfers of German populations from the territories east of the Oder and Western Neisse,

---

[104] Well aware of the weight of Polish arguments based on the recognition in practice by the Western Powers of the extent and territorial scope of transfers, revisionists strive to side-step this argument. With this in view, Professor Maurach (*op. cit.*, p. 123) erected the following juristic construction. He started from the premise that Germany, though still a subject of International Law, was nevertheless incapable of concluding legal acts, consequently, it is necessary to define who is entitled to "convalidate" the transfers of German populations. Maurach denies this right to both the Allied Control Council and the Council of Foreign Ministers. He believes the parties to the Potsdam Agreement *as a whole* are entitled to do so. These Powers — he believes — have assumed sovereign authority over Germany and only a unanimous declaration of the will of their authorized organs can "convalidate" the transfers effected by Poland (Maurach, *op. cit.*, pp. 125—126).

Leaving aside the question as to whether assumption by the Great Powers of supreme authority with regard to Germany did or did not mean assumption of sovereign authority, there remains the essential question as to why should the Great Powers again express their agreement to the transfers, once they had settled the problem in the Potsdam Agreement. Supreme authority with regard to Germany was assumed by the Great Powers at the moment of the Declaration of June 5, 1945, and the Potsdam Agreement was concluded in August 1945. The right to make decisions concerning German territory and population fell within the scope of the Great Powers' supreme authority over Germany (as Maurach himself admits), and, therefore, the Powers did not, and did not have to, "convalidate" the transfers.

[105] *Parliamentary Debates, House of Lords*, vol. C. XXXIX, p. 81.

there now exist two conflicting viewpoints: the German one, challenging these foundations, and the Polish one, defending them. It is worth noting that the Great Powers, though occasionally expressing doubts as to the final character of the present Polish-German frontier, have never attempted to query the legal foundations of the transfers effected.

The Polish juristic viewpoint is supported by the fact of agreed co-operation in the transfers by all the Great Powers. German revisionists scorn to explain the agreement of the Great Powers to, and their active cooperation in, the transfers. They even admit it. One of their representatives, Hoffmann, felt compelled to confess:

"If, in spite of this (supposed protests by Bevin and Churchill — B. W.), agreements were subsequently concluded which promised, and settled, acceptance of those expelled in the British zone of occupation, it is today still difficult to demonstrate by documentary evidence (*kann heute noch nicht aktenmässig belegt werden*) what were the motives which prompted the Western Powers to do so"[106].

Some West German scholars strive to shift responsibility for the transfers on to the Soviet and Polish Delegations by alleging that these falsely informed the delegations of the Western Powers that most of the German population had already fled from the territories east of the Oder and Western Neisse[107]. This allegedly false information — they claim — induced the Heads of Government of the Western Powers to agree to the transfers. This is obviously an attempt to present decisions concerning transfers as the outcome of a subterfuge or of fraudulent manoeuvres by the Soviet and Polish Delegations, which would make it legitimate to invalidate the norms laid down in Section XIII of the Potsdam Agreement[108]. It is quite likely that the parties attending the Potsdam Conference were not fully informed of the extent to which the German population had fled from the territories captured as a result of the Red Army's offensive

---

[106] Hoffmann, *op. cit.*, p. 16.
[107] Wagner, *op. cit.*, pp. 159—160; F. Zipfel, "Vernichtung und Austreibung der Deutschen aus den Gebieten östlich der Oder-Neisse Linie", *Jahrbuch für die Geschichte Mittel- und Ostdeutschlands*, Tübingen, vol. III, p. 155.
[108] On error, mistake or subterfuge in international agreements see J. Makowski in his textbook, p. 413.

in the winter and spring of 1945. It is a fact, however, that the flight and evacuation (ordered by the German authorities) involved almost the entire German population inhabiting those territories[109].   Indeed, the parties to the Potsdam Agreement might have been to some limited extent in the dark as to the number of the Germans still left on the territories that were to pass under Polish authority, but all this is completely irrelevant and it neither could nor did affect decisions on the transfers since the actual idea of transferring the German population from the territories Poland was to take over after the war adopted as early as 1943, precisely by the British and American Governments, and was confirmed on numerous subsequent occasions in declarations by leading statesmen of the Western Powers.

Furthermore, if in the German revisionist claim — irrelevant as it all is — there were a grain of truth, if there had been some subterfuge, trickery, fraud or misrepresentation on the part of the Soviet and Polish Delegations in supplying essential information, and if the British and American Delegations had been so gullible as to accept as *bona fide* such information without checking it independently, and had allowed themselves be deceived and lured into making decisions affecting the fate of millions of people — the Western Powers would certainly have been appalled by the unexpected and overwhelming influx of Germans transferred to the west which they would not have been prepared to receive, and it is quite obvious that they would have lodged at least formal notes of even the most half-hearted protest. On the other hand, it would certainly have given rise to controversies within the Combined Repatriation Executive. Why did nothing of the sort happen? Obviously the answer is simple. The principle of transfer of Germans from *all* post-war Polish Territory had been conceived and accepted by the Western Powers beforehand, and final decisions on the transfers were a foregone conclusion at the Potsdam Conference, a matter of mere formality.

The giving effect to the decisions on the transfer conclusively reaffirmed the essence of the decisions whereby the Polish-German frontier was settled as being along the Oder and Western Neisse line.

---

[109] *Die Vertreibung*, pp. 23E—24E.

CHAPTER VIII

THE QUESTION OF THE RECOGNITION OF THE FRONTIER ON THE ODER AND WESTERN NEISSE

1. RECOGNITION OF TERRITORIAL CHANGES IN INTERNATIONAL LAW

International doctrine and practice have only relatively recently concerned themselves with the question of recognition of territorial changes. In 1932, the American Secretary of State Stimson — referring to the annexation of north-east China (Manchuria) by Japan — declared that the Government of the United States "does not intend to recognize any situation, treaty or agreement which may be brought about by means contrary to the covenants and obligations of the Pact of Paris"[1] (Briand—Kellogg's Pact). Since that time, reference is made in International Law to the principle of non-recognition, by some authors termed Stimson's doctrine. The formulation of the principle of non-recognition has affected international practice[2].

The principle of recognition or non-recognition of territorial changes has not yet been exhaustively dealt with in International Law doctrine.

---

[1] For the relevant quotations from Stimson's declaration, see K. Marek, *Identity and Continuity of States in Public International Law*, Genève 1954, p. 556.

[2] For relevant clauses in international conventions, see K. Marek, *op. cit.*, p. 557.

[*Ed. note*: This opinion calls for some explanation. After the publication of the first English language edition of the present work, Wiewióra made a further contribution in his comprehensive monograph *Uznanie nabytków terytorialnych w prawie międzynarodowym* (The Recognition of Territorial Accessions in International Law) Poznań 1961, 243 pp. In this monograph Wiewióra presented the conception of recognition of territorial accessions as also the content and role of such recognition on the basis of documents and the contemporary achievements of international law. He confronted the results of his theoretical study with the territorial changes made after the Second World War and analysed the recognition of the Czechoslovak-German frontier, the Polish-German frontier and the frontier between the two German States. The monograph includes an English summary (pp. 230—236). So far this is the only thorough and comprehensive analysis of the problem.]

It is generally held that recognition of territorial accessions is being considered only in relation to an illegal action as a result of which a given State has secured these accessions, or when the legal basis of the accessions is obscure or doubtful. In such instances, recognition removes the doubts or the illegal character of such action, and makes acquisition of the given territory legal in the eyes of the State expressing recognition[3]. In literature, however, stress is laid on the fact that the principle of non-recognition is in legal and practical respects limited. It is rightly said that non-recognition of territorial accessions fails, *per se*, to produce *restitutio ad integrum*, does not change the existing situation, and although perhaps annoying to the actual possessor of the given territory — cannot force him to withdraw[4]. The function of the principle of non-recognition is merely to keep the legal status in suspense pending a final settlement which may involve either a restitution of the *status quo ante*, or an adaptation of the legal situation to the changed practical situation[5].

The essence of non-recognition is, as regards territorial changes, "the refusal, on the part of the non-recognizing Power, to regard the sovereignty of the dispossessed Power as superseded by that of

---

[3] Oppenheim-Lauterpacht, *op. cit.*, vol. I, p. 137; H. Lauterpacht, *Recognition in International Law*, Cambridge 1948, p. 411.

[4] K. Marek, *op. cit.*, p. 561.

[5] T. C. Chen, *The International Law on Recognition*, London 1951, p. 441.

the dispossessing Power, and to give to the acts of the latter the effects attaching to the acts of a rightful sovereign"[6].

In western International Law literature there is also a tendency to ascribe great importance to the principle of effectiveness. This is based on the argument that legal norms depend to a large extent on their effectiveness in practice. The best conditions for the existence of a legal system are said to be those in which the norms have a high — though not necessarily absolute — degree of effectiveness in relation to facts[7].

When the principle of non-recognition is compared with that of effectiveness, there ensue certain complications, since the doctrine of International Law admits the possibility that facts considered as illegal may nevertheless produce certain legal consequences[8]. There are acts and situations which may be considered as highly defective legally, but which are legally not altogether ineffective[9]. This is occasionally the interpretation of the principle *ex factis jus oritur*[10].

2. RECOGNITION OF THE ODER-NEISSE FRONTIER
(IN GENERAL)

The foregoing remarks are to some extent introductory to an analysis of the recognition of the frontier on the Oder and Western Neisse. There are several aspects of the question: 1) whether there is a necessity for a recognition of the Oder-Neisse frontier; 2) who is required to recognize it, and 3) how can recognition be expressed?

If we agree that recognition of the post-war Polish-German frontier is necessary, we must assume that Polish rights to the Recovered Territories are either derived from an illegal action, or are at least doubtful and obscure. The first possibility is ruled out: the objections on grounds of lawlessness would have to apply to,

---

6 Langer, *op. cit.*, p. 96.
7 K. Marek, *op. cit.*, pp. 554, 563 (based on Kelsen).
8 *Ibid.*, p. 564; H. Lauterpacht, *op. cit.*, pp. 420—421.
9 R. Laun, *op. cit.*, p. 25.
10 K. Marek, *op. cit.*, p. 564.

and challenge, the right of the Great Powers to make the Potsdam decisions, by virtue of which Poland acquired the Recovered Territories. The legality of the decisions of the Great Powers as regards the States vanquished in the Second World War was distinctly confirmed in Article 107 of the Charter of the United Nations, the fundamental act of contemporary International Law.

The point remaining to be considered is, therefore, whether Polish rights to the Recovered Territories are doubtful or obscure. This is the point at which the Governments of the Western Powers and German revisionists concentrate their attempts to undermine the legal foundations of the post-war Polish-German frontier. Both query the extent and permanence of Polish rights to the lands east of the Oder and Western Neisse.

First of all, we have to note the legal and political differences between the standpoints of, on the one hand the Western Powers and on the other the Government of the German Federal Republic. The United States, Great Britain and France never challenged the principle that Poland should obtain territorial accessions in the west. Debatable from the viewpoint of the Western Powers has been merely the extent of such accessions. In the course of relevant controversies which arose as between the Soviet Government and the Governments of the Western Powers concerning the settling of the Polish-German frontier on the Oder and Western Neisse, the Western Powers eventually queried the final character of the Potsdam decisions as concerning the western frontier of Poland. Thus we are dealing here with non-recognition in the formal sense, with an attempt to cause definitive legal settlement of the Polish-German frontier to fall into abeyance.

The Western Powers' reservations became especially noticeable in 1951, when — in connection with the Paris Conference, preparatory to the German Federal Republic's adherence to the European Defence Community — Chancellor Adenauer strove hard to persuade the Western Powers to support German territorial claims in the east. Adenauer even went so far as to declare to a group of deputies of the Christian Democratic Union, that the Western Powers had given a written undertaking to recognize the territories east of the Oder and Western Neisse as part of German land[11]. This was countered by an official dementi by the Allied High Commissioner, and Dr. Lenz, Under-Secretary of State in the West German Government, had to concoct explanations.

In spite of this, Adenauer promised (October 17, 1951) to German repatriates, that he would request the Western Powers shortly to restore to Germany the territories lost to Poland, and, moreover, he permitted himself to declare that even if the Western Powers recognized the frontiers of 1937, this would not bar possibilities of making further demands, as for instance for "a new agreement on the corridor enacted by the Versailles Treaty"[12].

The claims made by the West German Chancellor alarmed the Western Powers — not only public opinion, but also Government quarters. The British *Times* warned that it would be difficult for the Western Powers to maintain the exclusively defensive character of the Atlantic Pact if it were connected even in the most indirect way with German demands to restore to Germany her lost territories. Simultaneously, *The Times* suggested to Adenauer that he would be wise not to ask the Western Powers for any promise which would rule out altogether an eventual agreement with Russia. Such a promise would be "any declaration about the former German territories in Poland and Russia or any refusal to recognize the Oder-Neisse Line"[13].

Although Adenauer failed to obtain in November 1951 from the Western Powers any promises of support for the West German territorial claims, he was nevertheless successful in securing the inclusion of a formula in the 1952 Convention on relations between the Three Western Powers and the Federal Republic. Article 7 of the Convention, subsequently incorporated without modifications in the Paris Agreements of 1954, laid down that German frontiers are to be finally settled at the peace conference, and accorded to Germany the right to participate in defining the frontiers as a free partner. This formula is considered as the expression of the joint attitude

---

[11] Z. Jordan, *op. cit.*, (II), p. 16.
[12] *Manchester Guardian*, November 19, 1951.
[13] *The Times*, November 22, 1951.

of the Western Powers as regards the Polish-German frontier[14]. This was interpreted by Chancellor Adenauer as an opportunity to exert pressure concerning the settling of the frontier "in accordance with our (West German — B. W.) wishes"[15]. However, the Western Powers did not admit that the formula was expandable as to interpretation. When President Eisenhower declared on February 2, 1953 that the American Government "recognizes no kind of commitment contained in secret understandings of the past with foreign governments which permit . . . enslavement" of other nations, Adenauer announced at a press conference that West Germany now expected the United States to back German demands for the return of the Oder-Neisse territories turned over to Polish administration as a result of a decision of the Potsdam Conference[16]. The West German Chancellor thereby meant to intimate that appropriate assurances had been given to him by the United States Government. However, rumours to that effect were immediately refuted by the American Government. Conant, the American High Commissioner in Germany, declared that President Eisenhower had not spoken with Germany in mind, and that Germany's western frontiers would be determined in the final peace treaty, in the drawing up of which Germany would take part[17]. Having in mind the contingency of a conference on this subject, the Government of the German Federal Republic wants to preserve an unhampered right to oppose *any* changes in the pre-war Polish-German frontier.

Returning to our starting point — that is, to the question as to whether the Oder-Neisse frontier *needs* to be recognized, it may be said in general that once a State concerned queries territorial accessions as illegal or doubtful from the point of view of International Law, there obviously is a need for recognition. This, however, entails an additional question — namely, *who* is entitled to recognize this frontier?

If we admit that the Great Powers were legitimately entitled to decide the fate of Germany, we have to conclude that the only States

---

[14] Z. Jordan, *op. cit.*, (II), p. 17.
[15] *Manchester Guardian*, July 17, 1952.
[16] *New York Times*, February 7, 1953.
[17] *New York Times* and *Manchester Guardian*, November 13, 1953.

which may rightly consider themselves entitled to express recognition are: the United States, Great Britain, the Soviet Union and France.

Recognition of the Oder-Neisse frontier by Germany is a separate question. The problem is complicated only in that there are now two German States, both claiming to be the legal successors of the former Reich, and both considering themselves to be legitimately entitled to express their attitude as regards the Oder-Neisse frontier.

But, there is an essential difference between the attitudes of the two German States: the German Democratic Republic sees itself as *one of the two* existing German States, whereas the German Federal Republic claims *exclusive* title to represent Germany as a whole[18].

3. RECOGNITION BY THE GERMAN DEMOCRATIC REPUBLIC

One of the first acts of the Government of the German Democratic Republic[19] was recognition of the Oder-Neisse frontier as the settled

---

[18] The communiqué from the New York Conference of the three Western Powers (September 19, 1950) announced: "Pending the unification of Germany, the three governments (i.e. the United States, Great Britain and France — B. W.) consider the Government of the Federal Republic as the only German government freely and legitimately constituted and therefore entitled to speak for Germany as the representative of the German people in international affairs". B. Meissner, *op. cit.*, p. 232; similarly, in the Final Act of the London Conference (October 3, 1954) we also find the statement that the German Federal Republic is entitled to represent Germany. *Europa Archiv*, 1954, vol. 9, p. 6978. On the other hand, Dr. L. Bolz, Foreign Minister of the German Democratic Republic, declared in a public statement in August 1956: ". . .solange auf deutschem Territorium zwei deutsche Staaten bestehen, beide deutsche Staaten Nachfolgestaaten des ehemaligen Deutschen Reiches sind. Bis zur Wiedervereinigung Deutschlands ist deshalb auf internationalen Konferenzen, die Deutschland betreffende Fragen behandeln, die gleichberechtigte Teilnahme beider deutschen Staaten unerlässlich. Aus der Souveränität der DDR ergibt sich, dass keine Frage, die Deutschland betrifft, ohne Mitwirkung der DDR geregelt werden kann". *Neues Deutschland*, August 30, 1956.

[19] When, in September 1949, the German Federal Republic was established, progressive German political organizations represented in the German People's Council — which became transformed into the Provisional *Volkskammer* — asked the Soviet Government to agree to give effect to the previously accepted draft of the constitution of the German Democratic

and existing State frontier between Poland and Germany. Prime Minister Grotewohl declared in his first exposé, on October 12, 1949:

"The policies of peace and friendship are complete as regards the mutual relations with the People's Democracies, and above all with our neighbours — the new Poland and the Czechoslovak Republic — as well as with all peace-loving nations... To us, the frontier on the Oder and Neisse is a frontier of peace which will make possible friendly mutual relations with the Polish nation... Our political aims are in conformity with the purposes laid down in the Potsdam Agreement as binding upon Germany"[20].

[*Ed. Note*: The legal problems of the German Democratic Republic have been developed by Wiewióra in the monograph *Niemiecka Republika Demokratyczna jako podmiot prawa międzynarodowego* (The German Democratic Republic as a Subject of International Law), Poznań 1961, 175 pp. In the six chapters of that work he analysed and explained all the legal problems of the German Democratic Republic as one of the two German States. In Chapter II, dealing with the position of the G.D.R. as subject of international law, Wiewióra — availing himself of

Republic, and thereby to permit parliamentary and presidential elections to be held, and a Government of the German Democratic Republic to be set up. Simultaneously, Otto Grotewohl, candidate for Prime Minister of the German Democratic Republic, announced the future political principles of his Government, including the statement that the Democratic Republic "will act in complete harmony with the Potsdam Agreement and other declarations of the Allies with regard to Germany". Furthermore, he declared: "We shall strive to establish a democratic State and to rebuild peaceful and friendly relations with countries of the entire world". On October 10, 1949, General Chuikov communicated to the *Volkskammer* the Soviet Government's agreement. In this connection, the Soviet Government wound up the Soviet Military Administration and transferred its functions to the authorities of the German Democratic Republic. The Soviet Military Administration was superseded by a Soviet Control Commission "the task of which — declared General Chuikov — will be to examine the execution of the decisions of the Potsdam Agreement and of other joint decisions made by the Four Powers with regard to Germany". For text of the declarations by Prime Minister Grotewohl and General Chuikov, see Osmańczyk, *op. cit.*, pp. 28—29.

[20] *Zbiór Dokumentów* 1949, No. 10, pp. 893 ff. On the preceding day, Wilhelm Pieck, as President of the German Democratic Republic, declared: "Niemals werden wir es dulden, dass die Oder-Neisse-Grenze von den imperialistischen Interessenten an einem neuen Krieg zur Aufhetzung des deutschen Volkes gegen unseren Nachbarstaat missbraucht werden kann. Die Oder-Neisse-Grenze soll die Grenze des Friedens sein und niemals die freundschaftlichen Beziehungen zu dem polnischen Volke stören". W. Pieck, *Reden und Aufsätze aus den Jahren 1908—1950*, Berlin 1951, vol. II, p. 301.

documents — presented the process of East Germany's becoming a subject of international law and defined its capacity of functioning. The chapter also contains an analysis of the legal position of the German Democratic Republic in the light of the agreement concluded with the Soviet Union on September 20, 1955. In his analysis of the problem of recognition of States in the theory and practice of international law Wiewióra takes a determined stand and supports the declaratory theory which ascribes to recognition only quantitative functions, regarding it as an enlargement of the rights and privileges already possessed by a given State. Chapter IV, devoted to the recognition of the German Democratic Republic, includes many documents pertaining to the recognition of the German Democratic Republic by the Socialist countries. The Western countries' attitude to the German Democratic Republic is described by Wiewióra as based on the doctrine of legitimism which has been severely criticised by scholars as an intervention in the internal affairs of another State, an intervention made for temporary political purposes. It is from this point of view that Wiewióra examines what is called the Hallstein doctrine and its application by the Federal Government. He points out that that doctrine is of a repressive character with regard to third States and its main purpose is to keep the German Democratic Republic in political isolation. In Chapter V, Wiewióra analyses Eastern Germany's right to conclude international agreements. It should be stressed that this is the first Polish study dealing with the German Democratic Republic as a subject of international law.]

This declaration was confirmed on further occassions by Prime Minister Grotewohl[21]. Recognition of the frontier of the Oder and Western Neisse was a consequence of the acceptance by the German Democratic Republic of the Potsdam Agreement as a foundation for its foreign policies.

The peculiar, *programme-like character* of the Potsdam Agreement — in that it settled in advance of a peace treaty certain relations as between Germany and her neighbours and simultaneously outlined a programme for the transformation of Germany from an aggresive into a peaceful State[22] — makes part acceptance of it

---

[21] In an interview given to the Polish press on October 19, 1949, Prime Minister Grotewohl declared: "The Government of the German Democratic Republic neither has nor wants to have anything in common with the anti-Polish policies of former German Governments—Monarchy, the Weimar Republic, or Hitler... We wish to put an end once and for all to the policies of *Drang nach Osten*... We therefore believe... the frontier on the Oder and Neisse to be a frontier of peace, and anyone claiming a revision of the frontier to be an enemy of the German and Polish nations and a warmonger". *Zbiór Dokumentów* 1949, No. 10, pp. 943—944.

impossible; the Agreement is a complete and organic entity and as such must be either accepted or rejected as a whole, without discrimination against any particular decision. The attitude of the German Democratic Republic to the Polish-German frontier was the logical consequence of accepting the Potsdam programme as a whole.

The German Democratic Republic accepted the Potsdam Agreement as the legal foundation of Germany's territorial status, and accordingly signed frontier agreements with Poland.

4. NON-RECOGNITION OF THE ODER-NEISSE FRONTIER BY THE GERMAN FEDERAL REPUBLIC

The Government of the German Federal Republic was from the very beginning of its existence hostile to the Oder-Neisse frontier.

> [*Ed. note*: The legal problems of the German Federal Republic have been enlarged and developed by Wiewióra in a number of articles which have appeared since the publication of the first English language edition of the present book. Particularly worthy of mention is Wiewióra's condensed commentary to the discussion on *Das Östliche Deutschland*, a publication elaborated and produced by the Goettinger Arbeitskreis in 1959. This publication was commented upon by four Polish writers, Michał Sczaniecki, Bolesław Wiewióra, Zdzisław Nowak and Janusz Ziółkowski, in a collective article entitled "Manual of German Revisionism" (*Polish Western Affairs* 1960, No. 1, pp. 64—109). In his part of the article, entitled "The Law of Nations" (pp. 69—82) Wiewióra presented his views on the legal position of the German Federal Republic in international law. One of Wiewióra's last studies was an evaluation of the foreign policy of the Federal Republic in 1963. This study, entitled " The Aims of the Present Eastern Policy of the German Federal Republic", appeared posthumously (*Polish Western Affairs* 1963, No. 1, pp. 3—19).

We may ignore a multitude to attacks against Poland's western frontier at meetings of organizations of German repatriates, notice must be taken, however, of the violent attack, launched against this frontier by Dr. Hermann Pünder, Chairman of the "Administrative

---

[22] This question is dealt with in greater detail by A. Klafkowski, *Sprawa traktatu*, pp. 95 ff.

Council of Bizonia", as early as the spring of 1948[23]. Chancellor Adenauer declared even at the very first meetings of the Bundestag that his Government would never recognize the Oder-Neisse frontier and that he would strive to change it by "legal methods"[24]. The Federal Government has missed no opportunity to emphasize its revisionist attitude to Poland's western frontier[25].

Further evidence of Adenauer's persistently revisionist attitude towards the Oder-Neisse frontier will be found in the declaration he made on conclusion of the negotiations concerning entry into diplomatic relations with the Soviet Government. At a press conference in Moscow, on September 14, 1955, he declared that post-war German frontiers remain an open question pending final settlement to be accomplished in a peace treaty with Germany[26].

Changes in Poland in October 1956, after the VIII Plenary Session of the Central Committee of the Polish United Workers' Party, were thought by west German politicians to afford scope for various political speculations. The predominating notion was, however, that claims for a change of the existing Polish-German frontier should be upheld.

One might quote indefinitely revisionist claims made by West German politicians and Government representatives challenging the final character of the decisions regarding the Oder-Neisse frontier; for the purpose of this work, however, that is unnecessary. It need only be added that the revisionists by no means confine themselves

---

[23] See A. J. Kamiński in an article on the pedigree of Bonn's foreign policies, "Rodowód polityki zagranicznej Bonn", *Przegląd Zachodni* 1951, No. 5/6, p. 291.

[24] *Ibid.* The author legitimately points to analogies between Adenauer and Stresemann who prepared in the twenties the foundations for the renascence of German imperialism under the slogan of a revision of the eastern frontiers of the Reich. Stresemann professed in those days that he would strive by peaceful means to change the frontier with Poland since... "we are not strong enough to undertake any action against Poland".

[25] It is relevant to quote Chancellor Adenauer's note (1951) to the Western Powers, approved by the majority of the Bundestag, and claiming the Polish Recovered Territories. It is cited by the appeal of the German Democratic Republic's *Volkskammer* concerning reunification of Germany, and referred to as an "unheard of provocation". *Zbiór Dokumentów* 1951, No. 5, p. 1190.

[26] *Trybuna Ludu*, September 26, 1955, No. 256.

to challenging the Potsdam frontiers of Germany, but even claim the 1939 frontiers, and thereby strive to retrieve at least some of Hitlers' gains[27].

The attitude towards the Oder-Neisse frontier as formulated at various times by the German Federal Government shows certain differences. The following is a review of a number of formulations:

1) The Government of the German Federal Republic is prepared to engage in talks with the German Democratic Republic on the reunification of Germany on the condition that the return of territories beyond the Oder and Neisse be demanded[28].

2) No German Government will ever be able to recognize the frontier on the Oder and Western Neisse[29].

3) It is necessary to consider establishing a Polish-German condominium on the Recovered Territories[30].

4) The Polish-German frontier can be finally settled only in a peace treaty with Germany.

5) The time may come when the choice will have to be made "whether to renounce these other territories (east to the Oder and Neisse — B. W.) if thereby the 17 million Germans of the Soviet Zone can be freed, or whether this should not be done in order to

[27] For instance, Dr. Kather, Chairman of the Bund Vertriebener Deutscher, in the spring of 1957, *Volksbote* No. 16, 1957. During the 1957 election campaign, organizations of repatriates defined six main political principles, the first one arguing that *at least* the 1937 frontier should be claimed (*Die Welt*, July 22, 1957). Cf. also K. Rabl, "Rechtsgrundlagen deutscher Ostpolitik", *Der Europäische Osten* 1958, No. 1, p. 11: "Dem deutschen Staat steht also noch *de iure* die Gebietshochheit über das Memel- und das Sudetenland, sowie über die Oder-Neisse Gebiete zu. . ."

[28] October 6, 1951, Warburg, *Germany — Key to Peace*, Cambridge Mass. 1953, pp. 176—177.

[29] Chancellor Adenauer's memorandum to President Eisenhower May 29, 1953, quoted by H. Kraus, *Die Oder-Neisse Linie*, p. 12. This attitude was adopted again by Minister von Brentano in his speech in the Bundestag (January 31, 1957).

[30] *Trybuna Ludu*, September 12, 1953, No. 254. The idea of a Polish--German condominium on the Polish Recovered Territories was no novelty in the revisionists' stock-in-trade. It had been advanced by E. W. Meyer in *Die Grundlagen für den Frieden mit Deutschland*, Wiesbaden, p. 97. Wiskemann, *op. cit.*, pp. 206—207, reports that Adenauers' proposition met with strong opposition, and even with demonstrations by the *Landsmannschaften*, and had not been repeated since.

maintain our somewhat problematical title to these other territories [31].

6) Neither the Government of the German Federal Republic, nor that of the German Democratic Republic is entitled to settle the Oder-Neisse frontier. This is up to a future all-German Government. The Government of the German Federal Republic is, for its part, prepared to guarantee that it will not seek to change the existing *status quo* by force [32].

7) The Oder-Neisse frontier is a question for settlement between Poland and Germany [33].

8) If Poland joined the European Common Market and the European Coal and Steel Community, this would take much of the political edge off the problem of the Polish-German frontier [34].

There are differences between these formulations. Some are more definite, and others less so. Some were intimately connected with current prospects for a reunification of Germany. But they all have one feature in common, they all stem from negation of the existing Polish-German frontier.

The legal standpoint of the German Federal Government is based above all on a repudiation of the binding force of the Potsdam Agreement as regards Germany. It is also worth while to examine the legal arguments underlying the particular formulations. For instance, the thesis that the Polish-German frontier cannot be finally settled except in a peace treaty with Germany is based on such an interpretation of the Potsdam Agreement as would demand reconsideration of the problem at the peace conference. A completely different attitude is shown in the claim that the Polish-German frontier is a question to be settled between Poland and Germany. This concept, advanced

---

[31] Min. Brentano's statement at his press conference in London on May 1, 1956. The next day Brentano, under the pressure of mass protests by revisionists, explained that he referred to the poor possibilities of realizing those claims and not to the claims themselves being problematic; *Frankfurter Allgemeine Zeitung* of May 3, 1956.

[32] Declaration by Minister von Brentano at a press conference on November 30, 1956.

[33] This viewpoint was formulated in connection with the support given to the Oder-Neisse frontier by Yugoslavia in September 1957.

[34] A statement made by Chancellor Adenauer after the elections to the German Federal Republic's Bundestag in 1957.

in reply to the Yugoslav acknowledgement of the Oder-Neisse frontier, contradicts the preceding one, since it is impossible to deny to Yugoslavia, a former combatant in the war against Germany, the right to express an opinion on a problem to be discussed at the peace conference, in which, after all, Yugoslavia would have to participate. The concept that the Oder-Neisse frontier is the sole concern of Poland and Germány is tantamount to a repudation of the concept that it must be settled at the peace conference, and admits of such a settlement even at an earlier date. It is worth while to recall that Poland's judicial attitude maintains that the Polish-German frontier has been already settled and that it has been affirmed by the *German* State immediately adjoining to Poland — consequently most intimately concerned — the German Democratic Republic.

Finally, there is the German Federal Republic's reiterated offer to give guarantees that it will not seek to change the Polish-German frontier by force. Legally speaking, that offer is utterly void, since the German Federal Republic has already, in several legal acts, repudiated the use of force as a means of settling controversial problems; the German Federal Republic did this in the declaration of November 22, 1951, invoking the Charter of the United Nations, subsequently in Article 3 of the Convention on relations between the Three Western Powers and the Federal Republic also invoking the Charter, and, finally, in part V of the Final Act of the London Conference (October 3, 1954) in which the Federal Republic expressly "accepts the obligations set forth in Article 2 of the Charter of the United Nations" and in particular "undertakes never to have recourse to force to achieve the reunification of Germany or the modification of the present boundaries of the German Federal Republic, and to resolve by peaceful means any disputes which may arise between the Federal Republic and other States[35]. The offer to renounce the use of force as regards Poland means that either the German Federal Republic is not serious about her obligations following from the act signed at the London Conference, or that she seeks to sell as a political

---

[35] *The Times*, October 4, 1954.

concession what is in fact merely a logical consequence of the obligations she has incurred.

5. THE BINDING FORCE OF THE POTSDAM AGREEMENT AS REGARDS GERMANY

The negative attitude of the German Federal Republic towards
the Potsdam Agreement was adequately expressed during the trial
involving delegalization of the Communist Party of Germany, held
in the Constitutional Tribunal at Karlsruhe. In the course of this
trial, the Federal Government spokesman formulated the following
theses:

1) The Potsdam Agreement is not an international treaty but
merely an agreement between Heads of Government on principles
to govern the instructions to be given to military commanders and
their deputies in the Allied Control Council for Germany. This is
proved by the official name: Report on the Potsdam Conference.
As an intergovernmental agreement (*Regierungsabkommen*), the Potsdam Agreement is not binding upon States as a whole.

2) The Potsdam Agreement, as *res inter alios gesta*, is not addressed
to the German people and German constitutional organs. Consequently,
only the decisions of the Allied Control Council and Military Commanders of the zones are decisive for Germany and German organs.

3) The Potsdam Agreement determines the course of action of
the Occupying Powers with regard to Germany only during the
initial control period, hence the conclusion that it does not apply
to the subsequent period.

4) The Potsdam Agreement has become inapposite, part of the
decisions having been implemented, part having outlived their usefulness, and some are subject to substantial differences in interpretation as between the Great Powers. As an example of such differences,
the Government spokesman of the German Federal Republic quoted
the dispute between the Western Powers and the Soviet Union on
the final character of the Oder-Neisse frontier.

These theses call for a critical analysis[36]:

1) Legally speaking, there is no difference between agreements made as between governments and international treaties. Both kinds of agreements are equally binding; the kind of agreement does not influence its binding force. It is absurd to claim that the Potsdam Agreement is not binding upon "States as a whole", since Heads of Government sign agreements only as State organs: on behalf of the States and with legal consequences implied.

2) It is not true that the Potsdam Agreement is not addressed to the German nation. The contrary claim is refuted by the very text of the Agreement, addressed in Section II directly to the German nation in the following words: "If their own efforts (those of the German nation — B. W.) are steadily directed to this end (to a reconstruction on a democratic and peaceful basis — B. W.) it will be possible for them in due course to take their place among the free and peaceful peoples of the world"[37]. Other decisions of the Potsdam Agreement entail the necessity of co-operation by the German nation in carrying them into effect. The claim that the Potsdam Agreement is *res inter alios gesta*, and is not binding upon Germany, is contradictory to the rights of the Great Powers to decide Germany's fate. On the part of the German Federal Republic, the argument is advanced that the rights of the Great Powers with regard to Germany are not derived from the Potsdam Agreement but from the Declaration of June 5, 1945, made on the assumption of supreme authority with respect to Germany; but after all, the outcome of the assumption of supreme authority with respect to Germany is precisely the Potsdam Agreement; it defines in detail the programme for the reconstruction of Germany from an aggressive State into a peaceful and democratic one. The following correlation will be found to exist between the Declaration of June 5, 1945, and the Potsdam Agreement: the Declaration defines the essence, scope, and character of the authority of the Great Powers over Germany, while the Potsdam Agreement

---

[36] In polemics involving challenges to the binding force of the Potsdam Agreement, use is being made of the reply of Professor Kröger, the counsel for defence of the Communist Party of Germany quoted after the unofficial records of the Karlsruhe trial.

[37] *United Nations Documents, p.* 196.

defines the aims pursued in, and the means of, exercising such authority. Hence, there can be no question of the Potsdam Agreement
not being binding upon Germany: if the Government of the German
Federal Republic recognizes at all the rights of the Great Powers
in questions concerning the whole of Germany, it cannot deny binding force to the Potsdam Agreement, a manifestation of the execution of those rights. By denying legal consequences to the Potsdam
decisions, the Government of the German Federal Republic denies
the legal basis of the occupation of Germany in the years 1945—1949.

Legislation by the Allied Control Council and Commanders of
Military Zones is based precisely on the Potsdam Agreement. This
was confirmed by the Government of the German Federal Republic
in the memorandum of March 9, 1950, concerning the Saar, which
includes: "The fact that the Allied Control Council has ceased to
operate indefinitely is without legal consequence as long as the Potsdam Agreement has not been formally declared null and void" [38].

Consequently, to recognize legislation by the Allied Control
Council as binding upon Germany and at the same time to refuse
to recognize the binding force of the legal basis of such legislation
is a contradiction in terms.

Parenthetically, it should be added that the authority of the
Allied Control Council as regards foreign relations (assumption of
control over Germany's foreign relations) also confirms the right of
the Great Powers to decide the fate of Germany.

3) The aims defined in the Potsdam Agreement — viz., democratization, denazification, and demilitarization of Germany — were
permanent aims. In addition to these, the Potsdam Agreement also
defined short-term measures to be taken immediately — that is, in
the initial control period. The immediate measures included, for
instance, dissolution of the Nazi party, and liquidation of Nazi
military forces. The permanent aims of the Potsdam Agreement
should not be confused with immediate means of carrying them into
effect. It is hardly possible for anyone to claim that democratization or

---

[38] Excerpt from the memorandum quoted by Professor Kröger, the
German Communist Party's counsel for defence.

denazification are to be respected by Germany only during the initial control period.

4) In agreement with the principles obtaining in International Law, inappositeness, and consequently nullification, of the Potsdam Agreement would have to be declared by the parties themselvess — that is, by the Great Powers. But nothing of the kind has happened. On the contrary, at the Berlin Conference of Foreign Ministers in 1954, the Soviet Government unequivocally declared that the essence of the Potsdam Agreement still holds good, although a number of points have outlived their usefulness [39]. The Western Powers have also not challenged its binding force. And they have availed themselves of all the privileges granted to them under the Agreement. In notes to the Soviet Government of May 23, 1950, on the formation of the people's police forces in the German Democratic Republic, they even explicitly invoked the Yalta and Potsdam agreements as valid legal acts [40].

The very presence of occupation troops of the Western Powers in the German Federal Republic is also based on the decisions of the Potsdam Agreement. The Western Powers' recognition of the validity of the Potsdam Agreement is demonstrated by Article 2 of the General Agreement of 1952. The Article, as rewritten at the Paris Conference in October 1954, reads:

"Due to international situation, which up to the present renders impossible the reunification of Germany and the peace settlement for Germany, the three Powers reserve for themselves rights and obligations hitherto exercised or *incumbent upon them* (my italics — B. W.) in matters concerning Berlin and Germany as a whole, including reunification of Germany and the peace settlement"[41].

The Article refers to "rights and obligations . . . exercised or incumbent upon" the three Western Powers; these rights are derived

---

[39] Minister Molotov's declaration at the Berlin Conference of the Council of Foreign Ministers on February 1, 1954, *Konferencja Berlińska*, p. 135.

[40] *Zbiór Dokumentów* 1951, No. 1, pp. 170—171.

[41] *Verträge der Bundesrepublik Deutschland*, Carl Heymanns Verlag, Bonn-Köln-Berlin 1957, vol, 7, p. 8.

chiefly from the Potsdam Agreement as being an executive act of the authority wielded by the Great Powers in Germany.

But even assuming — purely hypothetically — that the Potsdam Agreement is renounced, Polish rights derived from this Agreement would not in any case be affected, since the decisions of the Tripartite Berlin Conference are of a territorial character, that is, they create by their execution a continuing state of fact. This point of view is adopted by the earlier[42] — as also by the most recent[43] — British doctrine on International Law. The main feature of the territorial rights is that once given and executed, they create a legal situation which could be changed only by a new agreement concerning the rights in question. As C. W. Jenks rightly points out, such agreements as treaties of cession are binding upon all comers. This principle:

"cannot be challenged without exposing both the community and all the parties concerned to the danger that any frontier dispute which has ever been settled by treaty may be reopened on the ground that some new state was not among the parties to the treaty by which it was settled. At this point the claims of stability overrule those of ease and adjustment to changing circumstances and it would seem imperative that the universal order should be uphold them"[44].

There are indeed controversies as to the interpretation of the contents of the Potsdam Agreement, duly reflected also in Article 7, paragraph 1 of the Convention of 1952, already referred to, which came into force together with the Paris Agreement concluded in October 1954. This Article declared that the final settlement of Germany's frontiers must be postponed[45], but this formal attitude of the Western Powers is contradicted by the practice of these States, discussed below.

Thus we arrive at the third question, that of forms in expressing recognition. In International Law, recognition may be expressed in

---

[42] J. Westlake, *International Law*, 2nd ed., 1910, Part I: Peace, pp. 60—62.

[43] C. W. Jenks, *The Common Law of Mankind*, London 1958, p. 94.

[44] *Ibid.*

[45] *Zbiór Dokumentów* 1952, No. 7—8, p. 2008.

two distinct forms: explicitly (for example, by making a suitable declaration), or implied (*per facta concludentia*)[46].

In the International Law doctrine it is stated that: "A Power that adopts a policy of non-recognition is bound to take certain measures in two spheres: in the field of its external relations, and in that of its domestic — judicial as well as administrative — activities"[47].

There is a characteristic contradiction in the practice of the Western Powers as regards the frontier on the Oder and Western Neisse. The contradiction is manifest in the disaccord between declarations and action. Let us analyse the practice of the particular Great Powers.

As to the attitude of the United States with regard to the western frontier of Poland, we have to recall the report already referred to on the Potsdam Conference given by President Truman on August 9, 1945. There we find the statement:

"The territory the Poles are to administer will enable Poland better to support its population. It will provide a short and more easily defensible frontier between Poland and Germany. Settled by Poles, it will provide a more homogenous nation".

This declaration clearly implies that President Truman at that time believed the Potsdam decisions on the Polish-German frontier to be final. After the Potsdam Conference, the American Military Governor General Clay, declared in a memorandum on the establishment of a federal republic in Germany that taking facts into consideration, the United States had permitted that certain German territories to be ceded to Russia, Poland and Czechoslovakia. He stated that recognizing that it was impossible to integrate those territories effectively with the respective States so long as their inhabitants were German, the removal of the whole German population had been agreed upon[48].

---

[46] H. Lauterpacht, *Recognition in International Law*, pp. 369 ff.

[47] Langer, *Seizure of Territory, The Stimson Doctrine and Related Principles in Legal Theory and Diplomatic Practice*, Princeton, New Jersey 1947, p. 101.

[48]) B. Meissner, op. *cit.*, p. 85.

However, within a year, the United States Government reversed its attitude. This became manifest in the speech made by Byrnes at Stuttgart on September 6, 1946. The American Secretary of State declared that the Western Territories had indeed been placed under Polish administration but that the decision on the Polish-German frontier was not final. The United States would support a revision of the pre-war Polish-German frontier in favour of Poland, but not as defined by the Potsdam Agreement[49].

The Byrnes speech calls for a somewhat more detailed consideration of the political background. The declaration was the outcome of a general charge of direction in American policies as regards Europe. The attitude to Poland was never one of the more important aspects in America's European policies[50], in which the most important role was played by Germany, especially when — after the termination of the Second World War — there appeared a rift between the Western Powers and the Socialist States[51].

About the middle of 1946, influential United States political circles believed it necessary to revise American policies in Germany. It was maintained that Soviet policies had begun to show a tendency towards achieving a dominant influence in Germany. The immediate occasion of the proposal to revise American policies was the Paris Session of the Council of Foreign Ministers, on July 10, 1946, where Molotov, the Soviet Foreign Minister, opposed certain French claims concerning West German territories.

---

[49] *Zbiór Dokumentów* 1946, No. 10—11, pp. 353—355.

[50] S. L. Sharp, *Poland's White Eagle on a Red Field*, Cambridge Mass. 1953, writes on page 7: "In political terms the attitude of the United States toward Poland can be understood primarily as being the by-product of American views on larger European issues and of relations with major Powers commensurable with this country".

[51] Sharp, *op, cit.*, p. 8, also wrote: "Poland became unimportant in World War II after serving for a while as inspiration of the world when interest in military cooperation with Russia outweighed the considerations of what is known as traditional friendship. When it appeared desirable to bring about the unconditional surrender of Nazi Germany it also seemed natural to encourage or, at least, acquiesce in — the acquisition of German lands by Poland. But when the postwar competition for German allegiance began between East and West, it appeared equally logical to question the extent and the finality of that acquisition if not the principle".

A group of State Department advisers submitted in August 1946 a memorandum on the question to Secretary of State Byrnes. The memorandum, concerning indirectly or directly the Polish-German frontier, declared that the main difficulty lay at the time in the fact that the French insisted on the revision of the Franco-German frontier before any steps were taken to rebuild Germany. The State Department advisers recommended that the United States should adopt a firm attitude against any revision of the Franco-German frontier.

The memorandum argued that since France did not contemplate mass transfers of the German population, a considerable number of Germans would come under French sovereignty; that would give rise, they maintained, to irredentism, and Germany, already deprived of her eastern "break-basket" would be unable to survive. The memorandum explained that the most cogent French argument for annexation was based on what had been permitted in the east. The Polish-Soviet annexations had transgressed the Atlantic Charter, and the mass expulsions and overcrowding of truncated Germany had caused pressures and hostile feelings, which were apt to provoke a new German aggression. Therefore — the French argued — having created such conditions, the Big Three must now finish the job, by depriving Germany of all such means as might possibly facilitate a future war, of which France would easily be the first victim. The State Department advisers declared that there was only one effective reply to the argument: *the United States must insist on re-opening* the problem of Germany's eastern frontier[52].

This view calls for rectification: it was not only the Soviet Union and Poland who transgressed the Atlantic Charter; the Western Powers, on numerous occasions, denied to Germany the right to appeal to the principles of the Charter. However, the memorandum suggests inescapable conclusions:

1) the recommendation that the United States should for political reasons *re-open* the question of Germany's eastern frontiers, implied *a contrario* that until that moment the question was considered closed;

---

[52] J. P. Warburg, *op. cit.*, pp. 25-26.

2) the change in the United States attitude was to be made for purely political reasons.

It can hardly be doubted that Secretary of State Marshall also was prompted by the same political motives[53] when he proposed in April 1947, at the Moscow Conference of the Council of Foreign Ministers, to revise the Oder-Neisse frontier and to settle the "final" Polish-German frontier with substantial departures, in favour of Germany, from the line agreed upon at Potsdam. Marshall's proposition boils down to the following points:

1) Poland would retain the part of East Prussia granted to her at Potsdam, together with Upper Silesia;

2) Upper Silesia would be subjected to a control system in "the interests of European economy";

3) the remaining territories east of the Oder and Western Neisse would be divided between Poland and Germany.

Marshall argued his propositions chiefly on grounds which were economic (loss of agricultural areas would cause a food crisis in Germany) and political (compressing of Germany within the Potsdam frontiers would produce a resuscitation of irredentist tendencies and would render impossible the democratization of Germany)[54]. This attitude was maintained by the United States also in the years which followed[55].

As regards Great Britain, Churchill — at the time leader of the opposition in the House of Commons — attacked the Potsdam decisions relating to the Polish-German frontier as early as August 1945. He referred to the frontier as "provisional" and complained that it deprived Germany of a quarter of her arable land. Decisions on the Oder-Neisse frontier, in the preparation of which he personally

---

[53] *Zbiór Dokumentów* 1947, No. 5, p. 213.
[54] *Zbiór Dokumentów* 1947, No. 5, pp. 214—219, 241.
[55] See, e.g., declaration by the United States High Commissioner on the Warsaw Declaration of June 6, 1950, *Kurier* (May 8, 1950), quoted by H. Kraus, *Die Oder-Neisse Linie*, pp. 37—38; Joint Declaration by the Foreign Ministers of the United States, Great Britain, and France, supported by the Government of the German Federal Republic, on November 22, 1951, *Zbiór Dokumentów* 1952, May 15, 1952 — *Zbiór Dokumentów* 1952, No. 4, p. 1401; No. 5, p. 1792. The American Government claimed in all these acts that the Potsdam Conference *did not* finally settle the frontiers of Germany.

took an active part, he described as a mistake and blamed them on the Polish Government[56]. On March 3, 1946 Churchill launched another attack against the western frontier of Poland. At Fulton, in a speech made in the presence of United States President Truman, he accused Poland of having made "wrongful inroads upon Germany" and deplored the "mass expulsion of millions of Germans"[57].

As regards to official declarations by the British Government, the attitude expressed in them in the first post-war years lacked clarity. In August 1945, Foreign Secretary Bevin still declared that there was an implied agreement as to Poland obtaining the Oder. As to the other territories, he suggested, in contradiction with the explicit wording of the Potsdam Agreement, that the frontier was settled on the Eastern Neisse[58]. In October 1945, Bevin declared that the settlement of the question of the Polish-German frontier depended on the policies of Poland[59]. But on February 21, 1946, Foreign Secretary Bevin declared during a debate in the House of Commons: "We acceded to the Oder and the Western Neisse at Potsdam; and so all you can do for Russia, Poland and the satellite States you have done"[60]. It may also be of some interest to quote Sir Hartley Shawcross, the chief British prosecutor at the Nüremberg Trial and at that time British Attorney General, who at a press conference in Warsaw in June 1946, expressed the view that Poland's frontiers were settled by that agreement (the Potsdam Agreement) on a solid basis and could not be queried even at the final peace conference[61].

However, in September 1946, in connection with Byrnes's Stuttgart speech, the British Foreign Office announced that they shared of the view of the American Secretary of State as regards the Polish-German

---

[56] *The War Speeches of the Rt Hon. Winston S. Churchill*, Compiled by Ch. Eade, London 1952, vol. III, p. 518.

[57] *Zbiór Dokumentów* 1946, No. 10—11, p. 305.

[58] *Parliamentary Debates, House of Commons, Official Report*, vol. 413, No. 1, p. 294

[59] Quoted after Hoffmann, *op. cit.*, pp. 15—16.

[60] *Parliamentary Debates, House of Commons, Official Report*, vol. 419, No. 87, p. 1351.

[61] *Kurier Codzienny*, June 18, 1946, quoted after A. Klafkowski, *Podstawy prawne*, p. 43.

frontier[62]. At the Moscow Conference of the Council of Foreign Ministers in April 1947, Foreign Secretary Bevin supported Marshall in his proposal to internationalize the industrial districts of Silesia, which the British Foreign Secretary then wanted to place in a situation analogical to that of the Saar[63]. In a report on the Moscow Conference, Bevin expressed doubts as to whether Poland was able to settle the extensive agricultural areas between Frankfurt on Oder and the Baltic, and made the final decision of the British Government contingent upon that question[64].

These vacillations in the British attitude to the western frontier of Poland were determined by political considerations. In 1948, the British Government adopted policy of ignoring the obligations they had incurred with regard to Poland. This is expressed in the notes of the British occupation anthorities of September 9, 1948[65], and of the British Government to the Polish Government of November 2, 1948[66], which emphasized that the British Government did not consider the Oder-Neisse frontier as final. All subsequent declarations by the British Government were co-ordinated with those of the United States Government[67].

As to the French attitude towards the problem of the Polish--German frontier two periods must be distinguished. In the initial post-war period it differed from that of the United States and Great Britain. Under the pressure of public opinion demanding safeguards against renewed German aggression, the then French Government recognized the Potsdam decisions concerning the Polish-German frontier as irrevocable. Referring to the Potsdam Agreement, the French Ministry of Foreign Affairs declared on August 3, 1945, that the French Government "has no essential objections to the

---

[62] The Swiss *Die Tat*, September 19, 1946, quoted by *Ost-Handbuch*, fascicle 6, p. 166.

[63] Quoted by Hoffmann, *op. cit.*, p. 20.

[64] *Parliamentary Debates, House of Commons, Official Report*, vol. 437, p. 1737.

[65] *Zbiór Dokumentów* 1948, No. 10, pp. 737—738.

[66] *Ibid.*, p. 740.

[67] See declaration by the British High Commissioner (June 6, 1950) on the Warsaw Declaration, *Kurier*, June 8, 1950, quoted by *Oder-Neisse*, p. 88, and H. Kraus, *Die Oder-Neisse Linie*, pp. 37—38; *Zbiór Dokumentów* 1951, No. 12, p. 2475; *Zbiór Dokumentów* 1952, No. 4, p. 1401; No. 5, p. 1792.

extension of Polish administration on the territories situated east of the Oder and Neisse"[68]. A similar statement is contained in the note from the French Ministry of Foreign Affairs to the Soviet Government (August 7, 1945)[69], while a note of the same date, addressed to the British Government, included:

> "With regard to the transfer of the German national minorities existing in Poland... the French Government has accepted the agreement made on that subject by the American, British, and Soviet Governments... The French Government does not in principle object to this transfer"[70].

The French attitude was also expressed in a declaration by the French Ambassador to Poland, M. Garreau, at a press conference in September 1945, to the effect that a change in Germany's frontier was the only means of avoiding a new assault. Furthermore, the French Ambasadors said:

> "From this viewpoint, the Oder-Neisse frontier is, I believe, the most sensible frontier, provided that not a single German shall have the right to stay east of this line. We have not infrequently had proofs that the German minorities are a pretext for a German aggression"[71].

The French interpretation of the Potsdam decisions as concerning the Oder-Neisse frontier follows from French Foreign Minister Bidault's declaration at the Paris Session of the Council of Foreign Ministers on August 10, 1946, in which he said:

> "Nothing serious can be achieved until the frontiers of post-war Germany are defined, and, to tell the truth, the occupation authorities cannot be expected to carry on a far-sighted policy until they know what territories will be German in the future. As regards the problem of east Germany, the Potsdam Conference reached an agreement, provisional in principle but essentially *fundamental* (my italics — B. W.), which agreement the French Government did not query..."[72].

---

[68] *Quellen*, p. 270. The French attitude is discussed by Z. Zaks, "Francja wobec uchwał jałtańskich i poczdamskich o polskiej granicy na Odrze i Nysie". *Zeszyty Naukowe S. G. S. Z.*, 1956, No. 2.

[69] *Quellen*, pp. 270—271.

[70] *Ibid.*

[71] *Dziennik Ludowy*, September 18, 1945, No. 21.

[72] *Zbiór Dokumentów* 1948, No. 1, p. 4.

With reference to Byrnes's Stuttgart speech, in which the Secretary of State undermined the definitive character of the Oder-Neisse frontier, the French Ambassador Garreau, declared:

"The Recovered Territories are Polish territory. The entire French nation considers the frontiers settled at Potsdam as a safeguard of the security of Europe, as well as of Poland and other Slav nations"[73].

We have already noticed how France — starting from the assumption that German frontiers ought to be settled *before a peace settlement* — claimed even in 1946 certain territorial accessions at the expense of Germany. France strove to sever from Germany the Saar and Rhineland, and to deprive Germany of the use of the Ruhr[74].

Even at the fifth (1947) session of the Council of Foreign Ministers in London, Foreign Minister Bidault thought it hard, in view of the ethnic changes[75], to imagine any alteration of the Oder-Neisse frontier[76], while at the fourth session he declared:

"In view of the enormous losses suffered during the war by Soviet Russia and Poland, France abandons any further discussion on this matter".

At a later period, the French Government consulted with the United States as to their attitude on that question[77]. French public opinion did not approve of the Government attitude, as was demon-

---

[73] *Journal Polonais*, September 11, 1946.
[74] B. Meissner, *op. cit.*, p. 85. According to J. P. Warburg, *op. cit.*, Cambridge Mass. 1953, French demands were the immediate cause of Byrnes's Stuttgart speech of September 6, 1946. By challenging the Polish-German frontier, the United States sought to deprive the French of the opportunity to invoke as a precedent the Potsdam decisions. Cf. also A. Klafkowski in an article on Germany as an object in International Law "Niemcy jako przedmiot prawa międzynarodowego". *Przegląd Zachodni* 1946, No. 4, p. 369.
[75] B. Meissner, *op. cit.*, p. 141.
[76] *Ibid.*, p. 108.
[77] This became manifest on July 7, 1950, in a declaration by the French High Commissioner in Germany, made with reference to the Warsaw Declaration of June 6, 1950. The French High Commissioner declared that France recognized the German territory within the 1937 frontiers. Quoted by Kraus, *Die Oder-Neisse Linie*, p. 38. For subsequent declarations see *Zbiór Dokumentów* 1951, No. 12, p. 2475, *ibid.* 1952, No. 4, 1401; No. 5, p.1792.

strated in November 1953, when during the foreign policy debate in the National Assembly, in connection with the ratification of the conventions concerning the so-called European Defence Community, a number of deputies, representing different parties, spoke in defence of the Oder-Neisse frontier[78].

It is clear, then, that the Western Powers did not immediately reach unanimity as regards non-recognition of the Oder-Neisse line as being the ultimate Polish-German frontier. The French attitude in the early post-war years has been referred to above. Orginally, the French Government had no doubt that the Potsdam decision settled once and for all the course of the Polish-German frontier, and that it had been settled *de jure* and *de facto* as definitive. A change appeared in the French attitude only at a later time and for political reasons.

As regards the Soviet Government, it has taken an unvarying, cleary defined and affirmative attitude towards the Oder-Neisse frontier. In reply to Byrnes and Churchill, who queried the frontier in 1946, Molotov declared on October 17, 1946, that the Polish-German frontier had been definitively settled at Potsdam[79]. The same was maintained by Stalin in an interview given to Hugh Baille on October 23, 1946[80]. In April 1947, at the Moscow Conference of the Council of Foreign Ministers, Molotov again opposed attempts by Marshall and Bevin to revise the western frontier of Poland. Molotov emphasized at the time two facts:

1) The Polish-German frontier had been discussed in great detail at two international conferences, the opinion of the Polish

[78] E.g., Herriot, President of the National Assembly (*Trybuna Ludu*, November 24, 1953, No. 327), Billoux, Communist Deputy (*Trybuna Ludu*, November 21, 1953, No. 324), General Aumeran, independent rightist Deputy (*Trybuna Ludu*, November 19, 1953, No. 322), Lebon, Gaullist Deputy (*Trybuna Ludu*, December 9, 1955, No. 342), etc. Moreover, the French Deputies who visited Poland in November 1953 emphasized on their return to France that the Oder-Neisse frontier was just, and that any violation thereof would undoubtedly lead to war. See, e.g. *Information*, interview with Jacques Soustelle (*Trybuna Ludu*, November 19, 1953, No. 352), and *Combat*, interview with the former French Prime Minister Edouard Daladier (*Trybuna Ludu*, January 13, 1954), in which Daladier declared that "The frontier on the Oder and Neisse is a frontier of peace for France also".
[79] Molotov, *op. cit.*, p. 244.
[80] *Zbiór Dokumentów* 1946, No. 10—11, p. 378.

Provisional Government of National Unity being heard before a decision was taken.

2) The decision on the Polish-German frontier was intimately linked with the decision on the transfers of the German populations from Poland within her new boundaries. Commenting upon these decisions, Molotov declared:

"The Governments who took the decision and *carried them into effect* (my italics — B. W.), could obviously not have believed that the resolution of the Potsdam Conference could in future be subjected to any revision. You cannot toy with such problems, let alone the fact that it would constitute an intolerable cruelty not only to Poles, but also to the Germans themselves".

3) Both the declarations by President Truman (August 9, 1945) and Bidault (July 10, 1946), had confirmed that the Potsdam decisions on the Polish-German frontier were considered as definitive.

Finally, Molotov declared: "The historical significance of the Potsdam resolution consists in that it settled new and equitable frontiers of the Polish State"[81]. At the same conference, Molotov firmly opposed attempts to submit Upper Silesia to international control[82].

The consistent standpoint of the Soviet Government towards the Oder-Neisse frontier was also demonstrated during the negotiations between the Great Powers concerned with post-war German problems and the possible peace treaty with Germany. The Soviet draft outline of the principles to be respected in a peace treaty with Germany, prepared in March 1952, provided: "German territory is defined by the frontiers laid down in the Potsdam decisions of the Great Powers"[83]. The inviolability of the Oder-Neisse frontier was the underlying premise of the Soviet draft of the peace treaty with Germany, based on the decisions of the Potsdam Agreement. This attitude of the Soviet Government was emphasized also in notes to the Western Powers on April 9, 1952[84], and May 24,

---

[81] Molotov, *op. cit.*, pp. 425—432.

[82] *Ibid.*, pp. 441—442.

[83] The note of the Soviet Government to the Governments of the United States, Great Britain and France, March 10, 1952, *Zbiór Dokumentów* 1952, No. 4, pp. 1355—1357.

[84] *Ibid.* p. 1408.

13

1952[85]. Furthermore, the Soviet Government again presented to the Western Powers on August 15, 1953, a draft of the basic principles for a peace treaty with Germany as defined on March 10, 1952[86], and did so yet again at the Berlin Conference of the Foreign Ministers of the Four Powers[87]. Finally, when on September 16, 1955, at a press conference in Moscow, Chancellor Adenauer raised his reservations with regard to Germany's frontiers, and said that in his view they had not yet been finally settled, the Soviet Government issued a communiqué again emphasizing their immutable attitude that the German frontiers had been definitively settled in the Potsdam Agreement[88].

This survey of the attitude adopted by the Great Powers to recognition of the Oder-Neisse frontier, must be supplemented by a survey of the practice of the Powers. When differences in interpretations appear, it is necessary to consider the practice of the States concerned, since only thus can be established the true will of the parties, free from subsequent distortions due to changes in foreign policies.

Practice is an *official interpretation* of an international agreement, wherein official interpretation is to be understood as the interpretation given to the agreement by the official organs of the contracting parties. This interpretation may be afforded by *practical application of the agreement in a manner indicating how it is really understood by the applying party (quasi-authentic or practical interpretation)*[89]. In applying this principle to the execution of the Potsdam Agreement, the following facts have to be considered:

1) On November 20, 1945, the Allied Control Council for Ger-

---

[85] *Ibid.* No. 5, pp. 1831—1832.

[86] Note from the Soviet Government to the Governments of France, Great Britain and the United States, August 15, 1953, *Trybuna Ludu*, August 18, 1953, No. 229.

[87] Supplement to *New Times*, No. 6, February 6, 1954, Documents II, pp. 11—12.

[88] Communiqué by the TASS press agency, see *Trybuna Ludu*, September 17, 1955, e., No. 257.

[89] L. Ehrlich, *Interpretacja traktatów* pp. 78—79. J. Makowski in his textbook maintains p. 499, that practice constitutes interpretation by usage, which is a form of authentic interpretation.

many prepared a detailed plan for the transfers of German populations. The plan was agreed upon with the Polish and Czechoslovak
Governments, and with the Allied Control Councils in Hungary
and Austria. It envisaged, among other things, the transfer of 3½
million Germans from Poland alone. The very figure of 3½ million
should suffice to prove that the territorial scope of transfers included
the territories east of the Oder and Western Neisse, for it would be
absurd to maintain that it might have referred to the number of
Germans inhabiting pre-war Polish lands[90].

2) On February 14, 1946, in consideration of the plan of transfers laid down by the Allied Control Council, an agreement on
technical points was made between the Polish representative Com-
mandor Konarski and the British representative Lt.-Col. Carroll,
both Members of the Combined Repatriation Executive. This is
plain evidence of the active co-operation of British occupation authorities with Polish authorities as regards transfers neither the territorial
scope of which, nor the number of people involved, were ever queried
at the time.

3) On December 11, 1945, the United States State Department
announced concerning German reparations and the peace-time economy of Germany that in defining the industrial potential of Germany's peace-time economy, as well as in calculating the nature
and extent of reparations, it must be assumed that the geographical
boundaries of Germany would be, in accordance with the decisions
of the Potsdam Agreement, the frontiers of the former Reich (*Altreich*),
without the territories east of the Oder-Neisse Line[91].

4) On March 8, 1946, the Allied Control Council prepared
a plan concerning determination of the level of Germany's industrial
production (in connection with the liquidation of the German arma-
ments industry, planned in the Potsdam Agreement). The first
fundamental premise of this plan assumed that German post-war

---

[90] This fact refutes the revisionist's claim that Poland was entitled to
transfer only the German population inhabiting pre-war Polish territories.
According to 1934 figures there were 740,000 Germans in Poland.

[91] J. W. Warburg, *Deutschland — Brücke oder Schlachtfeld*, Stuttgart
1949, p. 342, quoted by *Oder-Neisse* p. 94.

territory would be confined between the Oder-Neisse Line and the western frontiers existing at the time[92].

5) On February 25, 1947, the Allied Control Council issued Law No. 46, on the abolition of the Prussian State, which included:

"The Prussian State which from early days has been a bearer of militarism and reaction in Germany has *de facto* ceased to exist.

"Guided by the interest of preservation of peace and security of peoples and with the desire to assure further reconstruction of the political life of Germany on a democratic basis, the Control Council enacts as follows:

"Article I: The Prussian State together with its central government and all its agencies is abolished"[93].

Abolition of the Prussian State does *not* mean *merely* legalization of the changes of frontiers of the *Länder* in the American and British zones of occupation[94], nor even a repudiation of the programme for reconstructing Germany on Prussian lines[95], for it must be borne in mind that the Prussian State included also territories made over to Poland under the Potsdam Agreement. Abolition of the Prussian State, declared by Law No. 46 to have "*de facto* ceased to exist", implied also *confirmation by the Allied Control Council, and consequently by the Four Occupying Powers, of the permanent taking over by Poland of the lands formerly included in the Prussian State*. Special attention should be drawn to the argument quoted in Law No. 46: "Guided by the interest of preservation of peace and security of peoples". Abolition of the Prussian State ,"which from early days — in the words of the law — has been a bearer of militarism and reaction in Germany", constituted, as concerning the Occupying Powers responsible for international peace and security after the Second World War, an official condemnation of the German policies of conquest in the east. The political significance of the Law is emphasized by the fact that it was confirmed by the Council of Foreign Ministers at the Moscow Session in April 1947.

---

[92] Documents "Die Deutsche Wirtschaft seit Potsdam", published in *Europa Archiv*, vol. 1, p. 7.
[93] *Official Gazette of the Control Council for Germany*, No. 14, p. 81.
[94] A. Klafkowski, *Sprawa traktatu*, p. 66.
[95] *Ibid.*

An analysis of the facts referred to above warrants the conclusion that all the Great Powers, called upon to decide the fate of Germany, recognized the Oder-Neisse frontier *per facta concludentia*, by accepting the territorial scope and extent of the transfer of German population, and by describing in various legal acts the territory of Germany as excluding the lands east of the Oder and Western Neisse. For an evaluation of the attitude of the Great Powers, it is necessary and important to note that they confirmed in all the legal acts referred to above (international and internal administrative), that German territory did not include the lands east of the Oder and Western Neisse. Moreover, the Western Powers took measures proving beyond doubt that the Potsdam decisions were considered as definitive. With regard to the problem of recognition of the Oder-Neisse frontier, great significance attaches to the agreement reached between the British occupation authorities and Polish representatives concerning the technique of transferring Germans from Poland. In the theory of International Law it is said:

"... It would seem inconsistent with non-recognition, should a non-recognizing Power conclude with the dispossessing Power agreements regarding the occupied area, at least if this is done without explicitly adding that the transaction does not imply recognition"[96].

However, not only the agreement referred to above, but also the acts of the Allied Control Council for Germany bore distinct evidence that *all the Occupying Powers* recognized as definitive the Potsdam decisions relating to the Polish-German frontier.

On the German side, recognition of the Potsdam Polish-German frontier has been expressed by the German Democratic Republic, which has accepted without qualification the Potsdam programme for the rebuilding of Germany.

At a later time, some of the Great Powers queried the Oder-Neisse frontier as the definitive Polish-German frontier. This change of attitude is explained by specific political reasons. From the legal point of view, we may speak here rather of a withdrawal of recogni-

---

[96] Langer, *op. cit.*, p. 103.

tion due to political reasons, which obviously undermines the legal arguments of the Powers and qualifies their attitude as application in practice of the clause *rebus sic stantibus*, condemned in International Law[97]. Only thus can we explain the inconsistency between the official declarations of representatives of the United States, Great Britain, and France, and the actual practice of those Powers within the Allied Control Council for Germany until 1947. Wherever the eastern frontiers of Germany were involved, the practice of the Allied Control Council for Germany was invariably based — as has been shown above —on the assumption of the definitive character of the Oder-Neisse Line as the final Polish-German frontier, open to no subsequent changes. The latter assumption had wide currency in the western States[98], and the change of the attitude of the Great Powers in question is attributable exclusively to political reasons rooted in the general change in the world system of forces (antagonism between West and East). The practice of the Great Powers, as manifest in the joint decisions adopted by the Allied Control Council, represents an official interpretation of the Potsdam Agreement. It is very aptly emphasized in literature acknowledging the legal foundations of the Oder-Neisse frontier, that all the Great Powers — signatories to the Potsdam Agreement — have fully availed themselves of the

---

[97] The theory underlying this clause is that once the conditions attending the signing of the agreement are changed, the signatories are free to repeal or modify the agreement unilaterally. The clause was applied in practice in justifying aggressive policies. Invocation of the clause has been condemned on numerous occasions, as incompatible with respect for law in international relations—that is with the principle of *pacta servanda sunt*. See J. Makowski, *Podręcznik*, pp. 504 ff. where numerous examples are quoted. Unilateral and arbitrary application of the *rebus sic stantibus* clause has been objected to by numerous theoreticians of International Law: Ullmann, *Völkerrecht*, Tübingen 1908, pp. 285—286; Liszt-Fleischmann, *op. cit.*, p. 264; Lauterpacht, *Règles générales du droit de la paix*, Recueil des Cours, 1937, vol. IV, pp. 302 ff. ; *Harvard Law of Treaties*, pp. 1096—1126; A. *Ross, International Law*, 1947, p. 220. Among Polish authors: J. Makowski in his textbook, p. 509; L. Ehrlich, *Prawo narodów*, p. 257—258. The socialist doctrine of International Law is on principle opposed to the *rebus sic stantibus* clause—for example, Durdienievski, Krylov, *op, cit.*; Kozhevnikov, *op. cit.*, p. 76.

[98] See J. C. Campbell, "The European Territorial Settlement", *Foreign Affairs*, vol. 26, No. 1, October 1947, p. 200. Cf. also the declarations by representatives of the French Government, already referred to.

rights accorded to them by the Agreement[99]. Furthermore, as in other fields of law, conflicting declarations of will are inadmissible in International Law. In view of the principle, and confronted with the recognition *in practice* of the Oder-Neisse frontier as final, the Western Powers' contention that there exist a right and an obligation definitively to determine the Polish-German frontier at the peace conference, constitutes an abuse of law[100].

It is to be emphasized, however, that — although applying in their practice on Poland's western frontier the clause *rebus sic stantibus* — the Great Powers have never officially denounced, or even queried, the binding force of the Potsdam Agreement. This has been throughout the essential difference between their attitude and that of the German Federal Republic.

In drawing a final conclusion from the analysis of the question of recognition of the Oder-Neisse frontier, it should be made clear that:

1) Because of the definite legal status of the Recovered Territories, as stated in Potsdam and confirmed by the co-operation of the Powers in executing its decisions[101] the formal recognition of the new frontier by the Western Powers has no legal but important political significance. From the legal point of view any attempts to raise the question of recognition of Polands' title to the Recovered Territories are devoid of all foundation, since under International Law there is no need for an additional recognition of decisions that have not only been made, but even *implemented*. As regards the necessity of a recognition on the part of Germany, this is of secondary significance in view of the Great Powers' right to decide Germany's fate. In view of the right of the Great Powers to decide the future of Germany in the post-war period — a right established in such legal acts as the Declaration on the Assumption of Supreme Authority with respect to Germany (June 5, 1945), and the Yalta and Potsdam Agreements,

[99] M. Lachs, in an article on imperialist tendencies in bourgeois doctrine on International Law, "Imperialistyczne tendencje burżuazyjnej nauki prawa międzynarodowego", *Państwo i Prawo* 1951, N. 3, p. 424.

[100] Meister, *op. cit.*, p. 61.

[101] France had no part in formulating the Potsdam decisions, but she availed herself of the rights those decisions granted to her.

subsequently confirmed in Artlice 107 of the Charter of the United Nations, and emphasized in Article 2 of the 1952 Convention on relations between the Three Western Powers and the German Federal Republic (October 1954 version), as well as in Article 3 of the treaty with Austria of May 15, 1955[102], and repeatedly admitted by the Government of the German Federal Republic[103], — there is positively no need to ascribe to Germany's recognition of the Oder-Neisse frontier a constitutive sign ificance comparable to that attaching to the recognition by the Great Po wers.

2) The preceding conclusion also answers the question as to *who* primary is called upon to express recognition of the Oder-Neisse frontier. It shows beyond doubt that recognition by Germany has no *constitutive* but merely a *declaratory significance*. Consequently, the recognition of the frontier by the German Democratic Republic, which acknowledges the Potsdam Agreement as a legal act within the scope of the supreme authority of the Great Powers over Germany, is in agreement with International Law, whereas the lack of such recognition by the German Federal Republic conflicts with International Law and is inconsistent with that Government's own standpoint, since it contradicts the rights of the Great Powers with regard to Germany.

3) In view of the preceding two conclusions, we may dispense with an answer to the question as to in what form recognition of the

[102] Article 3 of the treaty entitled "Recognition by Germany of Austrian Independence" reads: "The Allied and United Nations will include into the peace treaty with Germany provisions *assuring the recognition by Germany* of Austrian sovereignty and independence and *renunciation by Germany* of all territorial and political claims towards Austria and Austrian territory" (my italics — B.W.), *Zbiór Dokumentów* 1955, No. 5, pp. 1012—1013. It clearly follows from this Article that — irrespective of any changes in the legal status of the two German States — the unqualified right of the Great Powers to make decisions affecting German territory still stands.

[103] In a memorandum on the reunification of Germany, addressed on September 7, 1956, to the Government of the Soviet Union, the Government of the German Federal Republic emphasized the obligations of the Great Powers with regard to Germany, and preservation of German unity in particular. *Trybuna Ludu*, October 25, 1956, No. 297. Without going into the essentials of the case, it must be said that this constitutes a recognition of the right of the Great Powers to decide the future of Germany. This conclusion is also suggested by the reference in the memorandum to the instruction given on July 23, 1955, by the Heads of the Government of the Four Powers.

Oder-Neisse frontier ought to be expressed. It merely remains to be observed that recognition of the frontier expressed in the practice of the States (*per facta concludentia*) occasioned the conception of the existence of a *de facto* Polish-German frontier[104]. This notion is resorted to by authors who do not believe the Polish-German frontier to be definitively settled in legal respects. The notion of a "*de facto* frontier" is alien to legal categories. However, the use of this term is by no means haphazard, since it emphasizes the irreversible fact which — some authors believe — are not entirely legal but have nevertheless certain legal consequences attaching to them. This is undoubtedly the result of comparing the principle of non-recognition with that of effectiveness (that is, the necessity to base legal status on facts). In this sense a definition of the frontier on the Oder and Western Neisse as a "*de facto frontier*" (*per analogiam* to a recognition *de facto* of a State or Government) is a manifestation of judicial and political realism, compelling a revision of the right attitude which ignores the thirteen years of Poland's sovereignty over the territories east of the Oder and Western Neisse.

---

[104] R. Laun, *op. cit.*, pp. 18—19; Wiskemann, *op. cit.*, p. 2; G. Barraclough in his review of Wiskemann's work, *International Affairs*, vol. 32, No. 4, October 1956; J. C. Campbell, *op, cit.*, p. 200.

CHAPTER IX

THE POLISH-GERMAN FRONTIER AND THE PEACE TREATY WITH GERMANY

1. TERMINATION OF WAR WITH GERMANY

In the preceding Chapters some reference has been made to the question of a peace treaty with Germany, with special reference to the final legal settlement of the Polish-German frontier. Revisionist literature — as already indicated — is unanimous in asserting that the frontier question can be legally settled only in a peace treaty with Germany[1]. This concept is also chosen as a basis for the present practice of the Western Powers who still maintain that final delimitation of the Polish western frontier should await the peace settlement.

No one would deny the important role of a peace treaty as a normal way of terminating a state of war between States; nevertheless, it must be emphasized that this is not the only way.

International Law makes a distinction between termination of hostilities and termination of state of war[2]. Literature quotes the following ways of terminating a state of war: 1) peace treaty, 2) termination of state of war *via facti* — that is, termination of hostilities and resumption of peaceful relations without a special agreement, 3) *debellatio* and annexation, 4) unilateral declaration[3].

The victorious Coalition of the United Nations intended to terminate the state of war with Germany by way of a peace settlement. As a legal act, the peace treaty with Germany would have to take

---

[1] Professor H. Kraus, already quoted, goes so far as to claim that for the peace treaty to confirm the Oder-Neisse frontier, would be incompatible with International Law.

[2] Oppenheim-Lauterpacht, *op. cit.*, vol. II, p. 597.

into account all the changes in the political system which took place during the course of the Second World War. That War demonstrated the peculiar responsibility of the Great Powers in ensuring world peace and security. It was essential to their purposes to achieve a harmonious co-operation of the Powers. Public opinion demanded that the Governments of the Great Powers should establish such a post-war system of international relations as would make impossible another aggression by any State, and by Germany in particular.

Under the pressure of public opinion, the Governments of the Great Powers laid down the principles of a new system of international relations calculated to ensure peace. The principles were incorporated in the Potsdam Agreements which became the legal foundation of post-war relations in Europe. This new system of relations was to be confirmed in the peace treaties with Italy and other Axis satellite States and in the peace settlement for Germany.

A peace settlement for Germany would be of immense importance not only to Germany, but to all the neighbour States as well. The principles of the peace settlement were determined in advance, in the Potsdam Agreement. Sections III, IV, V, VI, IX and XIII of the Agreement determined the political and economic principles on which Germany was to be re-established as a democratic and peaceful country, the principle of reparations and of arrangements concerning the German navy, Germany's post-war eastern frontiers, and population relations, Section I determined the procedure to be adopted in drawing up the peace settlement. Consequently, the Potsdam Agreement has, not without some reason, been at times regarded as the preliminary to a future peace-settlement for Germany[4]. It certainly is a fact that in preparing the ˏPotsdam Conference the Great Powers assumed that the decisions there reached would be of a preliminary character as regards a future peace

---

[3] Oppenheim-Lauterpacht, *op. cit.*, vol. II, p. 596; Durdieniev-ski and Krylov, *op. cit.*,; Guggenheim, *op. cit.*, vol. II, p. 820, J. Ma-kowski, *Podręcznik*, pp. 635—637.

[4] A. Klafkowski in his study on the question of the peace treaty with Germany *Sprawa traktatu pokoju z Niemcami*, pp. 23 ff. and A. Klaf-kowski, in an article on territorial cession *Cesja terytorialna*, pp. 15 ff. Klafkowski's thesis needs to be corrected in that the Potsdam Agreement did

conference[5]. The preliminary character of the Potsdam Agreement is stressed by the following formulation: " . . . the Council [of Foreign Ministers — B. W.]. . . shall be utilized for the preparation of a peace settlement . . . to be accepted by the Government of Germany"[6]. The possibility of a revision of the principles of the Agreement by the peace conference was excluded[7].

The preliminary character of the principles, as regards territorial decisions, set out in the Potsdam Agreement was stressed also by the Soviet draft covering the fundamentals of a peace treaty with Germany (March 1952), which declared: "German territory is defined by the frontiers settled at the Potsdam Conference of the Great Powers"[8]. This point of view was upheld in the Soviet Government's subsequent notes to the Western Powers[9] and at the Berlin Conference of the Foreign Ministers of the Four Powers[10].

The peace treaty with Germany has not been signed. Instead, the unity of Germany has been ruptured, and two States have been established on her territory: the German Federal Republic, and the German Democratic Republic. The two States have taken two diametrically opposed attitudes to the Potsdam Agreement as being a preliminary to a future peace treaty with Germany[11].

Developments between 1945 and 1955 have completely changed Germany's status. The state of war with Germany has, in fact, been completely liquidated, but that has not prevented the Great Powers

---

not, since it lacked Germany's signature, meet the *formal* requirements of a preliminary agreement. This does not alter the fact that the *substance* of the Potsdam Agreement had the character of peace preliminaries. The formal defect is explained by the contemporary status of Germany as being deprived of the capacity to conclude legal acts.

[5] Sherwood, *op. cit.*, vol. II, p. 881.
[6] Section I of the Potsdam Agreement.
[7] The obligatory nature of preliminaries to treaties are emphasized by: Hall, *op., cit.* p. 555, annotation 1; R. Foignet, *Manuel élémentaire de droit international public*, 1923 ed., p. 607; Liszt-Fleischmann, *op. cit.*, p. 557.
[8] *Zbiór Dokumentów* 1952, No. 4, pp. 1355—1357.
[9] *Zbiór Dokumentów* 1952, No. 4, p. 1408, and No. 5, pp. 1831—1832.
[10] Supplement to the Russian *New Times*, No. 6, February 6, 1954, Documents II, p. 11.
[11] For details on the subject, A. Klafkowski, *Sprawa traktatu*, pp. 29 ff.

from preserving some of the rights they acquired in relation to Germany at the moment of the termination of hostilities[12].

The foundations of those rights, however, have changed. For instance, military forces of the Great Powers are stationed on the territories of the German Federal Republic or German Democratic Republic, not on the basis of rights of occupation, but by virtue of agreements concluded by the Great Powers with one or other of the German Republics[13]. Furthermore, the German Federal Republic has signed, within the framework of the Paris Agreements of 1954, a convention concerning the regulation of problems created by the war and occupation, which settles most of the questions usually dealt with in peace treaties[14].

If it is agreed that the state of war with Germany has been terminated, it must be emphasized that this has been performed by unilateral declarations by particular States, parties to the Allied Coalition of the Second World War. The Declarations were not only made separately and at different times[15], but their practical consequences did not in any instance extend to both German States but only to one of them, — that is the German State recognized by the State declaring termination of the state of war. An exceptional position has been taken up only by the Soviet Union, which has entered into diplomatic relations with both German States[16]. Simultaneously,

---

[12] An analysis of the rights granted to the Western Powers by the Paris Agreement in relation to the German Federal Republic, is given by K. S k u b i-s z e w s k i in an article on Paris Agreements *Umowy Paryskie*, pp. 100 ff.

[13] For instance, the stationing of Soviet forces on the territory of the German Democratic Republic is envisaged in Art. 4 of the Agreement dated September 21, 1955, (*Trybuna Ludu*, September 22, 1955, No. 292), and in the Agreement of January 7, 1957, and was finally settled by the Agreement of March 12, 1957, on the stationing of Soviet Troops in the German Democratic Republic, *Neues Deutschland*, March 14, 1957, No. 63; the troops of the Western Powers are stationed in the German Federal Republic by virtue of the Paris Agreements of 1954, supplemented by a separate convention on the rights and obligations of foreign troops stationed in the German Federal Republic.

[14] Text in *Europa Archiv*, vol. 9, (1954).

[15] The three Western Powers abolished in 1951 the state of war between them and Germany, and in 1955 the state of war with Germany was liquidated by way of unilateral declarations by the Socialist States.

[16] In 1957 Yugoslavia attempted to enter into diplomatic relations with both the German States, but when she recognized the German Democra-

there has been, to an extent restricted to only one or other German State, a gradual liquidation of the consequences of war[17]. In some respects, liquidation of the consequences of war *preceded* termination of the state of war. An example may be found in the relations between Poland and the German Democratic Republic, in which the opening up of normal diplomatic relations, the signing of frontier agreements concerned with delimitation of the Polish-German frontier, and settlement of the question of reparations[18] took place *before* the termination of the state of war[19].

When it is added that both German States have concluded economic treaties with a number of other States formerly at war with Germany, that the two States have each joined different military groupings and participate in certain international organizations[20] and, finally, that military restrictions have in practice been abolished with respect to both States, it must be concluded that *most of the problems associated with the liquidation of the legal consequences of a state of war have been settled with regard to Germany in advance of the signing of a peace treaty*. However, it must be noted that this liquidation of the state of war is restricted in scope, and — with the exception of the Soviet Union — is confined to relations between particular States on the one hand and only one of the two existing German States on the other.

Consequently, the question arises as to what is the scope of problems left to be settled in a possible peace treaty with Germany.

---

tic Republic, the Government of the German Federal Republic broke off diplomatic relations with her.

[17] An analysis of the declarations by the Western Powers, see A. Klaf-kowski, *Sprawa traktatu*, p. 8.

[18] Declaration by the Polish Government, August 25, 1953, *Trybuna Ludu*, August 25, 1953, No. 236.

[19] Resolution of the Polish State Council, February 18, 1955, *Zbiór Dokumentów* 1955, No. 1, p. 305.

[20] See A. Klafkowski's article on the two German States in relation to U.N.O. and its specialist organizations "Dwa państwa niemieckie a ONZ i jej organizacje wyspecjalizowane", *Przegląd Zachodni* 1956, No. 9/10.

2. REUNIFICATION OF GERMANY AND THE
POLISH-GERMAN FRONTIER

Reunification of Germany has become the key problem of world peace. It has been frequently discussed at international conferences, but as yet without practical results.

This problem, still awaiting solution, is vital to the question of Poland's western frontier, since it may be asked whether the reunified German State will be bound by the Potsdam decisions on the Oder-Neisse frontier, and by the frontier agreements signed by Poland and the German Democratic Republic. In West German literature, the view is frequently advanced that the frontier agreements between Poland and the German Democratic Republic are legally invalid, or that their legal validity is restricted. Various reasons are quoted in support of this view. Some authors try to make it easy for themselves by simply denying that the German Democratic Republic is a State[21]. Others concede that the Governments of both the German Democratic Republic and the German Federal Republic are governments *de facto* but make the reservation that the agreements signed by these Governments will be valid only when ratified by the future Government of a Reunited Germany, which will be a government *de jure*. The territorial agreements, they maintain, signed by the German governments *de facto*, cannot be binding upon the future government *de jure*[22]. Still another view is based on the conception that both Governments represent, within the existing over-all German State *Teilordnungen* (fractional systems), and as such cannot forego rights that belong to the entirety[23]. Finally, there is a contention that Germany is in a condition analogical to a "cold civil war", and that the treaties signed by either

---

[21] U. S c h e u n e r, "Der derzeitige völkerrechtliche Status der Ostgebiete des Deutschen Reiches published in the collective work *Die Ostgebiete des Deutschen Reiches". Ein Taschenbuch.* Published by G. R h o d e, 2nd ed., Würzburg 1955, p. 161.

[22] A. A b e n d r o t h, "Die völkerrechtliche Bindung Gesamtdeutschlands durch Verträge seiner Staatenfragmente", published in *Gegenwartsprobleme des internationalen Rechtes und der Rechtsphilosophie,* Festschrift fur Rudolf Laun zu seinem 70. Geburtstag, Hamburg 1953, p. 84.

[23] H e y d t e, *op. cit.,* p. 84.

of the Governments embody the tacit condition that either the Government which signed it will triumph or the *status quo* will be perpetuated[24].

The official attitude of the Government of the German Federal Republic is rooted in the assumption that the Federal Government alone is entitled to speak on behalf of all Germany; that Government further invokes the attitude of the Western Powers as admitting this right. Thus, the German Federal Government goes much farther than some West German jurists who do not ignore the Socialist German State.

An analysis of the problem of the two German States does not appear essential to consideration of the legal foundations of the Oder-Neisse frontier. Merely as a marginal note, it may be pointed out that the theoretical conceptions advanced in West Germany bear no relations to facts and strive to brush aside the existence of the German Democratic Republic, the emergence of which has undoubtedly given rise to important legal consequences not minimized by the absence of recognition on the part of the Western Powers.

The answer to the question as to whether reunification of Germany may effect the legal position of the Oder-Neisse frontier is not to be sought in an analysis of the rights of this or that German State to dispose of German territory, since determination of the Oder-Neisse frontier was not affected by a bilateral frontier-agreement between Poland and the German Democratic Republic or, in fact, any German Government, but was settled in the Potsdam Agreement in consequence of a decision by the Great Powers which alone had at that time the unrestricted right to dispose of German territory. The right of the German Democratic Republic to conclude frontier agreement's with Poland is derived from that German Government's acceptance of the Potsdam Agreement as the foundation of their foreign policies. The Zgorzelec treaty manifestly refers to the "settled and existing State frontier between Poland and Germany", and to the Potsdam Agreement. It was the Potsdam Agreement of 1945, and not the Zgorzelec treaty, concluded 5 years later in 1950, which

---

[24] *Ibid.*, p. 83.

gave to Poland the right to extend her sovereign authority over the Recovered Territories. This does not mean that the frontier agreements between Poland and the German Democratic Republic were unnecessary; they gave effect to delimitation of the Polish-German frontier on the ground.

The determination of principles and conditions of German unity is a political problem. No political formulas concerned with the reunification of Germany can, however, ignore the rights Poland has acquired as regards the frontier on the Oder and Western Neisse. The decisions made in Section IX § B of the Potsdam Agreement were in perfect harmony with the propositions presented at the Potsdam Conference by the Delegation of the Polish Provisional Government of National Unity. When the Recovered Territories were granted to Poland, the Polish Government took over administration of these territories under the decree of November 13, 1945[25], extending over them Polish legislation (Art. 4 of the decree) and fitting them into the administrative system of the Polish State (Arts. 2, 5, and 7, of the decree)[26]. Furthermore the land reform and nationalization of industry involved the Recovered Territories, while Art. 9 of the decree ordered the Minister of National Defence to extend Polish military protection over those territories and to garrison them with Polish troops. The population of the Recovered Territories was put under the control of Polish authorities which, in conformity with Section XIII of the Potsdam Agreement and the decisions of the Allied Control Council for Germany, effected the transfer of the German population, replacing them with Polish population settled there alongside the indigenous inhabitants.

The process of population changes, essentially concluded in the years 1945—1947, made the substance of the Potsdam decisions also in fact irreversible as regards the Recovered Territories. This fact

[25] *Dziennik Ustaw* 1945, position 295.

[26] The Ministry of the Recovered Territories, set up by the decree of November 13, 1945, was not some separate or autonomous authority over the Recovered Territories. It was a Polish administrative organ created for a transitional period and charged to create such conditions as would promote the most rapid economic integration of the territories with the rest of Poland.

is appreciated also in some West German quarters[27]. Since the Potsdam Agreement granted to Poland, as a Third State, certain rights of which she availed herself, therefore from that moment on, any modifications of the rights acquired by Poland in relation to the Recovered Territories required — in conformity with existing principles of International Law — her consent.

The authority exercised by Poland over the Recovered Territories was from the very beginning of a sovereign character. This is in no way affected by the fact that the formula of the Potsdam Agreement placed the territories east of the Oder and the Western Neisse under Polish "administration", since the essence of that administration was in fact Polish sovereignty over those territories. Moreover, when in 1945 Poland assumed sovereign authority over the Recovered Territories, her right to do so was not challenged by any of the Great Powers entitled to make decisions concerning the fate of Germany. This was emphasized by the Foreign Ministers of Poland and Czechoslovakia, Rzymowski and Massaryk, at a press conference on November 14, 1946: "None of the signatories to the Potsdam Agreement protested at the settling of four million of Poles on the Recovered Territories"[28]. On the contrary, the active assistance and cooperation accorded by the occupation authorities of the Great Powers (including the western zones) in making the transfers of the German populations from these territories[29] prove that all the Great Powers recognized in 1945 Polish sovereign rights over the Recovered Territories.

An analysis of the relation between the future peace treaty with a Reunited Germany on the one hand, and the Polish-German frontier on the other, must inevitably lead to the conclusion that in 1945 Poland acquired from the victorious Allied Powers rights

---

[27]) E.g. W. Hubatsch, *Eckpfeiler Europas, Probleme des Preussenlandes in Europäischer Sicht*, Heidelberg 1953, p. 134, expresses doubts whether it is still possible "to begin further re-sorting of nations in east Central Europe".
[28] Keesing's *Archiv der Gegenwart*, 1946—1947, 924 E.
[29]) In a press statement (April 10, 1947), Minister Modzelewski lists among the legal justifications of Poland's right to the Recovered Territories, the agreement signed by the Polish Government and the Allied occupation authorites on the subject of the transfer of the German population to Germany. *Zbiór Dokumentów* 1947, No. 5, p. 222.

to the Recovered Territories, and that any changes in Germanys' legal status after 1945 are, as well as any changes which may occur in the future, utterly irrelevant in International Law, and cannot affect such rights in any way.

BIBLIOGRAPHY OF WORKS AND SOURCES

ACCESSIBLE TO THE AUTHOR

SOURCES

Beneš E., Memoirs of..., Boston (n.d.a.).

Bülow B., *Denkwürdigkeiten*, Berlin 1930. vol. I.

Conférence internationale de la Paix, La Haye, 18 Mai-29 Juillet 1899, La Haye 1907.

Cyprian T., Sawicki J., *Materiały Norymberskie* (Nuremberg Materials), Warszawa 1948.

Documents on American Foreign Relations, ed. by L. M. Goodrich and M. J. Carroll, London, vols. I—VIII (abbr.: *Documents*).

Dziennik Ustaw Rzeczypospolitej Polskiej (PRL) (abbr.: *Dziennik Ustaw*) (Journal of Laws of the Polish Republic).

Fleischmann M., *Völkerrechtsquellen*, Halle a/Saale 1905.

Foreign Relations of the United States. Diplomatic Papers. The Conferences at Cairo and Teheran 1943. Washington 1961 (abbr.: *Conferences at Cairo and Teheran*).

Foreign Relations of the United States. Diplomatic Papers. The Conferences at Malta and Yalta 1945, Washington 1955 (abbr.: *Conferences at Malta and Yalta*).

Freund M., *Geschichte des zweiten Weltkrieges in Dokumenten*, Freiburg 1953, vol. I.

Gelberg L., *Prawo międzynarodowe i historia dyplomatyczna. Wybór Dokumentów* (International Law and History of Diplomacy. Selected Documents), Warszawa 1954, vol. I.

Hull Cordell, *The Memoirs*, London 1948, vols. I—II.

The International Post-War Settlement. Report by the National Executive Committee of the Labour Party to be presented to the Annual Conference to be held in London from May 29 to June 2, 1944.

Internationales Recht und Diplomatie, 1956, Issue 3/4 (the statement of G.F.R. Secretary of State, Hallstein).

Die offiziellen Jalta-Dokumente des U.S. State Departments. Vollständige deutsche Ausgabe: Wien-München-Stuttgart-Zürich 1955 (abbr.: *Jalta--Dokumente*).

Keesing's *Archiv der Gegenwart*, 1946—1947.

Konferencja Berlińska (22 stycznia — 18 lutego 1954) (The Berlin Conference Jan. 22 — Feb. 18, 1954), Warszawa 1954.

The Constitution of the German Democratic Republic.

Leahy W. D., *I was there*, London 1950.

"Materiały syntetyczne do zagadnienia Ziem Odzyskanych" (Synthesis of Materials Concerning the Problems of the Recovered Territories) *Myśl Współczesna* 1947, No. 1.

Molotov W. M., *Voprosy Vnieshniey Politiki*, Moskva 1948.

National Socialism. Basic Principles, their Application by the Nazi Party's Foreign Organizations, and the Use of Germans Abroad for Nazi Aims. Prepared by R. E. Murphy, F. B. Stevens, H. Trivers, J. M. Roland, Washington 1943.

Oder-Neisse. Eine Dokumentation, comp. by R. Goguel, H. Pohl, Berlin 1956 (NRD), 2nd ed. (abbr.: *Oder-Neisse*).

Official Gazette of the Control Council for Germany. Ost-Handbuch, ed. Deutsches Büro für Friedensfragen, Stuttgart 1949, Issue 6.

Parliamentary Debates. House of Commons. Official Report, Hansard.

Parliamentary Debates, House of Lords. Official Report, Hansard.

Pieck W., *Reden und Aufsätze*, Berlin 1951, vols. I—II.

Pierepiska predsedatiela Sovieta Ministrov S.S.S.R. z prezidentami S.Sh.A. i premier-ministrami Vielikobritanii vo vremia otiechestvennoy voiny 1941— —1945 gg., Moskva 1957, vols. I—II.

Proceedings of the American Society of International Law at its 41 Annual Meeting, April 24—26, 1947, Washington 1947.

Publication de la Cour Permanente de Justice Internationale (abbr.: *C.P.J.I.*).

Quellen zur Entstehung der Oder-Neisse-Linie, ed. by G. Rhode u. W. Wagner, Stuttgart 1956 (abbr.: *Quellen*).

Rabenau F. von, *Seeckt. Aus seinem Leben 1918—1936*, Leipzig 1940.

The Refugee in the Post-War World. Preliminary Report of a Survey of the Refugee Problem, United Nations, Geneva 1951.

Sherwood R. E., *The White House Papers of Harry L. Hopkins*, London 1949, vols. I—II.

Sprawozdania stenograficzne z posiedzeń K.R.N. (Records of the Proceedings of the Polish National Council), Session V—VIII, Warszawa 1945—1946.

Stenogram nieoficjalny z procesu o delegalizację K.P.D. przed Trybunałem Konstytucyjnym N.R.F. w Karlsruhe (Unofficial Records of the K.P.D. Delegalisation Trial Held before the G.F.R. Constitution Tribunal in Karlsruhe).

Stettinius E. R., *Roosevelt and the Russians, The Yalta Conference*, London 1950.

Unconditional Surrender of Germany, Germany No. 1 (1945), His Majesty's Stationery Office, London.

United Nations Documents 1941—1945, Institute of International Affairs, London-New York 1946.

United Nations Treaty Series.

Die Vertreibung der deutschen Bevölkerung aus den Gebieten östlich der Oder-Neisse, Bundesministerium für Vertriebene vol. I/1 and I/2, (abbr.: *Die Vertreibung*).

Vnieshnaya polityka Sovieckovo Soyuza v pieriod vielikoy otiechestvennoy voiny, Moskva 1946, vol. II.

Vnieshnaya polityka Sovieckovo Soyuza, 1947, Moskva 1952.

Vyshinski A. J., *Voprosy Miezhdunarodnovo Prava i Miezhdunarodnoi Politiki*, Moskva 1949.

War and Peace Aims of the United Nations, ed. by L. W. Holborn, Boston 1943—1945, vols. I—II (abbr.: *War and Peace Aims*).

The War Speeches of the Rt Hon. Winston S. Churchill. Compiled by Ch. Eade, London 1952.

Winiarski B., *Wybór źródel do nauki prawa międzynarodowego* (Selected Sources to the Science of International Law), Warszawa 1938.

Die wirtschaftliche und soziale Struktur Deutschlands — Anl. V zu Reparationen, Sozialprodukt, Lebensstandard. Versuch einer Wirtschaftsbilanz, Bremen 1947.

Zbiór Dokumentów (Collection of Documents), editor J. Makowski, Warszawa.

DICTIONARIES AND ENCYCLOPAEDIAS

Cobbett Pitt, *Cases and Opinions on International Law*. London 1909.

Dictionnaire Diplomatique, ed. by A. F. Frangulis, Paris.

Lapradelle-Niboyet, *Répertoire de droit international*, Paris 1930.

Strupp K., *Wörterbuch des Völkerrechts und der Diplomatie*, Berlin 1924—1929, vols. I—III.

Strupp-Schlochauer: *Wörterbuch des Völkerrechts*, t. I, Berlin 1960, t. II Berlin 1961.

TEXTBOOKS

Despagnet., *Cours de droit international public*, ed. IV, 1910.

Durdienievsky V. N. and Krylov S. B. (editors), *Miezhdunarodnoye Pravo*, Moskva 1947.

Ehrlich L., *Prawo Narodów* (The Law of Nations), Kraków, ed. III.

Fenwick Ch. G., *International Law*, ed. III. New York 1948.

Foignet R., *Manuel élémentaire de droit international public*, ed. 1923.
Gould W. L., *An Introduction to International Law*, New York 1957.
Guggenheim P., *Lehrbuch des Völkerrechts*, Basel 1948, vols. I—II.
Hall W. E., *A Treatise on International Law*, Oxford 1909.
Hyde Ch. Ch., *International Law. Chiefly as Interpreted and Applied by the U.S.*, ed. II, Boston 1945.
Kozhevnikov F. I., (editor). *Miezhdunarodnoye pravo*, Moskva 1957.
Liszt-Fleischmann F., *Das Völkerrecht*, Berlin 1925, ed. XII.
Makowski J., *Podręcznik prawa międzynarodowego*, (A Handbook of International Law), Warszawa 1948 (abbr.: *Podręcznik*).
Muszkat M., (editor), *Zarys prawa międzynarodowego publicznego* (An Outline of Public International Law), Warszawa 1955—1956, vols I—II.
Oppenheim-Lauterpacht, *International Law*, London-New York-Toronto 1948 (vol. I.), 1952 (vol. II), ed. VII, 1955 (vol. I) ed. VIII.
Phillimore R., *Commentaries upon International Law*, London 1879, vol. I.
Pradier-Fodéré, *Droit international public*, Paris, vols. I—VIII.
Ross A., *International Law*, London-New York-Toronto 1947.
Rousseau Ch., *Droit international public*, Paris 1953,
Sibert M., *Traité de droit international public*, Paris 1951.
Ullmann E., *Völkerrecht*, Tübingen 1908.
Verdross A., *Völkerrecht*, Wien 1955.
Westlake J., *International Law*, ed. II, Cambridge 1910-3.

MONOGRAPHS AND ARTICLES

Abendroth, "Die völkerrechtliche Bindung Gesamtdeutschlands durch Verträge seiner Staatsfragmente" in: *Gegenwartsprobleme des internationalen Rechtes und der Rechtsphilosophie*. Festschrift für Rudolf Laun zu seinem 70. Geburstag, Hamburg 1953.
Barsegov J. G., *Tierritoriya v miezhdunarodnom pravie. Yuridichieskaya priroda tierritorialnego vierkhovienstva i pravoviye osnovanya rasporiazhenya tierritoriey*, Moskva 1958.
Berezowski C., *Terytorium, instytucje wyspecjalizowane, współpraca międzynarodowa, obszary kolonialne i zależne, wojna powietrzna* (Territory, Specialized Institutions, International Co-operation, Colonial and Depended Territories, War in the Air), Warszawa 1957.
Bieberstein W. F., Marschall von, *Zum Problem der völkerrechtlichen Anerkennung der beiden deutschen Regierungen*, Berlin 1959.
Bierzanek R., "Stanowisko wielkich mocarstw w prawie międzynarodowym" (The Status of the Great Powers in International Law), *Państwo i Prawo* 1946, No. 5/6.

Bloomfield L. P., *Evolution or Revolution. The U.N. and the Problem of Peaceful Territorial Changes*, Cambridge Mass. 1957.

Boratyński S., *Dyplomacja okresu drugiej wojny światowej. Konferencje międzynarodowe 1941—1945* (Diplomacy during the Second World War. International Conferences 1941—1945), Warszawa 1957.

— —, „Karta Atlantycka a uchwały poczdamskie o granicy polsko-niemieckiej" (The Atlantic Charter and the Potsdam Decisions Concerning the Polish-German Frontier), *Przegląd Zachodni* 1956, No. 9/10.

Bramson A., *Z zagadnień prawnych granicy nad Odrą i Nysą* (Some Legal Problems of the Frontier on the Oder and the Neisse), (The book in commemoration of Julian Makowski on the 50th anniversary of his scientific work), Warszawa 1957.

Briggs H. W., "The Leader's Agreement of Yalta", *American Journal of International Law* 1946.

Campbell J. C., "The European Territorial Settlement", *Foreign Affairs* 1947, October, vol. 26, No. 1.

Chen T. C., *The International Law of Recognition*, London 1951.

Claude Jr. I. L., *National Minorities. An International Problem*, Cambridge Mass. 1955.

Cruttwell C. R. M. F., *A History of Peaceful Changes in the Modern World* London-New York-Toronto 1937.

Cyprian T., Sawicki J., *Siedem wyroków Najwyższego Trybunału Narodowego* (Seven Verdicts of the Supreme National Tribunal), Poznań 1962.

— —, *Sprawy polskie w procesie norymberskim* (Polish Problems at the Nuremberg Trial), Poznań 1956.

Datner S., *Zbrodnie Wehrmachtu na jeńcach wojennych w II wojnie światowej* (The Crimes of the Wehrmacht against Prisoners-of-War in the Second World War), Warszawa 1961.

Decker G., *Das Selbstbestimmungsrecht der Nationen*, Göttingen 1955.

Ehrlich L., *Interpretacja traktatów* (Interpretation of Treaties). Warszawa 1957.

— —, *Karta Narodów Zjednoczonych* (The United Nations Charter), Kraków 1946

— —, "Suwerenność Polski na Ziemiach Odzyskanych. Zagadnienia prawne" (Poland's Sovereignty in the Recovered Territories. Legal Problems), *Zeszyty Naukowe U.J.* Prace prawnicze fasc. 6, Kraków 1959.

— —, *Suwerenność Polski na Ziemiach Zachodnich i Północnych. Zagadnienia prawne*. Śląski Instytut Naukowy, Biuletyn nr 34 (Poland's Sovereignty in the Western and Northern Territories. Legal Problems), Katowice 1962.

Ekspansja wschodnia Niemiec w Europie środkowej. Studia nad tzw. niemieckim "Drang nach Osten", praca zbiorowa pod red. G. Labudy (Germany's

Eastern Expansion in Central Europe. Studies on the so-called German Drang nach Osten, collected work edited by G. Labuda), Poznań 1963.

Gelberg L., "Tendencje we współczesnej niemieckiej literaturze prawa międzynarodowego" (The Trends in the Contemporary German Literature Dealing with International Law), *Państwo i Prawo* 1949, No. 1.

Giertych J., *Poland and Germany*, London 1958.

Goodrich L. M., Hambro E., *Charter of the United Nations*, London 1949.

Grzybowski K., *Ustrój Polski współczesnej 1944—1948* (The Political System of Contemporary Poland 1944—1948), Kraków 1948.

Gumkowski J., Kułakowski T., *Zbrodniarze hitlerowscy przed Najwyższym Trybunałem Narodowym* (Nazi War Criminals before the Supreme National Tribunal), Warszawa 1961.

Guradze H., *Der Stand der Menschenrechte im Völkerrecht*, Göttingen 1956.

"Harvard Research in International Law. Draft Convention on the Law of Treaties", *American Journal of International Law* 1935, Supplement (abbr.: Harvard Law of Treaties).

Heydte F. A. Frh. von der, "Völkerrechtliche Lage der deutschen Ostgebiete"; in: *Der deutsche Osten. Referate des ersten Ostseminars der Hochschule für politische Wissenschaften*, München 1956.

Hoffmann F., *Die Oder-Neisse Linie. Ihre politische Entwicklung und völkerrechtliche Lage*. Frankfurt a/Main 1949, Nachtrag für 1950.

Hubatsch W., *Eckpfeiler Europas. Probleme des Preussenlandes in europäischer Sicht*, Heidelberg 1953.

Ireland G., *Boundaries, Possessions and Conflicts in Central and North America and the Caribbeans*, Cambridge Mass. 1941.

Jänicke W., "Refugees: Bavaria 1947", *The Annals of the American Academy of Political and Social Science*, November 1948.

Jellinek H., *Der automatische Erwerb und Verlust der Staatsangehörigkeit durch völkerrechtliche Vorgänge*, Berlin 1951.

Jenks C. W., *The Common Law of Mankind*, London 1958.

Jennings R. Y., "Government in Commission", *British Yearbook of International Law*, 1946, vol. 26.

Jones S. B., *Boundary-Making*, Washington 1945.

Jordan Z., *Oder-Neisse-Line. A Study of the Political, Economic and European Significance of Poland's Western Frontier*, London 1952 (abbr.: Jordan I).

— —, *Granica Polski na Odrze i Nysie. Linia Odry i Nysy w polityce Zachodu*. Skrypt Szkoły Nauk Politycznych i Społecznych w Londynie (Poland's Frontier on the Oder and the Neisse. The Oder-Neisse Line in the Policy of the West. Mimeographed Lectures of the London School of Political and Social Sciences), Londyn 1954 (abbr.: Jordan II).

Kaczmarczyk Z., "Polska granica zachodnia w perspektywie tysiąca lat historii". (The Polish Western Frontier in the Perspective of a Thousand Years of History), *Przegląd Zachodni* 1960, No. 6.

Kamiński A. J., "Rodowód polityki zagranicznej Bonn" (The Origin of the Foreign Policy of Bonn), *Przegląd Zachodni* 1951, No. 5/6.

Kaufmann E., *Deutschlands Rechtslage unter der Besatzung*, Stuttgart 1948.

Kercea N., *Die Staatsgrenze in den Grenzflüssen. Völkerrechtliche Abhandlung. Ein Beitrag zu der Lehre von der Staatsgrenze.* Inaugural-Dissertation, Berlin 1916.

Klafkowski A., Morawiecki W., "Bezpieczeństwo zbiorowe a sprawa Niemiec"; in: *Zagadnienia bezpieczeństwa zbiorowego w Europie* (Collective Security and the Problem of Germany; in: The Problems of Collective Security in Europe), Materials of Polish Academy of Sciences Session, Warszawa 1955.

Klafkowski A., "Cesja terytorialna a traktat pokoju na tle granicy Odra-Nysa Łużycka" (Territorial Cession and the Peace Treaty against the Background of the Oder-Lusation Neisse Frontier), *Przegląd Zachodni* 1957 ,No. 1.

— —, "Konstrukcja jednolitego państwa niemieckiego w okupacyjnych aktach prawnych" (The Structure of a Uniform German State in the Occupation Legal Acts), *Przegląd Zachodni* 1948, No. 7/8.

— —, "Niemcy jako przedmiot prawa międzynarodowego" (Germany as an Object of International Law), *Przegląd Zachodni* 1946, No. 4.

— —, *Okupacja niemiecka w Polsce w świetle prawa narodów* (The German Occupation in Poland in the Light of the Law of Nations), Poznań 1946.

— —, *Podstawy prawne granicy Odra-Nysa na tle umów: Jałtańskiej i Poczdamskiej* (The Legal Foundations of the Oder-Neisse Frontier in the Light of the Yalta and Potsdam Agreements), Poznań 1947 (abbr.: *Podstawy prawne*).

— —, "Podstawy prawne wysiedlenia ludności niemieckiej z Polski" (The Legal Foundations of the Eviction of German Population from Poland), *Administracja i Samorząd na Ziemiach Odzyskanych*, S. A. Issue 7/8, 1947.

— —, *Sprawa traktatu pokoju z Niemcami* (The Problem of a Peace Treaty with Germany), Warszawa 1953, (abbr.: Sprawa traktatu).

— —, "Zagadnienie Administracji kościelnej na Ziemiach Odzyskanych w aspekcie prawa międzynarodowego" (The Problem of Church Administration in the Recovered Territories in the Light of International Law), *Życie i Myśl* 1955, No. 1.

— —, *Umowa poczdamska z dn. 2 VIII 1945. Podstawy prawne likwidacji skutków wojny polsko-niemieckiej* (The Postdam Agreement of August 2, 1945. The Legal Basis for the Liquidation of the Effects of the Polish-German War), Warszawa 1960.

Kozhevnikov, "Niekotoryie voprosy tieorii i praktiki miezhdunarodnovo dogovora", *Sovietskoye gosudarstvo i pravo* 1954, No. 2.

Kraus H., *Die Oder-Neisse-Linie. Eine völkerrechtliche Studie*, Köln-Braunsfeld 1954.

— —, "Das Selbstbestimmungsrecht der Völker" (treatise published in the collective work: *Das östliche Deutschland. Ein Handbuch*), Würzburg 1959.

Król M., *Wykładnia traktatów międzynarodowych* (Interpretation of International Treaties), Wilno 1932.

Krylov S. B., *Materialy k historii Organizatsi Obiedinionnykh Natsyi*, Moskva 1949.

Labuda G., "The Territorial, Ethnical and Demographic Aspects of Polish-German Relations in the Past (X—XX centuries)", *Polish Western Affairs* 1962, No. 2.

Lachs M., "Imperialistyczne tendencje burżuazyjnej nauki prawa międzynarodowego" (The Imperialist Trends in the Bourgeois Science of International Law), *Państwo i Prawo* 1951, No. 3.

— —, *Układy indochińskie, Genewa 1954. Zagadnienia prawne walki narodowo-wyzwoleńczej* (The Indochina Agreements, Geneva 1954. Legal Problems of the National Liberation Struggle), Warszawa 1955.

— —, "Zagadnienie jednomyślności wielkich mocarstw" (Aspekty prawne) (The Problem of Unanimity of the Great Powers), *Myśl Współczesna* 1947, No. 12.

Langer R., *Seizure of Territory. The Stimson Doctrine and Related Principles in Legal Theory and Diplomatic Practice*, Princeton, New Jersey 1947.

Lapradelle P. de, *La frontière*, Paris 1928.

Laun R., "Le droit des peuples à disposer d'eux-mèmes", *Annuaire de l'Association des Auditeurs et Anciens Auditeurs de l'Académie de Droit International de la Haye* 1958 (No. 28).

— —, *Das Recht auf die Heimat*, Hannover-Darmstadt 1951.

Lauterpacht H., *The Development of International Law by the International Court*, London 1958 (abbr.: Lauterpacht, *Development*).

— —, *Private Law Sources and Analogies of International Law*, London 1927.

— —, *Recognition in International Law*, Cambridge 1948.

— —, *Règles générales du droit de la paix*, Recueil des Cours, 1937, vol. IV.

Leriche A., "Quelques réflexions sur la Charte de l'Antlantique", *Revue Générale de droit international public*, vol. XLVIII-1 (1941—1945).

Liczbańska A., "Organizacje przesiedleńców niemieckich", (The German Refugees' Organizations), *Przegląd Zachodni* 1957, No. 1.

McNair, *Legal Effects of War*, ed. III, Cambridge 1948.

Makowski J., "Charakter prawny umów zawartych podczas drugiej wojny światowej" (The Legal Character of the Agreements Concluded during the Second World War), *Państwo i Prawo* 1948, No. 5/6 (abbr.: Charakter prawny umów).

Marek K., *Identity and Continuity of States in Public International Law,* Genéve 1954.

Maurach R., Seraphim P. H., Wolfrum G., *Ostwärts der Oder und Neisse,* Juridical part compiled by R. Maurach, Hannover 1949 (abbr.: R. Maurach).

Meissner B., *Russland, die Westmächte und Deutschland. Die sowjetische Deutschlandspolitik 1943—1953,* Hamburg 1954.

Meister R., *Das Völkerrecht garantiert die Friedensgrenze an Oder und Neisse,* Leipzig-Jena 1955.

Menzel E., "Das Annexionsverbot des modernen Völkerrechts und das Schicksal der deutschen Ostgebiete" (in the collective work *Das östliche Deutschland. Ein Handbuch*), Würzburg 1959.

Meyer W. E., *Die Grundlagen für den Frieden mit Deutschland,* Wiesbaden (n.d.a.)

Mosely Ph., "Dismemberment of Germany. The Allied Negotiations from Yalta to Postdam", *Foreign Affairs,* April 1950.

Muszkat M., Sawicki J., "Odpowiedzialność Niemiec a nasze prawa do Ziem Odzyskanych" (Germany's Responsibility and Our Rights to the Recovered Territories), *Państwo i Prawo* 1957, No. 2.

Muszkat M., "Rola obrony w procesie przeciwk KPD" (The Role of the Defence Counsel in the Trial Against K.P.D.), *Państwo i Prawo* 1955, No.6.

Nadolny R., *Völkerrecht und deutscher Friede,* Hamburg 1949.

Nahlik St., "Sprawozdanie z prac Sekcji Prawa Międzynarodowego Polskiego Instytutu Spraw Międzynarodowych" (Proceedings of the International Law Section of the Polish Institute for International Affairs), *Rocznik Prawa Międzynarodowego* 1949.

Namysłowski W., "Granice zachodnie Polski z punktu widzenia prawa międzynarodowego" (Poland's Western Frontiers from the Standpoint of International Law), *Przegląd Zachodni* 1946, No. 10.

Osmańczyk E., *Niemcy 1945—1950* (Germany 1945—1950), Warszawa 1951.

Ost-Handbuch, Deutsches Büro für Friedensfragen, Stuttgart 1949, Issue 15.

Pan S. C.Y., "Legal Aspects of the Yalta Agreement", *American Journal of International Law* 1952.

Pereterski I. S., "Znachenie miezhdunarodnovo dogovora dla tretievo gosudarstva", *Sovietskoye gosudarstvo i pravo* 1957, No. 4.

Phillipson Coleman., *Termination of War and Treaties of Peace,* London 1916.

Piwarski K., "Polskie Ziemie Zachodnie w rozwoju historycznym". (The Polish Western Territories in their Historical Development) included in the collective work *Polskie Ziemie Zachodnie,* Poznań 1959.

Polen, Deutschland und die Oder-Neisse Grenze (ed. R. Goguel), Berlin 1959.

Pospieszalski K. M., *Documenta Occupationis,* vols. I-VII, Poznań 1946—1959.

Pospieszalski K. M., *Polska pod niemieckim prawem 1939—1945 (Ziemie*

Zachodnie) (Poland under German Law 1939—1945 [The Western Territories]), Poznań 1946.

Rabl K., "Rechtsgrundlagen deutscher Ostpolitik", *Der Europäische Osten*, 1958, No. 1.

Reece Carroll, *On German Provinces East of Oder-Neisse Line, and Economic, Historical, Legal and Political Aspects Involved*, Washington 1957.

Rhode G., "Die Deutschen im Osten 1945", *Zeitschrift für Ostforschung* 1953, Issue 3.

Ross A., *Constitution of the United Nations. Analysis of Structure and Functions*, New York 1950.

Roxburgh R. F., *International Conventions and Third States*, London 1917.

Sasse H. G., "Die Ostdeutsche Frage auf den Konferenzen von Teheran bis Potsdam", *Jahrbuch für die Geschichte Mittel- und Ostdeutschlands*, Tübingen 1953, vol. II.

Sauerman H., "Demographic Changes in Post-War Germany", *The Annals of the American Academy of Political and Social Science*, November 1948.

Schechtman J. B., *European Population Transfers 1939—1945*, New York 1946.

Scheuner U., "Der derzeitige völkerrechtliche Status der Ostgebiete des Deutschen Reiches"; in: *Die Ostgebiete des Deutschen Reiches. Ein Taschenbuch.* Herausgeg. von G. Rhode, 2nd ed., Würzburg 1955.

Sharp S. L., *Poland's White Eagle on a Red Field*, Cambridge Mass. 1953.

Skubiszewski K., "Umowa poczdamska jako jedyna podstawa prawna układu terytorialnego Niemiec" (The Potsdam Agreement as the Only Legal Basis for the Territorial Status of Germany), *Przegląd Zachodni* 1952, No. 7/8.

— — "Umowy paryskie z 24 października 1954" (The Paris Agreements of October 24, 1954), *Przegląd Zachodni* 1955, No. 5/6 (abbr.: Umowy paryskie).

— — "Zagadnienie państwa niemieckiego w prawie międzynarodowym" (The Problem of the German State in International Law), *Przegląd Zachodni* 1950, No 5/6 (abbr.: Zagadnienie państwa).

Slavin G. M., *Borba Sovietskovo Soyuza za diemokraticheskoye rieshenie polskovo voprosa v nachale 1945 g.*, Moskva 1952.

Stalin J. V., *O Vielikoi Otiechestviennoi Voinie Sovietskovo Soyuza*, Moskva 1952.

Stefko K., "Glossa do wyroku Sądu Najwyższego z 5 IX 1946. Stan prawny na Ziemiach Odzyskanych z dn. 13 XI 1945", (A Gloss to the Verdict of the Supreme Court of September 5, 1946. Legal Status in the Recovered Territories as of November 13, 1945), *Państwo i Prawo*, 1947, No. 2.

Szafrański J., "Straty biologiczne i gospodarcze", w pracy zbiorowej: *Straty wojenne Polski w latach 1939—1945*, (Biological and Economic Losses, in the collective work: Polands War Losses in the Years 1939—1945), Poznań—Warszawa 1962.

Tunkin G. I., *Voprosy tieorii miezhdunarodnovo prava*, Moskva 1962.

Vattel E. de, *The Law of Nations or the Principles of Natural Law*, Washington 1916.

Wagner W., *Die Entstehung der Oder-Neisse-Linie*, Stuttgart 1953.

Wambaugh S., *A Monograph on Plebiscites*, New York 1920.

Wambaugh S., *Plebiscites since the World War*, New York 1933.

Warburg J. P., *Germany — Key to Peace*, Cambridge Mass. 1953.

Waszak St., "Bilans walki narodowościowej Greisera" (The Balance Sheet of Greiser's Anti-National Fight), *Przegląd Zachodni* 1946, No. 6.

— — "Zagadnienie Niemiec przeludnionych i Niemiec wymierających" (The Question of the Over-Populated and the Dying-Out Ger- many), *Państwo i Prawo* 1949, No. 1.

Wehberg H. *Die Stimson Doktrin. Grundprobleme des Internationalen Rechts.* Festschrift für Jean Spiropoulos, Bonn 1957.

Wheeler-Bennett, *The Nemesis of Power. The German Army in Politics 1918—1945*, London 1949.

Winiewicz J., *Mobilizacja sił niemieckich w Polsce* (Mobilization of German Forces in Poland), Warszawa 1939.

Wiskemann E., *Germany's Eastern Neighbours. Problems Relating to the Oder-Neisse Line and the Czech Frontier Regions*, London-New York--Toronto 1956.

Wolfke K., *Great and Small Powers in International Law from 1814 to 1920 (From the Prehistory of the United Nations)*, Wrocław 1961,

Zaks Z., "Francja wobec uchwał jałtańskich i poczdamskich o polskiej granicy na Odrze i Nysie" (France's Attitude to the Yalta and Potsdam Agreements Concerning the Polish Frontier on the Oder and the Neisse), *Zeszyty Naukowe Szkoły Głównej Służby Zagranicznej* 1956, No. 2.

Zipfel F., "Vernichtung und Austreibung der Deutschen aus den Gebieten östlich der Oder-Neisse-Linie", *Jahrbuch für die Geschichte Mittel- und Ostdeutschlands*, Tübingen 1954, vol. III.

BIBLIOGRAPHY OF THE MOST IMPORTANT WRITINGS BY B. WIEWIÓRA

MONOGRAPHS

Granica polsko-niemiecka w świetle prawa międzynarodowego (The Polish--German Frontier in the Light of International Law), Poznań 1957.

— do, Russian translation, *Polsko-germanskaya granitsa i miezhdunarodnoye pravo*, translated by E. Y. Braynin, edited by Y. G. Bersagov, Candidate of Legal Sciences Moskva 1959, Izdatelstvo Inostrannoy Litieratury.

— do, revised and enlarged English translation: *The Polish-German Frontier from the Standpoint of International Law*, with a preface by Professor Dr A. Klafkowski, Poznań-Warszawa 1959.

Granica na Odrze i Nysie Łużyckiej w polityce Zachodu (The Frontier on the Oder and the Lusatian Neisse in the Policy of the West), Poznań 1958.

Niemiecka Republika Demokratyczna jako przedmiot prawa międzynarodowego (The German Democratic Republic as a Subject of International Law), Poznań 1961.

Uznanie nabytków terytorialnych w prawie międzynarodowym (Recognition of Territorial Accessions in International Law), Poznań 1961.

TREATISES AND ARTICLES

"Zagadnienie przesiedleńców niemieckich w świetle prawa międzynarodowego" (The Problem of German Resettlers in the Light of International Law), *Przegląd Zachodni* 1952, No. 7/8.

"Umowy graniczne między Polską a Niemiecką Republiką Demokratyczną" (The Frontier Agreements between Poland and the German Democratic Republic), *Przegląd Zachodni* 1953, No. 4/5.

"Umowy międzynarodowe w świetle Konstytucji PRL. Zagadnienia wybrane" (International Agreements in the Light of the Constitution of the Polish People's Republic. Selected Problems). (Co-authors: A. Klafkowski and K. Skubiszewski). Published in the collective work *Zagadnienia prawne Konstytucji PRL* (The Legal Problems of the Constitution of the Polish People's Republic), Warszawa 1954, vol. II.

"Poczdamskie decyzje o granicy Odra-Nysa Łużycka. Studium z prawa międzynarodowego" (The Potsdam Decisions Concerning the Oder--Lusatian Neisse Frontier. Studies in International Law), *Przegląd Zachodni* 1955, No. 5/6.

"Granica na Odrze i Nysie Łużyckiej jako element stabilizacji pokoju i bezpieczeństwa w Europie" (The Frontier on the Oder and the Lusatian Neisse as an Element for the Stabilization of Peace and Security in Europe), *Przegląd Zachodni 1955*, No. 9/12.

"Organy reprezentujące państwo za granicą "(The Organs Representing the State Abroad) in the collective textbook edited by M. Muszkat *Zarys prawa międzynarodowego publicznego* (An Outline of Public International Law), Warszawa 1956, vol. II.

"Niektóre zagadnienia delimitacji i demarkacji granicy polsko-niemieckiej" (Some Problems Concerning the Delimitation and Demarcation of the Polish-German Frontier), *Zeszyty Naukowe UAM* No. 3 (Prawo), 1957.

"Problem nawiązania stosunków dyplomatycznych między Polską a Niemiecką Republiką Federalną. Zagadnienie prawa międzynarodowego" (The Problem of the Establishment of Diplomatic Relations between Poland and the German Federal Republic. A Problem of International Law), *Przegląd Zachodni* 1957, No. 3.

"Sprawa uznania Niemieckiej Republiki Demokratycznej przez Jugosławię" (The Recognition of the German Democratic Republic by Yugoslavia), *Przegląd Zachodni* 1957, No. 6.

"Sprawa granicy polsko-niemieckiej w korespondencji między szefami rządów ZSRR, Wielkiej Brytanii i Stanów Zjednoczonych" (The Problem of the Polish-German Frontier in the Correspondence between the Heads of the Governments of the U.S.S.R.., Great Britain and the United States), written in collaboration with J. Krasuski, *Przegląd Zachodni* 1958, No. 1.

"Tzw. «Recht auf die Heimat». Przyczynek do studiów nad zachodnio-niemiecką doktryną prawa międzynarodowego" (The so-called "Recht auf die Heimat". A Contribution to the Study of the West German Doctrine of International Law), *Przegląd Zachodni* 1958, No. 5.

"Niemiecka Republika Demokratyczna — sojusznik Polski Ludowej" (The German Democratic Republic — An Ally of People's Poland), *Przegląd Zachodni* 1959, No. 5.

"Status prawny Berlina" (The Legal Status of Berlin), *Przegląd Zachodni* 1959, No. 5.

— do, a summary in French, "Le statut juridique de Berlin", *L'U.R.S.S. et les Pays de l'Est, Revue des Revues*, No. 2/3, Decembre 1960.

"Nawiązanie stosunków konsularnych a zagadnienie uznania .(Sprawa utworzenia konsulatu generalnego NRD w Kairze)" (The Establishment of Consular Relations and the Problem of Recognition [In connection with the opening of the Consulate General of the German Democratic Republic in Cairo]), *Ruch Prawniczy i Ekonomiczny* 1960, No. 2.

"Zagadnienie uznania NRD a doktryna Hallsteina" (The Problem of Recognition of the G.D.R. and the Hallstein Doctrine), *Przegląd Zachodni* 1960, N. 5.

"Zagadnienia rewizjonizmu zachodnioniemieckiego na XV sesji Zgromadzenia Ogólnego ONZ" (The Problems of West German Revisionism at the 15th Session of the U.N. General Assembly), *Przegląd Zachodni* 1960, No. 6.

"Zachodnioniemieckie roszczenia wobec Polski a prawo międzynarodowe" (The West German Claims against Poland and International Law), *Państwo i Prawo* 1960, No. 12.

"West German Territorial Claims against Poland and International Law", *Polish Western Affairs* 1961, No. 1.

"Międzynarodowa Konferencja prawników w sprawie problemu niemieckiego" (The International Lawyers' Conference Devoted to the German Problem), *Przegląd Zachodni* 1961, No. 6.

"Völkerrechtliche Aspekte der polnischen Westgebiete" (Summary of a paper), *Polen im Wort und Bilde*, Wien, No. 1/42, März 1962.

"Problem niemiecki po drugiej wojnie światowej. Podstawowe umowy międzynarodowe. Powstanie dwóch państw niemieckich" (The German Problem after the Second World War. The Basic International Agreements. The Establishment of the two German States. In the collective work concerning the German Problem), *O problemie niemieckim*, Warszawa 1962.

"NRD w stosunkach międzynarodowych. Sytuacja polityczna Berlina zachodniego" (The G.D.R. in International Relations. The Political Status of West Berlin) [Annex], In the collective work edited by B. Gruchman and B. Wiewióra *Monografia Niemiec Współczesnych, Niemiecka Republika Demokratyczna* (A Monograph on Contemporary Germany, vol.I: The German Democratic Republic), Poznań 1963.

"Współczesna polityka wschodnia w Niemieckiej Republice Federalnej" (The Present Eastern Policy of the German Federal Republic) in the collective work edited by G. Labuda *Wschodnia ekspansja Niemiec w Europie środkowej. Zbiór studiów nad tzw. niemieckim "Drang nach Osten"* (Germany's Eastern Expansion in Central Europe. A collection of studies on the so-called German Drang nach Osten), Poznań 1963.

"The Aims of the Present Eastern Policy of the German Federal Republic", *Polish Western Affairs* 1963, No. 1.

"Nawiązanie pełnych stosunków dyplomatycznych między Kubą a NRD" (The Establishment of Full Diplomatic Relations between Cuba and the G.D.R.), *Przegląd Zachodni* 1963, No. 1.

"Zachodnia granica Polski na tle sytuacji międzynarodowej w latach 1945—1961" (Poland's Western Frontier against the Background of the International Situation in the Years 1945—1961), paper prepared for the National Congress of Polish Historians. (Given to press for the Polish Historical Society — Warszawa, 34 type-written pages).

"Zmiany terytorialne po II wojnie światowej" (Territorial Changes after the Second World War), *Przegląd Zachodni* 1963, No. 3.

"Prawne aspekty problemu Berlina zachodniego" (The Legal Aspects of the Problem of West Berlin), *Miezhdunarodnoya Zhizn*, 1963, No. 4. (col. with I. Łukaszuk.